KAREN BROWN'S

California

Country Hotels & Itineraries

KAREN BROWN'S

California
Country Hotels & Itineraries

Written by

CLARE BROWN   JUNE BROWN   KAREN BROWN

Illustrations by Barbara Tapp

Cover Painting by Jann Pollard

Travel Press

Karen Brown's Country Inn Series

Travel Press editors: Karen Brown, June Brown, Clare Brown, Susanne Lau Alloway,
Iris Sandilands; Technical support: William H. Brown III; Aide-de-camp: William H. Brown

Illustrations: Barbara Tapp; Cover painting: Jann Pollard
Maps: Susanne Lau Alloway—Greenleaf Design & Graphics

Written in cooperation with Town & Country-Hillsdale Travel, San Mateo, CA 94401

Distributed USA & Canada: The Globe Pequot Press
Box 833, Old Saybrook, CT 06475-0833, tel: (203)395-0440, fax: (203) 395-0312

Distributed Europe: Springfield Books Ltd., tel: (0484) 864 955, fax: (0484) 865 443
Norman Road., Denby Dale, Huddersfield HD8 8TH, W. Yorkshire, England,
A catalog record for this book is available from the British Library

Distributed Australia: Little Hills Press Pty. Ltd., tel: (02) 437-6995, fax: (02) 438-5762
1st Floor, Regent House, 37-43 Alexander St, Crows Nest NSW 2065, Australia

Distributed New Zealand: Tandem Press Ltd., tel: (0064) 9 480-1452, fax: (0064) 9 480 1455
P.O. Box 34-272, Birkenhead, Auckland 10, New Zealand

Library of Congress Cataloging-in-Publication Data

Brown, Karen.
  [California country inns & itineraries]
  Karen Brown's California country inns & itineraries / written by
 Clare Brown, June Brown & Karen Brown. -- Rev. 3rd ed.
     p. cm. -- (Karen Brown's country inn series)
  Includes index.
  ISBN 0-930328-08-6: $14.95
  1. Bed and breakfast accommodations--California--Guidebooks. 2. Hotels--
California--Guidebooks. 3. California--Guidebooks. I. Brown, Clare. II. Brown, June, 1949-
 . III. Title. IV. Title: California country inns & itineraries. V. title: Karen Brown's
California country inns and itineraries. VI. Title: California country inns and itineraries. VII. Series.
TX907.3.C2B76 1994
647.9479401--dc20   93-29582
                    CIP

KAREN BROWN TITLES

California Country Inns & Itineraries

English Country Bed & Breakfasts

English, Welsh & Scottish Country Hotels & Itineraries

French Country Bed & Breakfasts

French Country Inns & Itineraries

German Country Inns & Itineraries

Irish Country Inns & Itineraries

Italian Country Bed & Breakfasts

Italian Country Inns & Itineraries

Spanish Country Inns & Itineraries

Swiss Country Inns & Itineraries

Contents

INTRODUCTION   1–8

ITINERARIES
    San Francisco to Los Angeles via the Coast   9–28
    Leisurely Loop of Southern California   29–44
    Yosemite, the Gold Country & Lake Tahoe   45–60
    San Francisco to the Oregon Border   61–74
    Wandering Through the Wine Country   75–92

PLACES TO STAY
    Hotel Descriptions, listed alphabetically by town   93–241

MAPS
    Key Map   243
    Maps showing Places to Stay   245-257

INDEX   259–268

Introduction

Golden Gate Bridge

California the Golden State, is a fascinating state of dramatic scenery, exciting places to visit, and appealing places to stay. There is almost too much—it can be confusing to decide the most important sights to see and the most special inns to choose. This book is written to help you through the maze: we have done your homework for you. The first section of the book includes five driving itineraries that spider-web across the state. The second section features our personal recommendations of places to stay written with the sincere belief that where you lay your head each night makes the difference between a good and a great vacation. Every inn in this guide is one we have seen and enjoyed. We encourage you to buy new editions of our guides and throw away old ones—you will be glad you did because we add new discoveries and delete inns that have not maintained standards. We don't want you to spend one night of your precious vacation time at an inn we no longer include, or not know about a wonderful new recommendation.

ABOUT DRIVING ITINERARIES

Five driving itineraries map a route through the various regions of California so that you can choose one that includes the area you have your heart set on visiting. Each itinerary is preceded by a map that shows the routing and all the towns in which we have a recommended inn. Each routing can easily be tailored to meet your own specific needs by leaving out some sightseeing if time is limited, or linking several itineraries together if you wish to enjoy a longer vacation.

CAR RENTAL: The itineraries are designed for travel by automobile. If you are staying in San Francisco it is not necessary to pick up a car rental until you leave the city since the public transportation system is so convenient and this is a wonderful town for walking. However if your vacation begins in Los Angeles you will need a car within the city to get from place to place and should pick it up on arrival at the airport.

DRIVING TIMES: California is a large state, approximately one thousand miles from tip to toe. If you stay on the freeways you can quickly cover large areas of territory, but if you choose to savor the beauty of the coast along California's sensational Highway 1 or dip into the countryside along scenic back roads, plan on travelling about thirty miles in an hour and remember to allow extra time for stopping to enjoy countryside vistas.

MAPS: Each itinerary has a map outlining the suggested routing and detailing sightseeing and overnight stops. Alternate places to stay are also marked. The maps are an artist's rendering and do not show every road and highway—you need to supplement them with more comprehensive commercial maps. Another tip: before your trip, secure street maps of the larger cities and pinpoint your hotel's exact location.

PACING: At the beginning of each itinerary we suggest our recommended pacing for the itinerary to help you decide the amount of time to allocate to each region.

OREGON

● *Trinity Center*

Ferndale ●

4

● *Mendocino*

5 ● *Calistoga*

● *Napa*

Sonoma ●

Inverness ●

Nevada City

Lake Tahoe NEVADA

● *Sutter Creek*

Sacramento ●

● *Jamestown*   Yosemite National Park

San Francisco ●

3

● *Carmel*

1

● *Cambria*

Santa Barbara ●

● *Palm Springs*

2

● *Los Angeles*

● *Julian*

San Diego ●

1 San Francisco to Los Angeles via the Coast
2 Leisurely Loop of Southern California
3 Yosemite, the Gold Country & Lake Tahoe
4 San Francisco to the Oregon Border
5 Wandering Through the Wine Country

Overview of Itineraries

WEATHER: At the beginning of each itinerary a brief note is given on what you can expect to encounter weather-wise in the various regions. In California a whole new climate emerges by travelling just a short distance. The idea that the entire state is sunny and warm year-round can all too quickly be dispelled when the summer fog rolls into San Francisco or three feet of winter snow falls in the High Sierras.

ABOUT INN TRAVEL

We use the term "inn" to cover everything from a simple bed and breakfast to a sophisticated resort. A wide range of inns are included in this guide: some are great bargains, others very costly; some are in cities—others in remote locations; some are quite sophisticated—others extremely simple; some are decorated with opulent antiques—others with furniture from grandma's attic; some are large hotels—others have only a few rooms. The common denominator is that each place has some special quality that makes it appealing. The individual descriptions are intended to give you an honest appraisal of each property so that you can select accommodation based on personal preferences. To help you appreciate and understand what to expect when travelling the "Inn Way," the following pointers are given:

AIR CONDITIONING: Regions of California can be hot during the summer months. Many inns are in older buildings and do not have the luxury of air conditioning. Inquire in advance about air conditioning if you are concerned with the heat.

BATHROOMS: It is not standard that every inn recommended in this book has a bathroom for every accommodation. The situation is unique to each inn. For example, some inns will offer guest rooms that share a bath with other guest rooms, or guest rooms that enjoy private baths but they are located down the hall. We specify under each description how many of the guest rooms have private or share bathrooms. We do not detail whether the bath is equipped with shower, tub-shower, tub or Jacuzzi. Inquire as to what the term, "*with bath*" means when making your reservation.

BREAKFAST: Breakfast is almost always included in the room rate. If breakfast is NOT included in the room rate it is mentioned. However, know that breakfast can range from a gourmet feast to a simple roll and a cup of coffee. Some inns will serve breakfast to the room as well as offer it in the dining room. When there is no dining room, sometimes the only option is breakfast in the guest room. Again, ask the individual inns about their morning repast.

CANCELLATION POLICIES: Inns are usually more stringent than chain hotels in their cancellation policies: understand their terms when securing a reservation.

CHARM: It is very important that an inn has charm—ideally an inn should be a historic building, beautifully decorated, lovingly managed and in a wonderful location. Few inns meet every criteria, but all our selections have something that makes them special and are situated in enjoyable surroundings—we have had to reject several lovely inns because of a poor location. Many are in historic buildings, but remember that California is a relatively young state, so anything over fifty years in age is considered old—few inns date back further than the mid-19th century and many are new or reproduction-old buildings. Small inns are usually our favorites, but size alone did not dictate whether or not a hostelry was chosen. Most are small (one has only two guest rooms), but because California offers some splendid larger (one has seven hundred guest rooms) establishments of great character and charm—a few of these are also included.

CHECK-IN: Inns are usually very specific about check-in time—generally between 3:00 p.m. and 6:00 p.m. Let the inn know if you are going to arrive late and the innkeeper will make special arrangements for you, such as leaving you a door key under a potted plant along with a note on how to find your room. Also, for those who might arrive early, note that some inns close their doors between check-out and check-in times.

CHILDREN: Many places in this guide do not welcome children. They cannot legally refuse accommodation to children, but as parents, we really want to know and want to stay where our children are genuinely welcome. Under each description we have indicated the general policy of each inn, i.e. whether it is, or is not *appropriate* for children, but these are only guidelines. Many places will accept children with certain stipulations: they have the proper room available, the children are of a certain age, other families are going to be in residence or if it is a slow period.

CREDIT CARDS: Whether or not an establishment accepts credit cards is indicated at the bottom of each description—AX (American Express), MC (Master Card), VS (Visa), all major, or none accepted. Even if an inn does not accept plastic payment it will perhaps take your credit card number as a guarantee of arrival.

FOOD: The majority of places featured in this guide do not have restaurants. There are a few exceptions and these are noted under the hotel description. However, almost all of the accommodations do serve breakfast: quite often sumptuous ones. Frequently, in addition to breakfast, tea or wine and hors d'oeuvres are served afternoons. Sometimes, if you request in advance, a picnic lunch can also be prepared.

PROFESSIONALISM: All the inns we selected are run by professional innkeepers. There are many homes that rent out extra bedrooms to paying guests but this was not what we were looking for and they are not included in our guide. We have recommended only inns that have privacy for the guests and where you do not have to climb over little Freddie's tricycle to reach the bathroom.

RESERVATIONS: The best way to make a reservation is to just pick up your phone and call. Often each bedroom has its own personality, so it is very helpful to discuss the various differences in accommodation available. As a courtesy to the innkeepers, however, keep in mind that staff is often limited to one or two people, and during certain periods of the day they are busier than others, such as the breakfast hour. Also, inns are often homes as well, and you might be waking up the innkeeper if you call late evenings or early mornings. When planning your trip be aware that the majority of inns in this guide require a two-night stay on weekends and over holidays.

RESPONSIBILITY: Our goal is to outline itineraries in regions that we consider of prime interest to our readers and to recommend hotels that we think are outstanding. All of the hotels featured have been visited and selected solely on our merits. Our judgments are made on the charm of the hotel, its setting, cleanliness, and above all the warmth of welcome. No hotel ever pays to be included. However, no matter how careful we are, sometimes we misjudge a hotel's merits, or the ownership changes, or unfortunately sometimes hotels just do not maintain their standards. If you find a hotel is not as we have indicated, please let us know, and accept our sincere apologies. The rates given are those quoted to us by the hotel. Please use these figures as a guideline and be certain to ask at the time of booking what the rates are and what they include.

ROOM RATES: It seems that many inns play musical rates, with high season, low season, midweek, weekend and holiday rates. We have quoted the 1994 high season, general range of rates for two people occupying a bedroom, (singles usually receive a very small discount), to the most expensive suites. We have not discussed "special" rooms such as those that can accommodate three people travelling together. Discuss with the innkeeper rooms and rates available before making your selection. Please be aware that taxes are not included in the rates quoted and usually the hotel taxes are very high—frequently over 10%. Breakfast is included in the rates quoted. Of course, several hotels are exceptions to our guidelines and whenever this is the case we mention the special situation (such as breakfast not being included in the rate).

SMOKING: Ask about smoking policies if this is important to you—best to be forewarned rather than frustrated. Most inns prohibit smoking, a few permit smoking in restricted public areas or outside.

SOCIALIZING: Inns usually offer a conviviality rarely found in a "standard" hotel. The gamut runs all the way from playing "cozy family" around the kitchen table to sharing a sophisticated, elegant cocktail hour in the parlor. Breakfast may be a formal meal served at a set hour when the guests gather around the dining room table, or it may be served buffet-style over several hours where guests have the option of either sitting down to eat alone or joining other guests at a larger table.

Then again, some inns will bring a breakfast tray to your room, or perhaps breakfast in the room is the only option. Another social opportunity is the cocktail hour. In the evening some establishments provide hors d'oeuvres and wine, and guests meander in and out mixing or not mixing with other guests as they choose. Sometimes there are more formal cocktail parties, often with the innkeeper presiding. What you need to do is choose the inn that seems to offer the degree of togetherness, or rather, privacy that you desire.

WELCOME: The warmth of reception is extremely important in making a stay at an inn a happy experience, so we paid particular attention to the sincerity of an innkeeper's welcome.

San Francisco to Los Angeles via the Coast

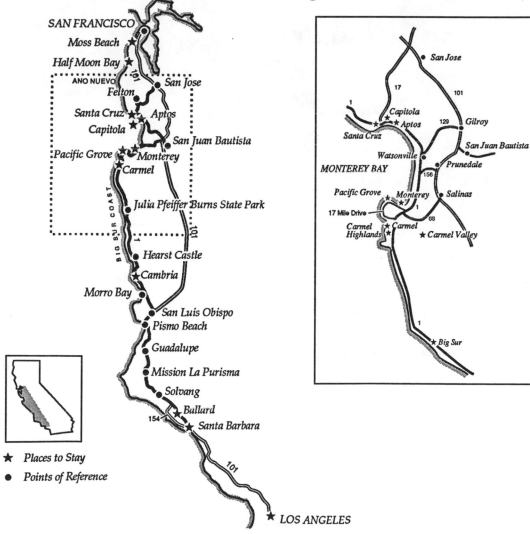

SAN FRANCISCO
Moss Beach
Half Moon Bay
ANO NUEVO
Felton
San Jose
Santa Cruz
Aptos
Capitola
San Juan Bautista
Pacific Grove
Monterey
Carmel

BIG SUR COAST

Julia Pfeiffer Burns State Park

Hearst Castle
Cambria
Morro Bay
San Luis Obispo
Pismo Beach
Guadalupe
Mission La Purisma
Solvang
Bullard
154
Santa Barbara

101

LOS ANGELES

★ Places to Stay
● Points of Reference

San Jose
17
101
1
Capitola
Aptos
129
Gilroy
Santa Cruz
San Juan Bautista
Watsonville
Prunedale
MONTEREY BAY
156
Salinas
Pacific Grove
Monterey
17 Mile Drive
68
1
Carmel
Highlands
Carmel
Carmel Valley
1
Big Sur

San Francisco to Los Angeles via the Coast

San Francisco Cable Car

You can drive between San Francisco and Los Angeles in a day or fly in an hour. But rather than rushing down the freeway or hopping aboard an airplane, drive leisurely along the coast between these two metropolises and enjoy the solitude of redwood forests, the quaintness of Carmel, the charm of Santa Barbara, the splendor of the Big Sur Coastline, the opulence of William Randolph Hearst's hilltop castle, and the fun of experiencing a bit of Denmark in Solvang. Also intertwined in this itinerary are stops to appreciate a piece of California's colorful heritage—her Spanish missions. This routing roughly follows the footsteps of the Spanish padres who, in the 1700's, built a string of missions (about a day's journey by horse-back apart) along the coast of California from the Mexican border to just north of San Francisco. Today many of these beautiful adobe churches and their surrounding settlements have been reconstructed and are open as museums, capturing a glimpse of life as it was lived by the Spaniards and the Indians in the early days of colonization.

OUR RECOMMENDED PACING: We recommend a minimum stay of two or three nights in San Francisco, affording two full days for a quick introduction to the city, and definitely more time if your schedule allows. San Francisco is a beautiful city and there is much to explore and enjoy. From San Francisco, if you take the direct route, you can easily drive to Carmel in about three hours. However, located just south of San Francisco is the Año Nuevo Reserve, where you can observe the enormous elephant seals in their natural habitat. It takes several hours to walk to and from the secluded beaches where the seals congregate, so if you want to visit the reserve en route to Carmel, we recommend an early start from the city. Plan on at least two to three nights (or again, if possible, more) in the Carmel, Pacific Grove or Monterey area. One day can easily be devoured exploring the Monterey Bay Aquarium, Cannery Row and the wharf. Another full day is needed to drive the gorgeous Seventeen Mile Drive, walk the spectacular Point Lobos State Park, visit the beautiful Carmel Mission—and we have yet to even discuss shopping downtown Carmel. From Carmel, one can drive the dramatic coastline of Big Sur and on to Santa Barbara in four to five hour's time, but plan to overnight in Cambria if you want to include even just one of the tours of Hearst Castle and visit the cute artist's town of Cambria—it's too much to do in one day. Santa Barbara is a beautiful, charming city with an expanse of lovely beach. You'd be disappointed if you didn't plan at least two nights in the area before continuing on to Los Angeles.

WEATHER WISE: San Francisco and the coast are often foggy during June, July and August. The further south you go the earlier in the day the fog burns off. The northern California coast is cool and rainy during the winter. In southern California the weather is warmer year round and traditionally less rain falls during the winter. Smog is a problem in certain parts of the Los Angeles area during the summer.

When you ask travellers around the world, "What is your favorite city?," many times the answer is "San Francisco." And it is no wonder. San Francisco really is very special, a magical town of unsurpassed beauty—spectacular when glistening in the sunlight, equally enchanting when wrapped in fog. But the beauty is more than skin deep: San

Francisco offers a wealth of sightseeing, fabulous restaurants, splendid shopping and a refreshing climate.

There are many large, super-deluxe hotels in San Francisco and we recommend a marvelous selection of small, intimate inns. Study our various recommendations to see what most fits your personality and pocketbook. Be advised that hotel space is frequently tight, so make reservations as far in advance as possible.

A good way to orient yourself with San Francisco is to take a half-day city sightseeing tour (brochures on these tours should be available at your hotel) and then return to the destinations that most catch your fancy. If you like to study before you arrive, there are entire guide books devoted to San Francisco and the Visitors' Bureau will send you an information packet on what to see and do. (San Francisco Visitors' Bureau, P.O. Box 6977, San Francisco, CA 94101, telephone (415) 391-2000). To keep you on the right track here are some of our favorite sights:

ALCATRAZ: A visit to the abandoned prison island in the middle of San Francisco Bay is a fascinating excursion and affords a magnificent view of the city skyline—if you don't have a friend with a yacht this is the next best thing! The lonely, concrete, fortress-like structure of Alcatraz was deemed escape-proof until a couple of prisoners (yet to be found) dug their way out of the fortress with a spoon. The tour of the prison involves lots of walking, so be sure to wear sturdy, comfortable shoes and don't forget your camera or woolly sweater because the views are gorgeous and it is cold on this windswept rocky island. This excursion is very popular. For further information call: (415) 546-2700.

CABLE CARS: You cannot leave San Francisco without riding one of the colorful little trolleys that make their way up and down the breathtakingly steep city hills. Rather than touring by cab or bus, plan your sightseeing around hopping on and off cable cars. One can travel easily from the shopping district of Union Square past Chinatown, the "crookedest street in the world"—Lombard, and on to the Ghiradelli Square-Fisherman's Wharf area. For a behind-the-scenes look at this charmingly antiquated transit system visit the Cable Car Museum at the corner of Washington and Mason Streets. Here you can view the huge cables that pull the cars from below the streets and a historical display that includes the first cable car.

CHINATOWN: Just a few short blocks from Union Square enter beneath the dragon arch (at the corner of Bush Street and Grant Avenue) into another world: street signs in Chinese characters, tiny grocery stores displaying Chinese vegetables and delicacies, apothecary shops selling unusual remedies, spicy aromas drifting from colorful restaurants, older women bustling about in traditional dress, the surrounding hum of unfamiliar phrases. Of course the streets are jammed with tourists and there are is a plethora of rather tacky, but fun to explore, souvenir shops. Don't limit your exploration of Chinatown to the main thoroughfare of Grant Avenue: poke down the intriguing little alleys and side streets. Plan a visit to 56 Ross Alley, the Golden Gate Fortune Cookie Factory. Down another alley, at 17 Adler Place, is the Chinese Historical Society of America—a small fascinating museum, portraying the story of the Chinese immigration. The Chinese Cultural Center, housed in the Holiday Inn at Kearny and Washington streets, offers fascinating docent-led heritage and culinary walks affording a glimpse of the "real Chinatown." For information call: (415) 986-1822. The Cultural Center also has a wonderful small museum that offers an ever-changing schedule of exhibits.

COIT TOWER: Coit Tower, located at the top of Telegraph Hill, is a relic of old San Francisco and fun to visit—not only because of the great view, but because its story is so "very San Francisco". The money to construct the watch tower, which resembles the nozzle of a fire hose, was willed to the city by the wealthy Lillie Hitchcock Coit, a volunteer fireman, (or should we say firewoman), who dearly loved to rush to every blaze wearing her diamond-encrusted fire badge. A mural on the ground floor provides a vivid depiction of early California life.

FISHERMAN'S WHARF: Fisherman's Wharf, where San Francisco fishermen haul in their daily catch, has long been a favorite with tourists. However, it is difficult to find even the heart of Fisherman's Wharf behind all the plastic trinket-filled souvenir shops and tacky tourist arcades. But look carefully, and sure enough you will see the colorful fishing boats bobbing about in the water at the waterfront between Jones and Taylor Streets. Nearby, Fish Alley, a small pier extending out into the harbor, affords a good view of the fishing fleet and the aroma of fresh fish mingling with the salty air. Snug on Fish Alley is the excellent Ascona fish restaurant. At Pier 43 you find the three-masted Scottish merchant ship, the Balclutha, which is open as a museum. Pier 39 is lined with newly constructed New England-style shops; nothing authentic, but a popular shopping and restaurant arcade complete with a beautiful two tier carousel. Pier 39 is now also home to some boisterous sea lions—at first considered a nuisance, now a wonderful and valued attraction.

FORT POINT: Nestled at the base of the Golden Gate Bridge's south pier, Fort Point, built in 1861 as one of the west coast's principal points of defense, provides both a fascinating insight into military life during that period and a most stunning and memorable view of the famous bridge. For more information call: (415) 556-1693.

GHIRADELLI SQUARE: Ghiradelli Square is located a few blocks from Fisherman's Wharf, in a wonderful old brick building that used to house the Ghiradelli Chocolate Factory—an appealing place to browse. The complex consumes one full square block that climbs steeply up a hillside, adding much variety to the design of the interior. Tucked within you will find a wealth of things to buy in the more than eighty little shops. Then, when you get hungry, there are more than a dozen excellent restaurants. Flower gardens and free entertainment add to the allure of shopping.

GOLDEN GATE PARK: Unless you are an enthusiastic jogger, you will need to take a bus or taxi to Golden Gate Park, but don't miss it. The park encompasses over one thousand acres, so large you really cannot hope to see it all, but many attractions are located within a manageable proximity. So, if you take a cab, ask to be let out at one attraction, and you can walk to the others. Visit the Japanese Tea Garden, the De Young

Museum, the Steinhart Aquarium and the Planetarium in the Academy of Sciences. If you have a car, explore the entire park, a treasure of lakes, gardens and green lawns.

LOMBARD STREET: Lombard is an ordinary city street—except for one lone, brick-paved block between Hyde and Leavenworth where the street goes crazy and makes a series of hairpin turns as it twists down the hill. Pretty houses border each side of the street, and banks of hydrangeas add color. Start at the top and go down what must be the crookedest street in the world: it is lots of fun. The Hyde Street cable car makes a stop at the top of the hill.

Lombard Street, San Francisco

MISSION SAN FRANCISCO DE ASSISI: This mission is frequently referred to as the Mission Dolores. If you are interested in California missions you will find a visit here worthwhile. It was on this spot that San Francisco was born when Father Francisco Palou founded his mission here in 1776. At one time this was a large complex of warehouses, workshops, granaries, a tannery, soap shop, corrals, Indian dwellings and even an aqueduct. Today, all that is left is the chapel and next to it the garden where gravestones attest to the fragility of life. Although small, the chapel is beautiful in its simplicity with four-foot-thick adobe walls and massive redwood timbers.

NATIONAL MARITIME MUSEUM: This ship-shaped building at the foot of Polk Street in Aquatic Park has displays on the history of water transportation from the 1800's to the present, including some marvelous photos of old San Francisco and exquisite exhibits of scrimshaw. Closed on Mondays and Tuesdays.

THEATER: For theater buffs, San Francisco offers a wonderful offering of entertainment. Most theaters are located in the heart of San Francisco within walking distance of Union Square. In addition, San Francisco has fine opera and ballet. The San Francisco Visitors' Bureau (415) 391-2000 can send you a packet with information on what is going on in the city. You can also call the "hot line" (415) 391-2001 for a recording of all current events.

TIBURON: An enjoyable excursion is to take the ferry from Pier 1 in San Francisco to Tiburon, a small town on a tiny peninsula just across the bay. Tiburon is loaded with charm—appealing little shops, intriguing art galleries and wonderful restaurants tucked into a little New England-style village. As a bonus, en route you enjoy wonderful vistas of San Francisco. For information call the Red and White Fleet at (415) 546-2815.

UNION SQUARE: In the center of the city is Union Square, hallmarked by a small park around which tower deluxe hotels and fancy department stores. Do not tarry too long at the "biggies" because just a block or so away is an irresistible assortment of specialty stores. Some of our favorites are: FAO Schwartz, 180 Post Street; which caters to the child in all of us, Gumps, 250 Post Street; unique to San Francisco with a reputation for personal service and elegant gifts, Jeffrey Davies, 575 Sutter Street, beautiful silk flower arrangements and antiques, La Ville du Soleil, 444 Post Street; fun, whimsical shop with cook ware, gifts and antiques, Laura Ashley, 563 Sutter Street, country-English clothing and fabrics, Pierre Deux, 532 Sutter Street, French fabrics and gifts, Williams-Sonoma, 576 Sutter Street, gourmet cookware.

UNION STREET: Union Street (between Laguna and Steiner), lined with lovely restored Victorian houses, offers a wonderful variety of quaint gift shops, elegant boutiques, beautiful antique stores, small art galleries and excellent restaurants and a multitude of intriguing little shops hidden down tiny brick-paved lanes.

It's a two-hour drive south from San Francisco to Carmel taking the scenic Highway 280 to San Jose and Highway 17 and Highway 1 on to Carmel. But rather than head directly to Carmel we suggest you meander down the coast, enjoying a number of sights en route —a journey that will deserve a couple of days.

Leave San Francisco to the south on 19th Avenue to Highway 280 and take Highway 1 through Pacifica where the freeway ends and the road narrows to meander around the precipitous rocky promontory known as Devil's Slide. Just south of Devil's Slide is Moss Beach, a suburban coastal town home to Karen Brown and her inn, Seal Cove, named after the nearby crescent of golden sand. Seal Cove Inn is also neighbor to the Fitzgerald Marine Reserve and park, where a remarkable world of marine life and tidepools are exposed at low tide. Rangers are usually available to answer questions and can also advise you as to the best time for exploration—call: (415) 728-3584.

Just to the south of Moss Beach, Princeton's harbor is one of California's last true commercial fishing harbors with its mass of fishing vessels and sailboats. Sport fishing and whale-watching boats leave early mornings from Princeton. Bookings can be made through Huck Finn Sport Fishing, telephone (415) 726-7133.

Detour off the Coastal Highway to the east at Highway 92 and take it for one block making a right on Half Moon Bay's Main Street. Park just across the bridge and visit Half Moon Bay Feed and Fuel an authentic country store that sells saddles, rabbits, chickens, animal feed and farm implements. Poke your head in the various shops that line Main Street and you'll find excellent casual clothing at Buffalo Shirt Company and art galleries a plenty. Leaving Half Moon Bay continue down Main Street to rejoin Highway 1 to the south of town.

Lengthy expanses of sandy beach are accessible from the many state parks along the coastline. Pigeon Point Lighthouse is one of the tallest lighthouses on the west coast. Tours are only given on Sundays between 10:00 a.m. and 3:00 p.m.

Thirty miles south of Half Moon Bay is the Año Nuevo State Reserve, home to elephant seals whose huge males with their trunk-like snouts reach a whopping 6,000 pounds. From December to the end of March docents conduct a three-mile round trip hike to the breeding grounds of these car size mammals. Reservation lines open in October (800)-444-7275 for the following season. If you are not able to book several months in advance call the park directly, (415) 879-2025, and they may be able to advise you if last minute tickets are available. We have, in the past, secured tickets by arriving at 8:30 a.m. and queuing at the entrance booth for tickets for tours that day. Outside of the breeding season obtaining permits to view the seals (there are often a great many sea lions in residence) is not a problem, tickets are issued on arrival and you follow the well-marked path out to the distant beach where the seals are found. Outside of the breeding season the best time to visit is during July and August when the males return for their summer molt.

Santa Cruz is twenty-two miles south of Año Nuevo. Years ago this busy seaside town, with its bustling boardwalk and amusement park bordering a broad stretch of white sand beach, was a popular day-trip for workers in San Francisco. In recent years the rides and attractions have received a facelift, making it a pleasure to visit. The rides include a heart-stopping wooden roller coaster and a wonderful old-fashioned carousel. An effort is being made to make the adjacent fishing pier attractive with restaurants and shops. If you enjoy riding trains you may want to take the old fashioned diesel that departs from the boardwalk twice a day for the sixty minute ride to Roaring Camp Railroad, an old fashioned steam train that winds along narrow gauge tracks up into a redwood forest.

Roaring Camp Railroad, Felton

The train leaves several times a day from its main station in Felton, (except Christmas—call for departure times and directions, (408) 335-4400), along narrow gauge tracks built to carry lumber out of the forest. The conductor tells stories of the "old days" as the train circles up through the trees, making a brief stop at the "cathedral," a beautiful ring of redwoods that form a natural outdoor church, before heading back to the depot. It is possible to take a picnic with you, alight at the top, and take the next train back.

Leaving Santa Cruz take Highway 1 south for about twenty miles to Highway 129 where you head east. Continue on the 129 for approximately sixteen miles through small farms and rolling hills to San Juan Bautista and its most attractive mission. There is far more to see here than just an old church for an area of the town has been restored to the way it was one hundred and fifty years ago with the mission as its focus. Facing the square is the restored Plaza Hotel, now a museum where tickets are sold for admission to the attractions in the park. The focal point of the sightseeing is, of course, the mission, but do not end your touring there. Directly across from the mission is a most interesting house, nicely restored, and furnished as it must have looked many years ago. Adjacent to this is a blacksmith shop and stables where there is a colorful display of old coaches. Next door to the Plaza Hotel is another home now open as a museum with period furnishings. After seeing the mission complex, walk into the town of San Juan Bautista, which still maintains its 19th-century, small town ambiance.

Follow Highway 156 west for a couple of miles until it merges with Highway 101 going south to the Monterey Peninsula. As you pass through Prunedale, begin to watch for signs indicating a sharp right-hand turn on Highway 156 west to the Monterey Peninsula.

Along the way, fields of artichokes come into view as you near Castroville, the artichoke capital of the world. When you begin to smell the sea air, stay in the left lane following signs for Highway 1 south to the Monterey Peninsula. As you approach Monterey, dunes lining the sweep of the bay come into view.

The main sightseeing attractions in Monterey are in two areas: old town and the marina, and Cannery Row and the Monterey Bay Aquarium. A bayside walking and biking path runs from the Marina along Cannery Row to the Aquarium and beyond to the adjoining town of Pacific Grove. A fun way to explore Monterey is to rent a side by side bicycle near the aquarium and pedal to the Marina.

In Old Town a three-mile walking tour links the restored buildings of early Monterey. The old adobes are interesting and a sharp contrast to the bustle of nearby Fisherman's Wharf, a quaint wooden fishing pier lined with shops and restaurants. At the end of the pier huge sea lions vie for the fish cast off the fishing boats.

Cannery Row, once the center of this area's thriving sardine industry (the fish are long gone), and brought vividly to life by John Steinbeck in his novels featuring Doc and the boys, is now filled with small stores and tucked into an old warehouse are some outlet stores. The premier attraction in Monterey is the adjacent Monterey Bay Aquarium, for information call: (408) 375-3333. The centerpieces of the Aquarium are the huge glass tanks that showcase the underwater world of the local offshore marine life: one tank is populated by huge sharks and colorful schools of fish while another contains a mature kelp forest teeming with fish.

Monterey is all hustle and bustle (especially in summer) and it is quite a relief to continue to the neighboring, much quieter town of Pacific Grove. To reach Pacific Grove, follow the road in front of the Aquarium up the hill and make a right turn onto

Ocean View Boulevard, a lovely drive lined on one side with gracious Victorian homes and splendid views of the sea on the other. Besides being an affluent residential community, Pacific Grove is famous for the Monarch butterflies that return each October and cluster in the grove of trees next to Butterfly Grove Inn on Lighthouse Avenue. The butterflies return faithfully every year.

Carmel lies just a few miles beyond Pacific Grove and there is no more perfect way to arrive than along the famous Seventeen-Mile Drive that meanders around the Monterey Peninsula coastline between the two towns. The route is easy to find as the road that leads to the "drive" intersects Lighthouse Avenue and is appropriately called Seventeen-Mile Drive. The Seventeen-Mile Drive loops through an exclusive residential area of multi-million-dollar estates and gorgeous golf courses. Because the land is private, $5 per car is levied at the entrance gate, where you'll receive a map indicating points of interest along the way.

The scenic drive traces the low-lying shore, passes rocky coves where kelp beds are home to sea lions, sea otters, cormorants and gulls (remember to bring your binoculars) and meanders through woodlands where Monterey pines gnarled by the wind stand sentinel on lonely headlands. Along the drive is the famous Pebble Beach Golf Course, site of the National Pro-Am Golf Championship each January.

Note: Should you be so lucky as to be driving the Seventeen-Mile Drive in April, watch carefully for a real treat. This is the birthing time for the baby seals and there are designated places where you can watch the mothers with their little ones snuggled along side. Ask the ranger at the entrance where to stop for the best view—signs along the way say "Quiet: Nursery".

Carmel is one of California's most appealing towns—filled with Hansel and Gretel-style cottages nestled under pines and surrounded by flower-filled gardens. Tourists throng the streets lined with enticing boutiques, attractive art galleries, pretty gift stores, appetizing sweet shops, beckoning bakeries and a wonderful selection of restaurants.

The picturesque combination of fairytale cottages and a sparkling blue bay makes Carmel so very special. Its main street slopes gently down the hill to a glorious white sand beach crested by windswept sand dunes.

Just south of town is the Carmel Mission, established in 1770 by Father Junipero Serra. Beautifully restored and fronted by a pretty garden, the mission was Father Serra's headquarters. It is from here that the stalwart little priest set out to expand the chain of missions.

Carmel

A small museum shows the simple cell in which Father Serra slept on a hard wooden bed. The church itself, with its Moorish tower, star-shaped window and profusion of surrounding flowers, has a most romantic appearance.

Located just south of Carmel on Highway 1 is another place you must not miss, Point Lobos State Reserve, one of the loveliest spots on the California coast. A small admission fee entitles you to day use of the park. Drive through the woods to the headlands where rocky coves are home to sea lions and sea otters. Walking trails are well-marked and the times of guided nature walks are posted at the entrance gate. There are a number of idyllic spots to picnic.

Believe everything you ever read about the beauties of the Big Sur coastline: it is truly sensational. However, hope for clear weather, because on foggy or rainy days an endless picture of stunning seascapes becomes a tortuous drive around precipitous cliff roads. (If the weather is inclement you may wish to take the inland route to Cambria by following the picturesque Carmel Valley road east to Highway 101 where you then head south. When you come to Highway 46, turn west. The road intersects with coastal Highway 1 just south of Cambria.) As you drive south on Highway 1, an indication that you are approaching Big Sur when you see the road sign "Hill Curves—63 miles," which is exactly what the road does as it clings precipitously to the edge of the cliff. While the road is quite narrow, there are plenty of turn-outs for photo taking.

The highway passes over the much photographed long, concrete span of Bixby Creek bridge. A few miles later the rocky volcanic outcrop topped by the Point Sur Lighthouse appears. About forty miles south of Carmel is the Pfeiffer Big Sur State Park with its camping facilities and many miles of hiking trails amongst coastal redwood groves.

If you choose only one place to stop along the Big Sur drive, make it Nepenthe (about three miles south of the entrance to Pfeiffer Big Sur State Park). Nepenthe is a casual restaurant, with a sixties-style decor, perched on a cliff high above the ocean offering unsurpassed views (on a clear day) of the coast to the south. Even if you are not in the mood for a substantial meal you can enjoy coffee and dessert on the lower terrace at the Cafe Amorpha. Interestingly, at the heart of the complex is a cottage that Orson Welles bought for his then wife, Rita Hayworth.

Another stop along the way where you can gain a closer view of this magnificent coastline is at the Julia Pfeiffer Burns State Park. The parking area is to the left of the road. Leave your car and take the short walk leading under the Highway and round the face of the cliff that overlooks a superb small cove with emerald green water and a white sand beach. From the rocky bluff a waterfall drops directly into the ocean and the restless sea beats against a craggy point. After you pass the Ragged Point Inn, the bends become less frequent, and as the cliffs give way to the coastal plain, the driving becomes far less arduous. After the road begins to flatten out, watch for Hearst Castle shimmering in the heat haze high on a hill to your left. In 1919, William Randolph Hearst commissioned California's famous architect Julia Morgan to design a simple vacation home atop a hill on his estate overlooking the California coastline. Twenty-eight years and $10,000,000 later his one hundred room retreat, La Cuesta Encantada (the enchanted hill) was complete. Now more commonly known as Hearst Castle, the enchanted hill continues to delight it's millions of visitors. Next to Disneyland, Hearst Castle is the most popular visitor attraction in California.

The number of visitors allowed on the hill during any one day is limited, so it is essential that you make reservations in advance. Hearst Castle is open every day except Thanksgiving, Christmas and New Year's Day. Several different one hour and forty-five minute tours are available for purchase. On certain days an evening tour is offered that combines the highlights of the castle. The evening tour is tremendously popular and must be booked well in advance. All tours are available for purchase eight weeks in advance by calling (800) 444-7275. Plan on arriving at the Visitors' Center at the foot of the hill at least half an hour before your scheduled departure, as the tours depart with clockwork-like precision and do not wait for stragglers. If you arrive early, you can browse through the small museum located next to the departure depot where groups assemble by number for their turn to be taken up the hill by bus.

Tour 1, the overview of the castle, is the one recommended for first-time visitors. You walk through the gardens to the main house, La Casa Grande, to tour the rooms on the lower level. The sheer size and elaborate decor of the assembly room where Hearst gathered with his guests before dinner sets the opulent mood of this elegant establishment.

Hearst Castle

In the adjoining refectory Hearst and his guests dined in a re-created medieval banquet hall—the bottles of Hearst's favorite ketchup on the table seem rather out of place. In the theater a short home movie of Hearst and some of his celebrity friends gives you an idea of life at the castle during the 1930's. A feeling for the opulence of the guest accommodation is given as you tour the bedrooms of the guest house Casa del Sol. The indoor Roman Pool has over half a million Italian mosaic tiles, vast amounts of gold leaf and took over five years to complete. Tour 2 views suites of bedrooms, the kitchen and the swimming pools. Tour 3 shows you the guest wing of the castle, a guest house and the pools. Tour 4 is offered only in summer, does not go into the main house and focuses on the gardens.

From the Hearst-San Simeon State Historical Monument it is just an eight mile drive south to Cambria. Cambria was once a whaling station and a dairy town that shipped butter and cheese to San Francisco. Now the main town lies away from the coast and encompasses two streets of art galleries, gift shops, antique stores and restaurants.

Leave Cambria on Highway 1 going south. The road leaves the coast and travels through low-lying hills to San Luis Obispo, merging with Highway 101 travelling south. If you want to visit every mission en route, when you reach San Luis Obispo take the Broad Street exit and follow signs to the mission that lies at the heart of this busy town. (Although it is an interesting mission, the setting does not compare in beauty with others included in this itinerary.)

About ten miles south of San Luis Obispo Highway 101 returns to the coast at Pismo Beach where you take the exit for Highway 1 and Pismo Beach, a twelve mile arc of white sand beach backed in part by dunes. This is the home of the famous Pismo clam which has unfortunately in recent years become rather scarce. As you travel south on Highway 1, views of the beach are blocked by apartments and motels, but do not despair: two miles south of town, leave the freeway by turning right into Pismo Beach State Park. After paying the entrance fee, pass quickly over the soft sand. Once your tires hit the well-packed, damp sand, your way feels more secure as you drive along the beach, paralleling the crashing waves. From this vantage point you can really appreciate the beautiful sweep of this white sand bay. While it is possible to drive about five miles south on the beach, the auto exit ramp lies one mile to the south.

Leaving Pismo Beach, follow Highway 1 south, passing flat wide fields of vegetables and eucalyptus groves through Guadalupe, a rather poor agricultural town. The road becomes a divided two-lane highway as Highways 135 and 1 merge. After passing the gates of Vandenburg Air Force Base (on the approach to Lompoc), take a left turn onto Mission Purisma Road which leads to Mission La Purisma Concepcion founded in 1787 and now carefully restored and maintained by the State Park system. A self-guided tour offers you the opportunity to see how the Indians practiced mission crafts such as leather working, candle making and building. The simply decorated church with its sparse furnishings, rough floors and stenciled walls is typical of Spanish and Mexican churches of the period. One of the nicest aspects of La Purisma Concepcion Mission is its lovely setting—far in the countryside amidst rolling hills and meadows filled with flowers.

Leaving the mission, follow signs for Buelleton that has the redoubtable fame as the home of split pea soup. Standing just before Highway 246 crosses Highway 101 is Andersen's Pea Soup Restaurant. The menu has more to offer than soup, but it is still possible to sample a bowl of the food that put this little community on the map.

From Buelleton it is just a short drive into Solvang, a town settled originally by Danish immigrants that has now become a rather Disney-fied version of how the perfect Danish village should look—a profusion of thatch-like roofs, painted towers, gaily colored windmills and cobblestone courtyards. The shops house a plethora of calorific bakeries, fudge and candy stores interspersed with nifty-gifty Scandinavian craft shops. Interestingly enough, a large portion of the town's residents truly are of Danish descent. Even if you are not in the mood for shopping, the town merits a bakery stop.

Leaving Solvang, rejoin Highway 246 and follow signs for Santa Barbara. Just outside Santa Inez, Highway 246 merges with Highway 154 and the lush green valley gives way to hills as the road climbs through the mountains up the San Marcos Pass. Rounding the crest of the pass, you see Santa Barbara stretched out below, hemmed between the mountains and the sea. The red tile roofs and the abundance of palm trees add an affluent look to this prosperous town.

Santa Barbara is one of California's loveliest cities. The homes, commercial offices and public buildings show a decidedly Spanish influence and make such a pretty picture—splashes of whitewashed walls, red-tiled roofs and palm trees snuggled against the Santa Ynez mountains to the east and stretching out to the brilliant blue waters of the Pacific to the west. A pleasant introduction to Santa Barbara is to follow the scenic driving tour that is outlined in the brochure published by the Chamber of Commerce. You can probably pick a brochure up at your hotel or by calling the Chamber of Commerce at (805) 965-3023. The route is well marked and gives you an overall glimpse of the city as you drive by beaches, the wharf, the old downtown area and affluent suburbs. The brochure also outlines what is called the "Red Tile Walking Tour" that guides you through the beautiful streets of Santa Barbara. It will take discipline to stay on the path as you pass the multitude of shops filled with so many tempting things to buy, but do continue on, because Santa Barbara is a beautiful city whose public buildings are lovely. The highlight of the tour is the Santa Barbara County Courthouse, a magnificent adobe structure with a Moorish accent.

You definitely must not leave town without visiting the splendid Mission Santa Barbara that is located at the rise of the hill on the northern edge of town. This beautiful church with two bell towers faces a large park laced with rose gardens. As in many of the other missions, although the church's main purpose is for religious services, a museum is incorporated into the complex with examples of how life was lived when the Spaniards first settled in California.

When your allotted stay in Santa Barbara draws to a close, it is a little less than a one hundred mile drive to the greater Los Angeles area. The vast, often smog-filled, Los Angeles basin is criss-crossed by a mind-boggling network of freeways that confuses all but the resident Southern Californian. Frustrating traffic jams at the morning and afternoon rush hours are a way of life. Therefore, plot the quickest freeway route to your destination and try to travel during the middle of the day in order to avoid the worst traffic. Los Angeles does not offer a wide selection of inns, but there are many attractive, modern hotels where you can stay. The greater Los Angeles area has an incredible wealth of places to visit and things to do—something to suit every taste. Sightseeing suggestions are described in the next itinerary.

Leisurely Loop of Southern California

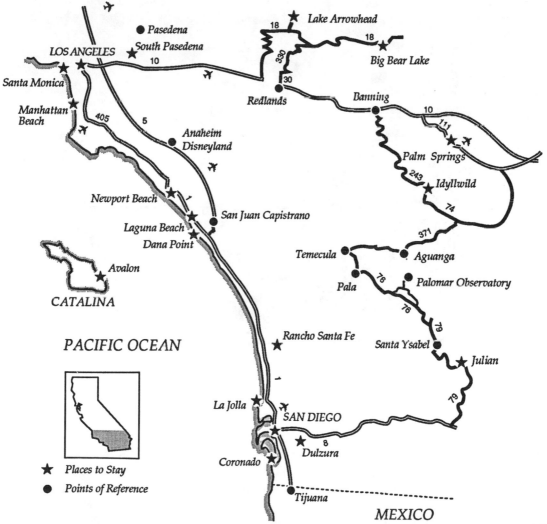

Lake Arrowhead

Pasedena

South Pasedena

LOS ANGELES

10

18

18

330

Big Bear Lake

30

Santa Monica

Redlands

Banning

Manhattan
Beach

405

5

10

111

Anaheim
Disneyland

Palm Springs

243

Idyllwild

Newport Beach

1

74

Laguna Beach

San Juan Capistrano

371

Dana Point

Temecula

Aguanga

Avalon

Pala

76

Palomar Observatory

CATALINA

76

79

Rancho Santa Fe

Santa Ysabel

PACIFIC OCEAN

Julian

79

La Jolla

SAN DIEGO

Coronado

Dulzura

8

Places to Stay

Points of Reference

Tijuana

MEXICO

Leisurely Loop of Southern California

Disneyland

Los Angeles and San Diego are popular destinations, attracting travellers from around the world to a wealth of sightseeing treats. But in addition to visiting these justifiably famous cities, we hope to entice you to venture out into the countryside to explore lesser known sightseeing gems: quaint Balboa Island with its handsome yachts, charming La Jolla with its idyllic beaches, picturesque Julian exuding its Gold Rush heritage, secluded Idyllwild nestled in the mountains, glamorous Palm Springs where movie stars still steal away, beautiful Arrowhead with its crystal clear lake. Perhaps nowhere else can you discover within only a few brief miles such a fabulous fabric of places to visit—all so different, all so appealing. White sand beaches, forests with towering pines, deserts rimmed with snow-peaked mountains, bountiful orchards, historical mining towns, and shimmering blue lakes—all await your discovery.

OUR RECOMMENDED PACING: Greater Los Angeles is an enormous metropolis of cities and suburbs, connected by an overwhelming maze of very busy freeways—during the commuter rush hours it can take hours to get from one side of the city to the other. Choose a hotel or motel close to the principal attraction you are visiting in Los Angeles and use it as a base for visiting the other attractions. If you are just visiting Disneyland stay in the area for two nights—the more attractions you want to include—the longer the recommended stay: if you include San Diego or La Jolla, add two nights; if you visit Palm Springs add another and possibly include one additional night for Lake Arrowhead.

WEATHER WISE: The weather along the coast is warm year round and there is very little winter rain. Julian has a more temperate climate—though sometimes in the summer they have the odd very hot day and in the winter the occasional snow fall. Palm Springs can be boiling hot, but a dry heat, during the summer, and is ideal in the winter with warm days and cool mountain desert nights. Lake Arrowhead is a mountain resort with warm summer weather and snow in the winter.

If you are going to be staying for an extended period of time in Los Angeles, supplement this guide with a book totally dedicated to what to see and do. There is also a wealth of free information available from the Los Angeles Visitors' Bureau: (213) 624-7300—they will send you a very useful packet of information. We are not going to attempt to detail all of Los Angeles' sightseeing possibilities, just briefly mention a few highlights.

DISNEYLAND: The wonderland created by Walt Disney needs no introduction. What child from two to ninety-two has not heard of this Magic Kingdom home to such lovable characters as Mickey Mouse, Donald Duck, Pluto and Snow White? The park is a fantasyland of fun, divided into various theme areas. You enter into Main Street U.S.A. and from there it is on to Tomorrowland, Fantasyland, Frontierland and Adventureland—each with its own rides, entertainment and restaurants. Disneyland is open every day of the year. The park is located at 1313 Harbor Boulevard in Anaheim. For further information call: (714) 999-4565.

HUNTINGTON LIBRARY, ART GALLERY AND BOTANICAL GARDENS: The home and two hundred and seven acre estate of the late Henry Huntington are open to the public and should not be missed by any visitor to the Los Angeles area. Huntington's enormous home is now a museum featuring the work of French and English 18th-century artists. What makes the museum especially attractive is that the paintings are displayed in a home-like setting surrounded by appropriately dramatic furnishings. Nearby, in another beautiful building, is the Huntington Library—a real gem containing, among other rare books, a 15th-century copy of the Gutenberg bible, Benjamin Franklin's handwritten autobiography and marvelous Audubon bird prints. The gardens of the estate merit a tour in themselves and include various sections such as a rose garden, a Japanese garden, a camellia garden, a cactus garden, an English garden and a bonsai garden. Located at 1151 Oxford Road in San Marino, the estate is open Tuesday through Friday from 1:00 p.m. to 4:30 p.m., and Saturday and Sunday from 10:30 a.m. to 4:30 p.m. For information on special events and shows call: (818) 405-2281.

J. PAUL GETTY MUSEUM: Even non-art enthusiasts enjoy the J. Paul Getty Museum, a replica of an ancient Roman villa from Herculaneum, dramatically set in ten acres of garden. The reflecting pool, bronze statues and marble columns add to the grandeur of this very special museum that features many Greek and Roman sculptures and an excellent collection of 18th-century European art. Either a taxi must drop you off at the front gate or you must call ahead to make a parking reservation—you cannot just walk or drive up to the museum. The museum is located at 17985 Pacific Coast Highway,

Malibu, open Tuesday through Sunday from 10:00 a.m. to 5:00 p.m. For information call: (213) 458-2003.

NBC TELEVISION STUDIOS: Los Angeles is the television capital of the world. To get an idea of what goes on behind the screen, visit the NBC Television Studios and take their one-hour tour that gives you a look at where the stars rehearse, how costumes are designed, how stage props are made and what goes into the special effects. The tour also visits some of the show sets. The Studios are located at 3000 West Alameda Avenue in Burbank. For further information call: (818) 840-3537.

THE NORTON SIMON MUSEUM OF ART: The Norton Simon Museum of Art is without doubt one of the finest private art museums in the world, set in a beautiful Moorish-style building accented by a reflecting pool and manicured gardens. Norton Simon and his actress wife, Jennifer Jones, share their incredible collection of art including paintings by such masters as Rubens, Rembrandt, Raphael, Picasso and Matisse. The museum, open Thursday through Sunday from noon to 6:00 p.m., is located at 411 West Colorado Boulevard in Pasadena. For further information call: (818) 449-3730.

PUEBLO DE LOS ANGELES: With all the tinsel of modern-day Los Angeles, it is easy to forget that this city grew up around a Spanish mission. You catch a glimpse of the town's history in Pueblo de Los Angeles, a little bit of Mexico where Hispanic people sell colorful Mexican souvenirs and operate attractive restaurants. The forty-two-acre complex of old buildings (some dating back to the 1780's) has been restored and is now a state park. Pueblo de Los Angeles is located at 130 Apse de la Plaza, Los Angeles. For further information call: (213) 628-1274.

THE QUEEN MARY: If you take Highway 710 west to Long Beach, the freeway ends at the waterfront. The Queen Mary is docked alongside: you can go aboard and wander through the biggest ocean liner ever built. A portion of the ship is a hotel, the rest a museum, re-creating the days of splendor when the Queen Mary was queen of the seas.

UNIVERSAL STUDIOS: Visiting Universal Studios, the biggest, busiest movie studio in the world, is like going to an amusement park. Included in the admission price is a two-hour tram journey that takes you around the four hundred twenty-acre lot, out of the real world and into make believe. Along the way *Jaws* tries to grab you, the Red Sea parts to let you pass, an Alpine avalanche almost engulfs you and you are attacked by robots. This is an entire day's outing for there is so much to see and do—stunt shows, animal shows, Streets of the World, Star Trek Adventure, and on and on. The studios are just off the Hollywood Freeway at the Universal Center Drive exit in Universal City. For further information call: (818) 508-9600.

It takes only a couple of hours to whip down the freeway between Los Angeles and San Diego; instead, follow our sightseeing suggestions and dawdle along the way to enjoy some of southern California's coastal attractions en route.

Drive south from Los Angeles on Highway 405, the San Diego Freeway, until you come to Highway 73, the Corona del Mar Freeway, which branches to the south toward the coast. Take this, then in just minutes you come to Highway 55, Newport Boulevard. Exit here and stay on the same road all the way to Newport Beach. Soon after crossing the bridge, watch for the sign to your right for Newport Pier. (In case you get off the track, the pier is at the foot of 20th Street.) Try to arrive mid-morning so that you can capture a glimpse of yesteryear when the Dory Fleet comes in to beach (just to the right of the pier). The Dory Fleet, made up of colorfully painted, open wooden fishing boats, has been putting out to sea for almost a hundred years. It is never certain exactly what time the fleet will come in (it depends upon the fishing conditions), but if you arrive mid-morning the chances are you will see the fishermen preparing and selling their catch-of-the-day from the back of their small boats. If seeing all the fresh fish puts you in the mood for lunch, walk across the street to the Oyster Bar & Grill—the food is excellent and the clam chowder truly outstanding. If you want to overnight in Newport Beach, Doryman's Inn, just steps from the pier, is highly recommended.

Newport Beach is on a long, thin peninsula. After seeing the Dory Fleet, continue south: the next community you come to is Balboa. In the center of town there is a clearly signposted public parking area adjacent to Balboa Pier: leave your car here and explore the area. The beach is beautiful—stretching the entire length of the long peninsula, all the way from the southern tip of and beyond Newport Pier to the north. Stroll along the beach and then walk across the peninsula (about a two-block span) to the Balboa Pavilion, a colorful Victorian gingerbread creation smack in the center of the wharf. Next to the pavilion are several booths where tickets are sold for cruises into the harbor. One of the best of these excursions is on the Pavilion Queen that makes a forty-five-minute loop of the bay. Buy your ticket and, if you have time to spare until the boat leaves, wander around the nostalgic, honky-tonk boardwalk with its cotton candy, Ferris wheel, saltwater taffy shops and penny arcade. But be back in time to board your boat because the Balboa harbor cruise should not be missed. Along the way is a boat fancier's dream: over nine thousand yachts moored in the harbor. Also of interest are the opulent homes whose lawns stretch out to the docks where their million-dollar cruisers are moored.

A block from the Balboa Pavilion is the ferry landing—you cannot miss it. After your cruise, retrieve your car and follow signs to the Balboa Ferry. You might have to wait in line a bit because the little old-fashioned ferry only takes three cars at a time. When your turn comes, it is just minutes over to Balboa Island, a delightful, very wealthy community. Park your car on the main street and poke about in the pretty shops, then walk a few blocks in each direction. The homes look quaint and many seem quite small and simple, but looks are deceiving—the price tags are very high.

From Balboa Island there is a bridge across the harbor to the mainland. Almost as soon as you cross the bridge, turn right, heading south on Highway 1 through the ritzy community of Corona Del Mar. Although there is still a quaintness to the area, exclusive boutiques, expensive art galleries, palatial homes and trendy shops hint at the fact that this is not the sleepy little town it might appear to be.

From Corona del Mar Highway 1 parallels the sea that washes up against a long stretch of beach bound by high bluffs. The area seems relatively undeveloped except for its beach parks. About eleven miles south of Corona del Mar the road passes through Laguna Beach, famous for its many art galleries, pretty boutiques and miles of lovely beach. In summer, from mid-July through August, Laguna Beach is usually packed with tourists coming to see the Pageant of the Masters, a tableau in which town residents dress up and re-create paintings. Two dozen living paintings are staged each evening and viewed by spectators in an outdoor amphitheater.

Continue south along the coastal Highway. Soon after passing Dana Point, take the turnoff to the east on Highway 5 to San Juan Capistrano. Watch for signs directing you off the highway to Mission San Juan Capistrano (just two blocks from the freeway). This mission, founded by Father Junipero Serra in 1776, has been carefully restored to give you a glimpse of what life was like in the early days of California. Although located in the center of town, the mission creates its own environment since it is insulated by lovely gardens and a complex of Spanish adobe buildings. Another point of special interest at San Juan Capistrano is that the swallows have chosen it as "home," arriving every March 19th (St. Joseph's Day) and leaving October 23rd. Visit the mission and then retrace your route to the Coastal Highway 1 and continue south to San Diego, about an hour's drive away.

The San Diego Visitors' Bureau, (619) 232-3101, will send you a packet of valuable information. Some of the favorite tourist attractions are:

BALBOA PARK: Balboa Park is without a doubt one of the highlights of San Diego. One of the most famous attractions within the park is the San Diego Zoo, one of the finest in the world. A good orientation of the zoo is to take either the forty-minute bus tour or else the aerial tramway. Most of the more than three thousand animals live within natural-style enclosures with very few cages. The Children's Zoo is especially fun, with a nursery for newborn animals and a petting zoo. Balboa Park offers much more than its splendid zoo. There are fascinating museums and exhibits within the fourteen hundred-acre park: the Museum of Man, the Aerospace Museum, the San Diego Museum of Art, the Timken Art Gallery, the Natural History Museum, the Reuben H. Fleet Space Theater and Science Center, the Hall of Champions, the Museum of Photographic Arts, the Lily Pond and the Botanical Building. Most of the museums are housed in picturesque Spanish-style buildings. For information call: (619) 234-1614.

CORONADO: While in San Diego take the bridge or the ferry over to Coronado, an island-like bulb of land tipping a thin isthmus that stretches south almost to the Mexican border. Here you find not only a long stretch of beautiful beach, but also the Coronado Hotel, a Victorian fantasy of gingerbread turrets and gables. The Coronado is a sightseeing attraction in its own right and makes an excellent choice for a luncheon stop.

THE EMBARCADERO: The Embarcadero is the downtown port area located along Harbor Drive. From here you can take a harbor cruise or visit one of the floating museums tied up to the quay. One of these, the Star of India, built in 1863, is a dramatic tall-masted ship that carried passengers and cargo around the world and the Medea, a turn-of-the-century luxury yacht. For information call: (619) 234-9153.

HERITAGE PARK: Just adjacent to Old Town is Heritage Park, where some of San Diego's Victorian heritage is preserved. Next to the spacious village green a street lined with fabulous Victorian houses slopes gently uphill. The houses were moved here from other areas of San Diego to save them from the bulldozers. These intricate creations now house small shops and offices (be sure not to miss the doll shop with a wonderful collection of doll houses and antique toys).

LA JOLLA: Be sure to visit La Jolla, "The Jewel"—a sophisticated suburb just north of San Diego. Classy shops line the streets and spectacular homes, secluded behind high walls, overlook the ocean. La Jolla is home to a branch of the University of California and within it's Scripps Institution of Oceanography is an excellent aquarium and museum featuring marine life from California and Mexico. However, what really makes

La Jolla so special are her beautiful white sand beaches sheltered in intimate little coves. If you prefer to stay here rather than in San Diego proper, The Bed & Breakfast Inn at La Jolla, is highly recommended.

MEXICO: Mexico lies just south of San Diego. Do not judge the many wonders of Mexico by its border town of Tijuana, but if you would like to have a taste of Mexico, take one of the "shopping and sightseeing" tours that leave from downtown for the short drive to the border. You can drive across the border, but the packaged bus tour takes all the hassle from the trip. United States citizens need only carry identification such as a driver's license if they are staying in Mexico for less than seventy-two hours. For further information call Gray Line Tours at (619) 491-0011.

Mission San Diego de Alcala

MISSION SAN DIEGO DE ALCALA: The oldest of the chain of missions that stretches up the coast is Mission San Diego de Alcala. The mission was originally closer to San Diego but was moved to its present site (10818 San Diego Mission Road) in 1774. To reach the mission head east on Highway 8 and it is signposted to the north of the highway beyond the intersection of Highway 15. Call For information: (619) 281-8449.

OLD TOWN: Old Town is where San Diego originated. Just southeast of the intersection of Highways 5 and 8 you see signposts for the oldest sections of San Diego. The area has been designated as a city park and several square blocks are accessible to pedestrians. Make the Historical Museum your first stop and orient yourself by viewing a scale model of San Diego in its early days. Although small in area, Old Town is most interesting to visit as many of the buildings are open as small museums, such as the Machado-Steward Adobe, the Old School House, and the Seeley Stables (an 1860's stage depot with a good display of horse-drawn carriages). If you are in Old Town at meal time, you will find many attractive restaurants. For further information call: (619) 291- 4903.

SEAPORT VILLAGE: Just a little way south of the Embarcadero is Seaport Village, a very popular tourist attraction and fun for adults and children alike. Situated right on the waterfront, it has little paths that meander through twenty-three acres of a village of shops and restaurants built in a colorful variety of styles from Early Spanish to Victorian. Street artists display their talents to laughing audiences. An old-time merry-go-round (an import from Coney Island) jingles its gay melody, irresistibly beckoning the child in all of us to climb aboard.

SEA WORLD: San Diego's marine display is in Mission Bay Park. Set in a one hundred-fifty-acre park, Sea World features one of California's famous personalities, Shamu, the performing killer whale who delights children of all ages with his wit and aquatic abilities. (Fans of Shamu will be happy to know there is a baby Shamu.) Penguin Encounter, is a particularly fun exhibit where you watch comical penguins waddling about in their polar environment. For further information call: (619) 226-3901.

WILD ANIMAL PARK: This is a branch of the San Diego Zoo thirty miles north of the city near Escondido—truly a zoo on a grand scale. The animals roam freely in terrain designed to match their natural habitat. You feel as if you are on a safari in Africa as you watch for lions and other animals while you tour the park on the Wgasa Bushline

Monorail tour. There are also several open theaters where animal shows are presented. For further information call: (619) 234-6541.

Leaving San Diego Highway 8 takes you east and winds through low shrub-filled canyons dotted with ever expanding housing suburbs. About thirty minutes after the highway leaves the city, watch for the sign for Highway 79 where you turn north toward Julian. The road weaves through an Indian reservation and the scenery becomes prettier by the minute as you climb into the mountains and enter the Cuyamaca Rancho State Park. There are not many opportunities to sightsee en route, but if you want to break your journey you can pause at the park headquarters and visit the Indian museum or the museum at the Old Stonewall Mine. Leaving the park, the road winds down into Julian.

Julian is a small town that can easily be explored in just a short time. What is especially nice is that, although it is a tourist attraction, the town is not "tacky touristy." Rather, you get the feeling you are in the last century as you wander through the streets and stop to browse at some of the antique shops, visit the small historical museum in the old brewery and enjoy refreshment at the soda fountain in the 1880's drug store. If you want to delve deeper into mining, just a short drive (or long walk) away on the outskirts of town is the Eagle Mine—founded by pioneers from Georgia, many of them soldiers who came here after the Civil War. Tours are taken deep into the mine and a narration gives not only the history of the mine, but the history of Julian.

If you are in Julian in the fall, you can enjoy another of Julian's attributes—apples. Although you can sample Julian's wonderful apples throughout the year (every restaurant has its own special apple pie on the menu), the apple becomes king during the fall at harvest time. Beginning in October and continuing on into November, special craft shows and events are held in the Julian Town Hall, and of course, apples are featured at every meal in every restaurant. You might also want to visit one of the packing plants on the edge of town where you can buy not only apples, but every concievable item that has apples as a theme.

It is only a short drive north from Julian on Highway 79 to Santa Ysabel where you turn right at the main intersection. At this junction you see Dudley's Bakery, a rather nondescript looking building that houses a great bakery. Loyal customers drive all the way from San Diego just to buy one of their twenty-one varieties of tasty bread. As you leave Santa Ysabel you come to Mission Santa Ysabel, a reconstructed mission that still serves the Indians. This is one of the less interesting missions but you may want to see the murals painted by the local Indians.

About seven miles after leaving the mission Highway 79 breaks off to the east and you continue north on Highway 76. In five minutes you come to Lake Henshaw. Just beyond the lake turn northeast (right) on East Grade Road that winds its way up the mountain to the Palomar Observatory. Just near the parking area is a museum where you learn about the observatory through photos and short films. It is a pleasant stroll up to the impressive white-domed observatory that houses the Hale Telescope—the largest in the United States. A flight of steps takes you to a glass-walled area where you see the giant telescope whose lens is two hundred inches in diameter, two feet thick and took eleven years to polish. You cannot see the telescope in operation because it is only used at night, but it is fun to imagine scientists scanning the heavens.

After viewing the observatory, loop back down the twisting road to the main highway and when it intersects with Highway 76 turn northwest (right), driving through hills covered with groves of avocado and orange trees. In about twelve miles you come to Pala and the Mission San Antonio de Pala, one of the few remaining active "asistancias" (missions built in outlying areas to serve the Indians). This particular one has been in operation since 1810. The mission is small, but the chapel holds great beauty in its rugged simplicity enhanced by thick adobe walls, rustic beamed ceiling and Indian paintings. A bell tower stands alone to the right of the chapel, a picturesque sight; to the left are a simple museum and souvenir shop.

From Pala it is about a ten minute drive north on S16 to Temecula. Just before you enter town the road intersects with Highway 79 and you head east for eighteen miles to Aguanga where Highway 371 takes you northeast for twenty-one miles to Highway 74. As you head north on 74 the mountain air becomes sweeter and the scenery increasingly prettier as you enter the forest. In about twelve miles you see signs for Idyllwild to the northeast. Turn here on Highway 243 and very soon you come to the small mountain resort tucked into the mountains high above Palm Springs. Homey little restaurants, antique stores and fascinating gift shops make up the town. If you are interested in handmade items stop at Maggie's Attic. Originally the store featured handmade items from fifteen local artisans. Now Maggie has seven hundred fifty suppliers, not only from every state, but from around the world. There is also a Christmas section with a marvelous selection of Santa Claus ornaments. The shop is located in an old six-room house at 54380 North Circle Drive.

Leaving Idyllwild, continue north on Highway 342 to Banning where you turn east (right) on Highway 10. In about twelve miles you come to Highway 111 where you turn right and follow signs to Palm Springs (about a ten-minute drive). Palm Springs was first discovered by the Indians who came to this oasis to bathe in the hot springs that they considered to have healing qualities. The same tribe still owns much of Palm Springs and rents their valuable real estate to homeowners and commercial enterprises. The hot springs are still in use today.

During the winter season the town is congested with traffic and the sidewalks are crammed with an assortment of people of every age, size and shape dressed in colorful sporty clothes. Palm Springs used to be deserted in summer when the days are very hot. However, more and more tourists are coming in June, July and August, attracted by the lower hotel rates. Although the temperature in the summer months is frequently well above 110° degrees, it is a dry heat and not unbearable in the mornings and balmy evenings. In fact, due to the altitude, evenings often require a sweater.

So, if your visit is in summer, plan your sightseeing for early and late in the day and spend midday in the comfort of your air-conditioned inn.

In addition to the pleasures of basking in the sun or playing on one of the many golf courses in the area, Palm Springs offers a variety of sightseeing. The most impressive excursion is to take the Aerial Tramway (located just north of town off Highway 111) from the desert floor up two and one half miles into the San Jacinto Mountains. In summer you go from sizzling heat to cool mountain forests while in winter you go from desert to snow. The weather atop the mountain is often more than forty degrees cooler than in Palm Springs so remember to take the appropriate clothing. At the top are observation decks with telescopes, a restaurant and miles of hiking trails.

Aerial Tramway, Palm Springs

If you enjoy deserts be sure not to miss the Living Desert Outdoor Museum (closed in summer) where six miles of trails wind through different types of desert found in the United States. Tour booklets are available at the entrance to assist you along the trails. If you are interested in the rich and famous, join a bus tour that takes you by the outside of their magnificent homes—many movie stars have second homes in Palm Springs.

Palm Springs is a convenient place to end this itinerary because it is a quick, easy freeway-drive back to Los Angeles. But, if time permits squeeze in one more contrasting destination, the exclusive alpine resort of Lake Arrowhead.

Leave Palm Springs and head north on Highway 111 for about ten miles to Highway 10 and turn west for Banning. Approximately twenty miles past Banning at Redlands, exit from the freeway on Highway 30 and drive north for a few minutes until Highway 38 travels into the hills. As the road begins to climb up from the valley the scenery becomes prettier with every curve—the dry desert brush is gradually left behind, replaced by evergreen trees. At the town of Running Springs turn west on Highway 18. This is called the "Rim of the World Highway," a road where sweeping vistas of the valley floor can be glimpsed through the clouds. Be aware that fog often hovers around this drive and instead of admiring beautiful views you creep along in thick gray mist.

Lake Arrowhead Village is a newly built cluster of restaurants and shops along the lakefront. The lake is bordered by magnificent estates for the wealthy from southern California. The magnet of Lake Arrowhead is not any specific sightseeing, but rather the out-of-doors. You can take leisurely walks through the forest, picnic in secluded parks, explore the lake by paddle boats or rent bicycles for a bit of fresh-air adventure. You also must take the hour-long ride on the nostalgic steamer that circles the lake—en route the narrator points out the many fabulous holiday homes of the rich and famous.

When it is time to complete your itinerary retrace your path back to the valley and follow Highway 10 back into Los Angeles. Unless you encounter unexpected traffic, the trip should take about two hours.

Yosemite, the Gold Country & Lake Tahoe

Malakoff Diggins
Grass Valley
Nevada City
20
I-80

Auburn
Tahoe City
Virginia City

Sacramento
Coloma
Georgetown
Lake Tahoe
Carson City

to San Francisco
I-80
Placerville
Emerald Bay
50

I-5
Amador City
Sutter Creek

SAN FRANCISCO
Jackson
Volcano

NEVADA

Stockton
Arnold

to San Francisco
580
205
Angels Camp
Murphys
Calaveras Big Trees State Park

120
Columbia

Chinese Camp
Jamestown

Groveland
Yosemite National Park

49
Yosemite Valley

Wawona
Glacier Point

Mariposa Grove

140

Merced
Oakhurst

41

★ Places to Stay
99

● Points of Reference
Fresno

to Los Angeles

45

Yosemite, the Gold Country & Lake Tahoe

Half Dome, Yosemite

This itinerary features two of California's most spectacular natural attractions, majestic Yosemite National Park and beautiful Lake Tahoe, and links them together by one of California's best kept secrets—the spirited, nostalgic, Gold Rush towns which string along the Sierra foothills. These colorful towns date back to 1848 when the cry went up that gold had been found at Sutter Creek, precipitating the rush to California by men eager to make their fortunes. Overnight boom towns sprang up around every mining camp, with a cluster of similar-style saloons, restaurants, hotels, dance halls and homes. Gold Rush fever quickly cooled and many of the towns were left, quietly forgotten, until tourists rediscovered their charm. Today these benignly neglected Gold Rush towns have been spruced up and bustle with activity: antique shops, art galleries, nifty boutiques, attractive restaurants and appealing inns are tucked into the old Victorian houses lining the sleepy streets. The highway that runs through the mother lode country is numbered 49 after the gold-seeking miners who were known as the Forty-Niners.

OUR RECOMMENDED PACING: We recommend a minimum of two nights in Yosemite and suggest that you try to stay at accommodation in the park (see page 48). Either before or after visiting Yosemite, it is a perfect opportunity to explore California's Gold Rush Country. Rather than backtracking, plan to progress through the region, spending at least one night in the south and at least one night in the north. From the northern region of the gold country it is a logical continuation on to Lake Tahoe. Many people enjoy Lake Tahoe as a resort, basking on its sandy beaches in the summer and skiing down the snow covered peaks that ring its waters in the winter. If you are visiting Lake Tahoe as a tourist we recommend a two-night visit.

WEATHER WISE: Heavy snow is the norm at Tahoe and Yosemite during the winter, while most of the Gold Rush towns are beneath the snow line and experience heavy winter rains. During the summer months the days are hot in Yosemite and Tahoe and several degrees warmer in the gold country.

As you read through this itinerary, please be aware that each of the areas featured could well be destinations in themselves. Yosemite and Lake Tahoe are especially popular resorts and an entire vacation could easily be dedicated to either one. If that is your desire, just extract from the itinerary the portion that suits your interests. However, the Gold Rush country is not as well known and makes a super link between Yosemite and Tahoe—or, for that matter, also a great destination in its own right.

Since Yosemite makes a most convenient first-night stop from either San Francisco or Los Angeles, driving directions are given from both so that you can tailor the trip to your own needs. Much of the first day of this itinerary is spent driving to Yosemite National Park, about a four to five-hour drive from San Francisco or a six to seven-hour drive from the greater Los Angeles area. A brief description of what to see and do during your stay in San Francisco begins on page 12 while the attractions of the much larger, more sprawling Los Angeles area begin on page 31.

From San Francisco to Yosemite National Park is about a four- to five-hour drive. Leave the city east over the Bay Bridge, in the direction of Oakland. Once across the bridge, stay in the middle lane and follow signs for Highway 580, heading east, signposted Stockton. Stay on Highway 580 for about forty-eight miles until you come to Livermore where Highway 580 meets Highway 205 that you take continuing east, following signs for Manteca. Near Manteca, take Highway 120 east, directly to the northern gate of Yosemite National Park. Total driving distance is about two hundred miles.

From Los Angeles to Yosemite is about a six- to seven-hour drive. Leave the city heading north on Highway 5 until you come to the junction of Highway 99 that you take north (signposted Bakersfield). Continue on Highway 99 to the north edge of Fresno where you take Highway 41 north, directly to the southern gate of Yosemite National Park. Total driving distance is about three hundred miles.

The main attractions of the over one thousand square miles of Yosemite National Park lie within the narrow seven-mile-long Yosemite Valley and if at all possible you should try to stay in the valley. A two- or three-night stay in the park is recommended. From hotels through tented cabins, all accommodations in Yosemite are controlled by the Yosemite Park and Curry Company—for information call: (209) 372-0265. Year round it is necessary to make reservations well in advance by phoning: (209) 252- 4848.

From the stately and very expensive Ahwahnee Hotel, through lodges, cabins, tented camps and campsites, Yosemite has accommodations to suit every pocketbook. If your taste in hotels runs to grand, stay at The Ahwahnee. Yosemite Lodge provides more moderately priced accommodations in both cabins and motel/hotel-type rooms. Still less expensive are the tented camps that provide canvas tents on wooden board floors (you do not need sleeping bags since beds and linens are provided). The budget choice is the campsites. But please remember—space is very limited in every category and reservations are essential.

While the attractions of staying in the valley cannot be denied, a more relaxed, serene, country atmosphere pervades at the Wawona Hotel, located within the park, but about a twenty-seven mile drive south on Highway 41. With its shaded verandahs overlooking broad rolling lawns, the hotel presents a welcoming picture. Bedrooms with private bathrooms are at a premium—most rooms use communal men's and women's bathrooms (sometimes situated quite a distance from your bedroom).

Yosemite Valley, an awe inspiring monument to the forces of nature, is bounded by awesome scraped granite formations—Half Dome, El Capitan, Cathedral Rock, Clouds Rest—beckoning rock climbers from around the world. And, over the rocks, cascading to the valley far below, are numerous high waterfalls with descriptive names such as Bridalveil, Ribbon, Staircase and Silver Strand. Below the giant walls of rock the crystal-clear Merced River wends its way through woodlands and meadows of flowers. Undeniably, this is one of the most beautiful valleys anywhere in the world.

A first stop should be the information center to obtain pamphlets, books and schedules. The park service offers a remarkable number of guided walks, slide shows and educational programs—look over the possibilities and select the ones that most appeal to you.

Once you are in the valley, park your car and restrict yourself to travel aboard the free shuttle buses as you can do most of your sightseeing by combining pleasant walks with shuttle-bus rides. Alternate modes of transportation are by guided horseback trips and by bike (bicycles can be rented in the park). Because the valley is flat, it has miles of paths for biking—a very non-strenuous, efficient way of getting around.

During the summer months Yosemite Valley is jammed with cars and people—spring and fall are much more civilized times to visit.

Within the park, but beyond the valley floor, are many areas of great natural beauty. Situated just inside the park's southern perimeter is the Mariposa Grove of giant sequoias. It was here that John Muir, the great naturalist who fathered the idea of the national park system, persuaded President Theodore Roosevelt to add the two hundred fifty acre grove of trees to the Yosemite park system. A tram winds through the grove of sequoias as the driver tells the stories of these giant trees—some of the largest in the world.

To the south of the valley Highway 41 climbs for about ten miles (stop at the viewpoint just before the tunnel) to the Glacier Point turnoff. It is a fifteen mile drive to a spectacular Glacier Point—a viewpoint over three thousand feet above the valley floor. From Glacier Point everything in the valley below takes on Lilliputian proportions: the ribbon-like Merced River, the forest, the meadows and the waterfalls all dwarfed by huge granite cliffs. Beyond the valley a giant panorama of undulating granite presents itself. At Glacier Point rangers offer evening interpretive programs. The ideal photographic time to visit is early in the morning or evening.

Leave Yosemite by the northern gate on Highway 120 to Groveland a handsome, old town shaded by pines. The nearby town of Big Oak Flat is little more than a couple of houses strung along the road. As Highway 120 drops steeply down five miles of twisting road to Highway 49, the shady pine forests of the mountains give way to rolling, oak-studded foothills, the typical scenery of the gold country. Heading north on Highway 49, detour into Chinese Camp, home to over five thousand Chinese miners in the 1850's and now almost a ghost town sleeping under a profusion of delicate Chinese trees of heaven.

The main street of Jamestown is off Highway 49 and therefore free of traffic. With its wooden boardwalks, balconies and storefronts, Jamestown has managed to retain much of the feel of the Gold Rush days. Inviting shops, particularly the emporium, merit a browse, the western-style saloons are full of local color and the Jamestown Hotel has been restored to a beauty such as the Gold Rush days never witnessed.

Just above Main Street on Fifth Avenue is The Railtown 1897 State Historic Park where visitors can see old freight and passenger cars, steam trains and the roundhouse. The park is open on weekends when tours of the roundhouse are conducted.

Leaving town, continue up the main street and cross Highway 49 onto a peaceful little road that takes you through the countryside to Columbia. Follow signs for Columbia or, wherever a junction is unmarked, continue straight. A fifteen-minute drive brings you to Parrot Ferry Road on the outskirts of the town.

In the 1850's Columbia was one of the largest towns in California, with many saloons, gaming halls and stores. Today the main street is closed to car traffic and has been restored as a state park to reflect the dusty, raucous days when Columbia was the "gem of the southern mines." The renovated buildings of Main Street are like exhibits that make learning fun.

Columbia State Historic Park

Be sure to visit the Wells Fargo office, fire station, candy store, mining museum, and concession shops where costumed citizens sell goods appropriate to the period. You can enjoy a cold sarsaparilla at the saloon, munch candy rocks at the Candy Kitchen and pan for gold at the mining shack. It is great fun to climb aboard a stagecoach for a ride through the town or take a tour to the Hidden Treasure Mine.

Both the Fallon and City Hotel have been restored (at vast expense) by the state of California to mirror the look of two of Columbia's hotels in Gold Rush days. The City Hotel on Main Street has a less ornate Victorian decor reflecting the Columbia of the 1860's.

Parrot's Ferry Road leads north from Columbia, crosses the dam and continues through hilly countryside in the direction of Murphys. If you would like to try your hand at rappelling into the largest cavern in California, the opportunity is afforded you at Moaning Cavern. (You can, of course, take the saner descent down a spiral staircase into a room capable of holding the Statue of Liberty.) The rappel is exciting, and with outfitting, instruction and a boost of confidence you descend through a small opening into the well-lit cavern—a most exhilarating experience.

From the caves a short drive brings you to Highway 4 where you turn east (right) for about a twenty mile drive to Calaveras Big Trees State Park, a six thousand acre preserve of forest including two magnificent stands of sequoia trees. A forty-five minute self-guided tour takes you through the North Grove and the nearby visitors' center provides information and history on these mammoth trees. If you have time and interest you can visit the more distant South Grove of giant sequoias.

Leaving the park, retrace your route down Highway 4 and detour into Murphys, a sleepy Gold Rush town sheltered under locust and elm trees where several old buildings and an Old Timer's Museum reflect it's Gold Rush heritage. Well signposted from the center of town is another cavern complex, Mercer Caverns, with rooms of stalactites, stalagmites and other interesting limestone formations.

At the junction of Highways 4 and 49 sits Angels Camp, a pleasant town with high sidewalks and wooden-fronted buildings. Today Angels Camp's fame results not from mining, but from the frog-jumping contests held every May. There is even a monument to a frog taking the place of honor on the main street along which almost all the shops sell items carrying a frog motif.

Leave Angels Camp travelling north on Highway 49 through San Andreas where nearly all evidence of Gold Rush days has been obliterated by modern shopping centers and commercial businesses. On the outskirts of the town Highway 49 makes a sharp turn to the east (right) that is signposted Jackson. A seven mile drive brings you to Mukulumne Hill which in its heyday was one of the more raucous mining towns, though now it seems to be quietly fading away. Turn off Highway 49 and loop through town past the impressive (though genteelly shabby) Hotel Leger and turn left in front of the crumbling I.O.O.F building, then through the residential area and back onto the main road.

Jackson still supports a population roughly the same of that it had during the Gold Rush—consequently modern shopping centers and sprawling suburbs are the order of the day. Turn right at the first stop sign in town and almost immediately left to the main street. Set above the old town in an impressive Victorian home is the Amador County Museum, 225 Church Street. The various rooms have rather eclectic exhibits from the Gold Rush days: for example, the kitchen is full of 19th-century cookware while a small upstairs bedroom displays Indian baskets. Set in an adjacent building is a scale working model of the North Star Stamp Mill that crushes tiny stones.

Retrace your route to where you turned off Highway 49 and turn left on Highway 88 signposted for Lake Tahoe and Pine Grove. Just outside Pine Grove turn left (signposted for your next two destinations, Indian Grinding Rock State Park and Volcano) and follow one of the gold country's prettiest backroads to Chaw'se Indian Grinding Rock State Park. A giant slab of limestone has over one thousand grinding mortars worn in it by Indian women grinding acorn meal. A typical Miwok village has been built nearby with a ceremonial roundhouse and various tree bark dwellings. The adjacent cultural center, built in the style of an Indian roundhouse, has interesting displays from several local Indian tribes.

Just a short drive takes you past the turnoff for Sutter Creek and into Volcano, one of the smallest (population one hundred), prettiest gold country towns that boasted the first lending library and theater group in the state. Now it is a tiny one-street town whose most impressive building is the three-storied, balconied St. George Hotel. Several weathered building fronts give an impression of what the town looked like in more prosperous days. Three miles beyond the town lies Daffodil Hill where over two hundred fifty thousand daffodil bulbs provide a colorful spring display.

Follow the narrow wooded ravine alongside Sutter Creek as it twists down to the town of the same name. Sutter Creek rivals Nevada City as the loveliest of the Gold Rush towns. Its main street is strung out along busy Highway 49 but somehow the noisy logging trucks, commercial and car traffic do not detract from its beauty. False wooden store fronts support big balconies that hang over the high sidewalks of the town. Today many of the quaint wooden buildings are home to antique, craft and gift shops.

Amador City and Drytown, the first two towns you encounter after leaving Sutter Creek as you head towards Placerville on Highway 49, have an old-world charm and are worth exploring. However, following are a string of commercial towns that offer nothing of attraction to the tourist although the intervening countryside is still most attractive. Follow Highway 49 as it weaves through the commercial sprawl of Placerville, crosses Highway 50 and climbs out of town.

It is an eight-mile drive along Highway 49, through apple orchards and woodlands, to Coloma where the Gold Rush began. Or you can make it a twenty-five mile drive by taking a right turn east just after leaving Placerville onto Highway 193, a narrow road that twists down a thickly forested canyon to Chili Bar (a popular spot for rafters to launch) and then does a spectacular weaving climb out of the valley through Kelsey and into Georgetown. Stop to explore Georgetown's shaded streets and then pick up Marshall Road (turn left behind the gas station) which takes you down to Highway 49 where you turn south into Coloma.

Set on the banks of the American River, the scant remains of the boom town of Coloma are preserved as Marshall Gold Discovery State Historic Park. It all began in 1848 when James Marshall discovered gold at Sutter's Sawmill. The remaining historic buildings are scattered over a large area, each separated by expanses of green lawn and picnic places along the banks of the American River. The residential part of town is a sleepy little village of attractive houses set back from the river—it is hard to believe that there was once a population of over ten thousand. The museum shows a short film on gold discovery and provides information for a self-guided tour. A duplicate of Sutter's original sawmill, looking like a big shed, sits on the bank of the river. If you would like a change of transportation, a number of companies offer one-day rafting trips on the American River from Coloma.

Auburn lies a further twenty miles north along Highway 49 that weaves through its suburbs, crosses Highway 80 and continues as a fast, wide road for approximately twenty-four miles into Grass Valley. An alternate, far more attractive and just a few miles longer route, is to take Highway 80 north to the Colfax-Grass Valley exit and follow Highway 174 through pretty woodlands and orchards into Grass Valley. (The following sightseeing suggestion, Empire Mine State Park, is signposted on your left as you near town.)

Grass Valley has a booming economy and sprawls far beyond its historic boundary. Its combination of old downtown buildings housing everyday stores attests to its prosperity. Save town explorations for adjacent Nevada City and concentrate on Grass Valley's Empire Mine State Park at the southern end of town. This hard-rock mine produced $100,000,000 of gold before it closed. An exhibition depicts the mining methods used by miners who came here from the Cornish tin mines in England. Park personnel offer tours of the mine buildings, the most interesting of which is the opulent home of William Bourne, the mine's original owner.

Nevada City

The adjacent town of Nevada City is as handsomely quaint as Grass Valley is functional. The old mining stores and saloons have been cleverly converted into pleasant restaurants, antique stores and the like. It is a most attractive town in which to wander. Many settlers came here from the east bringing with them the deciduous trees of their home states and thus Nevada City is one of the few places that has the glorious fall foliage.

As a conclusion to your gold country explorations, take a forty-five mile round trip to Malakoff Diggins where high-powered jets of water were blasted at a mountainside to extract gold. The method was very successful, but it clogged waterways for miles and left a lunar landscape where there had once been a forested mountainside. This is a very pleasant summer evening trip, but rather than run the risk of returning down narrow country roads in the dark, make the loop as you leave Nevada City for Lake Tahoe. The route is quite well signposted, but it gives you reassurance to have the map from Nevada City Chamber of Commerce, telephone: (916) 265-2692, in hand. Leave Nevada City going north on Highway 49, following it through wooded countryside for eleven miles to the marker directing you right to Malakoff Diggins (signposted Tyler Foote Crossing

Road). The narrow paved road leads you through the forest and, just as you are beginning to wonder quite where you are going, a signpost directs you right down a dirt road into North Bloomfield, a town of white painted houses and buildings set behind picket fences under forest shade. (The town is being restored by the park service and the museum/ranger station is a useful informational stop.) The road through town leads to the diggins proper, a vast lunar landscape of awesome scars. If the weather is inclement, turn back at this point and return to Nevada City by way of the paved highway. Otherwise, continue along the well-maintained dirt road (forking left and downhill at junctions) that wends you down through some lovely scenery to a narrow wood and metal bridge spanning a rocky canyon of the South Yuba River where you pick up the paved road that brings you back to Highway 49 on the outskirts of Nevada City.

Leave Nevada City on Highway 20 east, a freeway that soon becomes a two-lane highway passing through forests and along a high ridge that gives vistas of the Sierras. As Highway 20 ends, take I-80 towards Truckee, a fast freeway that climbs into the Sierra mountains through ever more dramatic rugged scenery.

The freeway climbs over Donner Pass and by Donner Lake named in honor of the group of settlers led by George Donner who in 1846 became snowbound while trying to cross the Sierra Nevada in late fall. Harsh conditions and lack of food took many lives and resulted in the survivors resorting to cannibalism.

Take Highway 89, the Tahoe City exit, and follow it alongside the rushing Truckee River to River Ranch, an inn where in summertime it is great sport to sit on the patio and watch rafters hurtling down the last stretch of their river ride and scrambling ashore. You may even be tempted join them—the Truckee is usually a very gentle river making rafting a fun adventure.

Follow the Truckee River to its source, Lake Tahoe. Tucked in a high valley, Lake Tahoe is a vast, blue, icy-cold lake ringed by pine forests and backed by high mountains. The lake has about seventy miles of shoreline, a maximum depth of 1,645 feet and a summer

Emerald Bay, Lake Tahoe

temperature of about sixty-five degrees. When people from the San Francisco Bay Area say they are "going to the mountains," Tahoe is usually where they're heading. While certain enclaves have their share of hot dog stands, MacDonalds and glitzy gambling casinos, there are many, many areas where this is frowned upon and you can enjoy the exquisite beauty of the lake and it's surrounding stunning scenery.

Tahoe City combines rustic, folksy shops, restaurants and everyday stores with two quite interesting tourist attractions: Fanny Bridge and the Gatekeeper's Cabin. Fanny Bridge is very close; just turn right at the supermarket, and there it is. You will see immediately the derivation of "Fanny" Bridge when you see the tourists leaning over the railing to watch the trout gobble up the food tossed to them. On the same side of the bridge where the fish feed, outlet gates are opened and shut to control the level of the lake—the entire flow of water exiting from Lake Tahoe is regulated here as the water runs into the Truckee River. The other attraction of Tahoe City, the Gatekeeper's Cabin, sits on the bank of the Truckee River. The rustic old cabin, once home to the man who controlled the river level, is now an attractive small museum operated by the local historical society.

Hugging the shoreline, Highway 89 opens up to ever more lovely vistas as the road travels south. Nine miles south of Tahoe City brings you to Sugar Pine State Park with its many miles of hiking trails, camping and picnic sites. In summer you can tour the nicely furnished Ehrman Mansion, once the vast lakeside summer home of a wealthy San Francisco family.You will know by the sheer beauty of your surroundings when you are at Emerald Bay. The road sits hundreds of feet above a sparkling, blue-green bay and miles of Lake Tahoe stretch beyond its entrance. Center stage is a small wooded island crowned by a stone tea house. A one and half mile trail winds down to the lake—it seems a lot farther walking up—and in summer you can tour Vikingsholm, the thirty-eight room lakeside mansion built in 1929 and patterned after a 9th-century Norse fortress. It is the finest example of Scandinavian architecture in America and is filled with Norwegian furniture and weavings.

Just below Emerald Bay a trail leads from the parking lot up a quarter mile steep trail to a bridge above the cascading cataract of Eagle Falls that offers fantastic views of Lake Tahoe. A mile farther up the trail is Eagle Lake, in an isolated, picture-perfect setting.

A memorable outing from Tahoe is a day trip to Nevada's silver towns: Virginia City and Carson City. Leaving Tahoe City, follow the northernmost shore of the lake across the Nevada state line and take Highway 431 from Incline Village over Mount Rose to the stoplight at Highway 395. Cross the highway and go straight ahead up the winding Geiger Grade, Highway 341, to Virginia City. Built over a honeycomb of silver mines, in its heyday Virginia City had a population of over thirty thousand. Its wooden sidewalks, colorful saloons (you must visit the Bucket of Blood Saloon) and false-front buildings with their broad balconies make it a town straight out of a John Wayne movie. The stores sell everything from homemade candy to western boots and several have been reconstructed as museums. You can walk up to the old cemetery, take a steam train ride or tour a mine.

Continue through town through Gold Hill and Silver Hill to Highway 50 where you turn south for the seven mile drive to Carson City, the state capital. The town itself has little of interest except for the Nevada State Museum—just across the street from the Nugget Casino on the main road. The highlight of the museum is the re-created silver mine in the basement. You walk along rail car lines in semi-darkness, past exhibits of miners at work and mine machinery—a lot safer than going down a working mine.

To return to Tahoe go south on Highway 395, the main street of town, to Highway 50 west. Turn right and when you come to Lake Tahoe turn right, following the lake to Tahoe City.

Leaving Lake Tahoe it is a fast four- to five-hour freeway drive, via Highway 80, to the San Francisco Bay area. If you are going to Los Angeles take Highway 80 to Sacramento and Highway 5 south to Los Angeles—a fast eight- to nine-hour drive.

San Francisco to the Oregon Border

OREGON

Crescent City

Ft. Jones · 3 · Yreka · Mt. Shasta

Etna · 3 · McCloud

Trinidad · Trinity Center

Eureka · 299 · Weaverville · Cassel

101 · Redding · Lassen Volcanic National Park

Ferndale · Avenue of the Giants

Scotia · Garberville · Drakesbad

Leggett

Ft. Bragg · Skunk RR · Willits

Mendocino · Little River

Albion · 128 · Ukiah

Elk · Boonville · Cloverdale

PACIFIC OCEAN · Geyserville · Healdsburg

Gualala · 116 · Guerneville

Ft. Ross · 1 · Santa Rosa · SACRAMENTO

Pt. Reyes Station · Occidental

Pt. Reyes Nat'l Seashore · 101 · Petaluma

Inverness · Muir Woods

Muir Beach · SAN FRANCISCO

★ Places to Stay

● Points of Reference

San Francisco to the Oregon Border

Mendocino Coast

If your heart leaps with joy at the sight of long stretches of deserted beaches, rugged cliffs embraced by wind-bent trees, gentle meadows of wildflowers, sheep quietly grazing near crashing surf, groves of redwoods towering above carpets of dainty ferns and mountain hideaways off the tourist route, then this itinerary will suit you to perfection. Nowhere else in California can you travel surrounded by so much natural splendor. Less than an hour after crossing the Golden Gate Bridge, civilization is left far behind you and your adventure into some of California's most beautiful scenery begins. The first part of this route includes many well-loved attractions: Muir Woods, the Russian River, Sonoma County wineries, the Mendocino Coast and the Avenue of the Giant Redwoods. Then the route becomes less "touristy" as it reaches the Victorian jewel of Ferndale and the remote coastal hamlet of Trinidad before climbing into the Trinity Alps with their beautiful mountains and lakes.

OUR RECOMMENDED PACING: One can cover the distance between Mendocino and San Francisco in a day's journey, although the drive is demanding and driving times are different depending on the route. It is approximately a four hour drive if travelling inland on Highway 101 and then cutting over at Cloverdale on Highway 128 west back to the coast just south of Mendocino. It is approximately a six hour journey if following Highway 1 as it hugs the coast all the way north. We recommend a route that follows Highway 1 for a short distance north of San Francisco and then winds back to Highway 101 to explore the northern Sonoma Valley before heading back to the coast and the final stretch on to Mendocino. If time allows, this trip would be most rewarding to spend one night just north of San Francisco near Point Reyes National Seashore (more if you want to take advantage of the expanse of hiking and biking trails); a night or two in the Sonoma wine region, at least two nights in or near Mendocino, a night in Ferndale and a night or two to rest in the Trinity Alps before crossing into Oregon.

WEATHER WISE: The weather along California's northern coast is unpredictable: beautiful summer days suddenly become overcast when the fog rolls in. Rain falls during the winter and spring; and fall, the nicest season, enjoys beautiful crisp clear days. In the Trinity Alps the summers are warm and snow falls during winter.

San Francisco, a city of unsurpassed beauty, is a favorite destination of tourists. And it is no wonder. The city is dazzling in the sunlight, yet equally enchanting when wrapped in fog. The setting is spectacular: a cluster of hills on the tip of a peninsula. San Francisco is very walkable and if you tire, a cable car, bus or taxi is always close at hand. Enough sightseeing suggestions to occupy several days begin on page 12.

Avoiding commuter hours and congestion leave San Francisco on the Golden Gate Bridge following Highway 101 north. After you cross this famous bridge pull into the view point for a panoramic view of this most lovely city. For another spectacular detour, take the very first exit after the view point, Alexander Avenue, turn left back under the freeway and continue as if you are heading back onto the Golden Gate Bridge, but instead, take a quick right to the Marin Headlands. Some of the city's most spectacular skylines are photographed from the vantage point of the headlands looking back at the city through the span of the Golden Gate. The headlands are windswept and rugged. The road continues through the park and eventually winds back to Highway 101. Information and maps are available at the Visitor's Tourist Center located in the old Fort Barry Chapel. Signs in the park direct you to the center which is open daily, 9:30 a.m. to 4:30 p.m., tel: (415) 331-1540. Not to be missed is the Marin Mammal Center, where injured seals are nursed back to health by a multitude of volunteers (telephone: (415) 289-7325).

After returning to Highway 101, continue on to the Mill Valley exit. Circle under the freeway and follow signs for Highway 1 north. As the two-lane road leaves the town behind and winds up through the trees, watch closely for a sharp right turn to Muir Woods. The road takes you high above open fields and down a steep ravine to the Muir Woods entrance and car park. A park volunteer gives out a map and information and there is no charge for admission to the park. Near the park entrance a cross section of a trunk of one of the stately giant coastal redwoods gives you an appreciation of the age of these great trees. Notations relate the tree's growth rings to significant historical occurrences during the tree's lifetime: 1066—the Battle of Hastings, 1215—the Magna Carta, 1492—the discovery of America, 1776—the Declaration of Independence. But this tree was only a baby—some date back over two thousand years. Your brochure guides you on the walk beneath the redwoods or you can take a guided tour with one of the rangers. Allow about an hour for the park, longer if you take a long walk or just sit on one of the benches to soak in the beauty.

Leaving the park continue west to the coastal road Highway 1. Turn left and then, almost immediately right. There is a small sign, marked Muir Beach, but it is easy to miss. Just before you come to the beach you arrive at the Pelican Inn, a charming recreation of an English pub that fortunately also offers lodging. The adjacent Muir Beach is a small half-moon beach bound at each end by large rock formations.

Return to Highway 1 and head north along a challenging, winding section of this beautiful coastal road. The road descends to the small town of Stinson Beach where by entering the state park you can gain access to a fabulous stretch of wide white sand, bordered on one side by the sea and on the other by grassy dunes. This is a perfect spot to stretch and enjoy a walk along the beach.

Leaving Stinson Beach, the road curves inland bordering Bolinas Lagoon, a paradise for birds, and then leaves the water and continues north for about ten miles to the town of Olema. At Olema you leave Highway 1 and take the road marked to Inverness, just a short drive away.

If the weather is fine, allow time to explore Point Reyes National Seashore, a spectacular wilderness area stretching along the sea. If you happen to be in Inverness on a weekend, call ahead to the park (415) 663-1200 to find out what special field trips (such as tidepool studies, bird watching and sights and sounds of nature) are being offered.

The Ranger Station, located in a handsome redwood building at the entrance to the park, has maps, leaflets, books, a museum, and a movie theater where a presentation gives interesting information on the park. Be sure to stop here before exploring the park to obtain a map and study what you want to see and do. A short stroll away from the ranger station is the "earthquake trail" where markers indicate changes brought about by the 1906 earthquake. Also within walking distance is Morgan Farm where horses are raised and trained for the park system.

If the weather is clear, a drive out to Point Reyes Lighthouse is a highlight that should not be missed. As you drive for forty-five minutes across windswept fields and through dairy farms to the lighthouse you realize how large the park really is. When you arrive, it is a ten minute walk from the parking area to the viewing area. From there, steep steps lead down to the lighthouse. Be prepared: it is like walking down a ten-story building and once down, you have to come back up! In winter and spring it is a perfect place from which to watch for migrating gray whales.

Point Reyes Lighthouse

After a visit to the lighthouse, look on your map for Drakes Bay, one of the many beaches along this rugged strip of coast, and named for explorer seeking lands for Queen Elizabeth I of England, who sailed into the bay on the Golden Hind, and christened it Nova Albion, meaning New England. If you are hungry, there is a cafe at Drakes Bay where you can have a bite to eat. Another interesting stop is at the Johnson Oyster Company on Sir Francis Drake Boulevard—a sign directs you to it on the left on the drive toward Point Reyes Lighthouse.

Stop to see the interesting demonstration of how oysters are cultivated in the bay for eighteen months before being harvested.

If you choose to continue on to the northern most point of the peninsula, travel Pierce Point Road that ends at the Tule Elk Range. Before 1860 thousands of Tule Elk roamed here. After an absence of almost a century, a herd has been returned to this wilderness. Trails lead through this wilderness and research area to the Tomales Point Bluff or a shorter distance down to McClures Beach and Elephant Rock.

Retracing your route through the park, from Point Reyes Station continue north on Highway 1. The road winds through fields of pastureland and creameries and then loops back and follows for a while the northern rim of Tomales Bay, providing lovely vistas across the water to the wooded hills and the town of Inverness. About a twenty minute drive brings you to the village of Marshall, and soon after, the road heads inland through rolling ranch land bound by picket fences—passing the towns of Tomales (the bakery here is worth noting—rivaling anything you would sample in France, the Tomales Bakery located in the old barbershop is open Thursday through Monday) and Valley Ford before turning west to Bodega Bay and the small town of Jenner. From here it is about a fifteen minute drive to Fort Ross. "Ross" means "Russian" and this is the site where the Russians, in the early part of the 19th-century, built a fort to protect their fishing and fur interests in California.

After browsing through the museum, follow the footpath through the woods and enter the courtyard bounded by the weathered wooden buildings where the settlers lived and worked. Be sure not to miss the pretty Russian Orthodox Chapel in the southeast corner of the compound. When you have finished roaming through the encampment, take the dramatic walk along the bluffs above the ocean.

Leaving the fort retrace your path to Jenner and follow Highway 116 inland along the banks of the Russian River. This is a tranquil stretch of road, passing through dense forests that open up conveniently to offer views of the very green water of the Russian River. (In winter after heavy rains the river can become a rushing torrent—no longer green and tranquil.) On weekends this road is very congested, but midweek and off season this is a very pretty drive. The largest resort along the river is Guerneville and just a few miles beyond the town you come to the Korbel Winery, a picturesque large building banked with flowers. The last guided tour usually leaves at 3:00 p.m.—to be safe, call to double check the schedule: (707) 887-2294. Korbel is famous for sparkling wines and the tour and video presentations are especially interesting. Three Korbel brothers came to this area from Bohemia to harvest the redwoods and ended up harvesting grapes. There is also a tour of the pretty rose garden nestled on the slope to the left of the winery.

Sampling champagne at Korbel will whet your appetite for additional wines from Sonoma County. Leaving the winery continue for a short distance along River Road watching for a left-hand turn for Westside Road (if you go over the bridge, you have gone too far). Westside Road winds its way to Healdsburg, past vineyards, meadows with cows grazing, pretty apple orchards and several wineries, including Hop Kiln Winery and the nearby J. Rochioli Winery that are open for tasting until 5:00 p.m. The architecture at Hop Kiln is very interesting with whimsical chimneys jutting into the sky. As the name implies, the winery was originally used for drying beer hops.

Nearby Healdsburg has an attractive main square lined with quaint shops and restaurants. Leaving Healdsburg follow Highway 101 north for the half-hour drive to Cloverdale where you take Highway 128 heading northwest toward the coast. At first the road twists slowly up and over a rather steep pass. After the summit, the way becomes more gentle as you head down into the beautiful Anderson Valley, well-known for its delicious wines. Whenever the hills spread away from the road, the gentle meadows are filled with vineyards. If time permits, stop at the Navarro Winery, housed in an attractive contemporary building where wine tasting is offered. As the road leaves the sunny open fields of grapes, the sun almost disappears as you enter a majestic redwood forest, so dense that only slanting rays of light filter through the trees. Upon leaving the forest, Highway 128 soon merges with the coastal Highway 1 (about a sixty mile drive from where you left Highway 101). Here you join Highway 1 north going north through Albion and Little River, and then on to Mendocino.

Mendocino is an absolute jewel: a New England-style town built upon the headlands that juts out to the edge of ocean. It is not surprising that the town looks as it was transported from the East Coast because its heritage goes back to adventurous fishermen who settled here from New England, and upon arrival, built houses like those they had left behind. (In fact, the "New England" setting, seen in the popular television series *Murder She Wrote*, is filmed here.) Tucked into the many colorful wood-frame buildings are a wealth of art galleries, gift shops and restaurants. Do not let your explorations stop at the quaint town, but venture out onto the barren, windswept headlands—a visit to Mendocino would not be complete without a walk along the bluffs. In winter there is an added bonus: spouts of water off the shoreline are an indication that a gray whale is present.

Mendocino makes a most convenient base for exploring the coast. However, if breath taking views are more important to you than quaint shops and restaurants, then overnight instead sixteen miles south of Mendocino in Elk, a tiny, old, lumber town hugging the bluffs along one of most spectacularly beautiful stretches of the sensational Mendocino coastline. Elk has several places to stay that are described in detail in the hotel section of this guide, each has its own personality, each has a magnificent ocean view. Note: If you choose to overnight in Elk instead of the town of Mendocino, when Highway 128 merges with Highway 1, go south to Elk instead of north to Mendocino.

Staying in this area you could most successfully be entertained by doing absolutely nothing other than soaking in the natural rugged beauty of the Mendocino Coast. However, there are some sightseeing possibilities. Just north of the town of Mendocino you come to Fort Bragg. This is a sprawling town that, when compared to the quaintness of Mendocino, has little to offer architecturally except for an extremely colorful fishing harbor. However, there is another well-known attraction in Mendocino, the Skunk Railroad that runs between Fort Bragg and Willits. During the summer months you can either take the all-day trip that makes the complete round trip to Willits, or choose a half-day trip leaving in the morning or the afternoon. The train follows the old logging route through the redwood forests. Frankly, you will have already seen lovelier glens of redwood trees than those you will view on the ride, but the outing is fun, especially if you are travelling with children. The train station is easy to find—it is in the center of town just after you pass over the rail tracks. Call ahead for reservations (707) 964-6371. You can make advance reservations.

Leaving the Mendocino area continue following the coast north and enjoy a treasury of memorable views: sometimes the bluffs drop into the sea, other times sand dunes almost

hide the ocean and at one point the beach sweeps right up to the road. At Rockport Highway 1 turns inland and twists and turns its way over the coastal range, passing through glens of redwood trees and forests. After about thirty miles you arrive at Leggett. Just before the junction with Highway 101 look for a sign to your right indicating a small privately owned redwood park where you can drive your car through a hole in a giant redwood tree.

From Leggett continue north along Highway 101 signposted for Eureka. Along the route you pass many small stores advertising every imaginable item made from redwood; so if you've always craved taking an eight-foot redwood Indian home to Aunt Tilda, this is a perfect opportunity to stop and buy one.

Rather than rush up Highway 101 follow the old highway, called The Avenue Of The Giants, that weaves through the Humboldt Redwoods State Park. This is a thirty-three mile long drive, but you can select the most beautiful section by skipping the first part and joining the Avenue of the Giants at Myers Flat. As you exit Highway 101 at Myers Flat, the two-lane road passes a few stores and then glides into a spectacular glen of redwoods. A particularly idyllic section of the forest is at Williams Grove where you must stop for a stroll.

Nearby are the Humboldt Park Ranger Station and a small museum whose dedicated volunteer staff answers questions and offers displays and a short slide presentation describing the park facilities.

Continue on the Avenue of the Giants. Pass under the freeway and follow signs to the left to Rockerfeller Forest, the oldest glen of redwoods left in the world—some dating back over two thousand years. The trees are labeled and a well-marked footpath guides you through the forest to the Big Tree, an astounding giant measuring seventeen feet in diameter and soaring endlessly into the sky, and also to the Flat Iron Tree (another biggie with a somewhat flattened-out trunk) located nearby in an especially serene grove of trees.

About ten minutes after rejoining Highway 101, exit to Scotia. Plan your day carefully because this is a must see. The entire town—homes, shops, school, hotel—is owned by the largest lumber company in the world. The picturesque little redwood homes are dominated by the Pacific Lumber Company. Drive into town to the museum—an all redwood building resembling a Grecian temple with redwood tree (bark and all) pillars instead of marble. During summer months, free passes are issued here along with a redwood shingle giving directions for the self-guided mill tour. You drive to the visitors' carpark and then, like Dorothy in Wizard of Oz, you follow the "yellow brick road," a well-marked trail, highlighted with yellow arrows, which guides you throughout the factory.

Your first stop is at the hydraulic de-barker where you watch through windows the bark stripped from the logs by high pressure water that sweeps back and forth over each log like a broom. Bits of bark and sprays of water cover the windows while the entire building rumbles as the giant logs are stripped naked.

The next stop is the saw mill where the log is pulled back and forth beneath a giant-sized rotary saw which slices it into large boards. Walking along the overhead ramp, you watch the entire process from the first touch of the saw until the various sized boards are neatly wrapped and bound tightly with straps.

Note: The Pacific Lumber Company mill is closed on weekends and holidays. Passes are given out for tours Monday through Friday, 7:30 a.m. to 2:30 p.m. It is best to check times in advance of your arrival by calling (707) 764-2222.

Returning to Highway 101, about a ten-mile drive brings you to the Ferndale exit. Ferndale's Main Street is lined with so many gaily painted Victorian houses and shops that you'd think Walt Disney had a hand in its design. Actually, the townspeople decided on the appropriate colors, and as a community project, painted the entire town. Not only does the town sparkle with color, but Main Street is a gem, lined with delightful little galleries and stores—a favorite being the irresistible candy shop where you view, through the window, hand-dipping of delectable chocolates. Many visitors enjoy the small theater on Main Street where some excellent plays are produced. Epitomizing the colorful character of the town is The Gingerbread Mansion.

Leaving Ferndale, retrace your way to Highway 101 and continue north through Eureka. About twenty miles beyond the town, take the exit to the coastal hamlet of Trinidad. Although the houses are now mostly of modern architecture, Trinidad Bay has an interesting history. It was first discovered by the Portuguese in 1595, claimed by the Spaniards in 1775, flourished in the 1850's Gold Rush as a supply port for the miners and was later kept on the map by logging. Now Trinidad is a sleepy little cluster of homes nestled on the bluffs overlooking a beautiful cove where a wonderfully unsophisticated, untouristy wharf stretches out into the bay. Next to the wharf is the Seascape Restaurant where you can dine on fish straight from the little fishing boats.

Ferndale

Stroll along the headlands enjoying the exceptionally lovely views then return to Highway 101 and retrace your route twelve miles south to Highway 299 heading east. For the first few miles a four-lane freeway cuts through large dairy farms, then the road narrows as it climbs up into the hills. The drive over the mountains is lovely. Especially outstanding is the portion as you head down the eastern side of the pass and follow the Trinity River into Weaverville. Along the river you often see fishermen lazily casting their fly rods and occasionally come across a few lone miners panning for gold.

About two and a half hours after leaving Highway 101 you come to the picturesque town of Weaverville, which seems like a stage set for an old John Wayne movie. The museum on Main Street is filled with memorabilia from the Gold Rush days and the Joss House belonged to the Chinese who journeyed here in the hopes of finding gold in the Trinity

Alps. Still in use today, the Joss House is the oldest continuously used Chinese temple in California. Adjacent to the Joss House is a small museum with many photographs that poignantly tell the story of the Chinese people in this part of California.

From Weaverville an hour's drive east on Highway 299 brings you to Redding where Highway 5 will whisk you north into Oregon or south for the five hour drive to San Francisco.

However, if you have time linger in the beauty of the Trinity Alps. Highway 3 travels north from Weaverville and winds back into the mountains. With glimpses of Trinity Lake on the right, travel to its north end to the small community of Trinity Center. A wonderful place to stay lies six miles beyond Trinity Center on Carrville Loop, the Carrville Inn. What a happy surprise to find such a wonderful little inn tucked into a small valley "in the middle of nowhere." Actually, this now remote spot once bustled with travellers on their way along the popular pass into Oregon, an extremely popular route because the Indians along the way were so friendly.

San Francisco to the Oregon Border

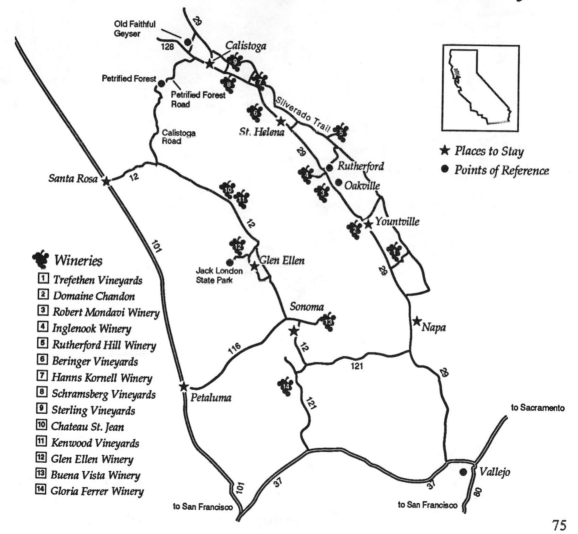

Wandering through the Wine Country

Old Faithful Geyser

Calistoga

Petrified Forest

Petrified Forest Road

Calistoga Road

St. Helena

Silverado Trail

Santa Rosa

Rutherford

Oakville

Yountville

Glen Ellen

Jack London State Park

Sonoma

Napa

Petaluma

to San Francisco

to Sacramento

Vallejo

to San Francisco

★ *Places to Stay*

● *Points of Reference*

🍇 *Wineries*

1. *Trefethen Vineyards*
2. *Domaine Chandon*
3. *Robert Mondavi Winery*
4. *Inglenook Winery*
5. *Rutherford Hill Winery*
6. *Beringer Vineyards*
7. *Hanns Kornell Winery*
8. *Schramsberg Vineyards*
9. *Sterling Vineyards*
10. *Chateau St. Jean*
11. *Kenwood Vineyards*
12. *Glen Ellen Winery*
13. *Buena Vista Winery*
14. *Gloria Ferrer Winery*

75

Wandering through the Wine Country

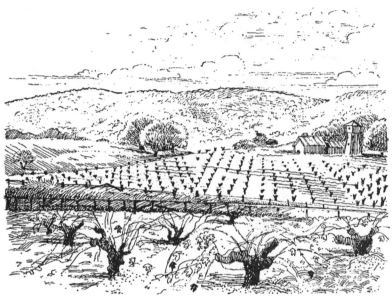

The Napa Valley

The Napa and Sonoma Valleys, just north of San Francisco, have earned a well-merited reputation for the excellence of their wines. Happily for the tourist, many of the wineries are open to the public for tours and tasting. But it is not only visiting the wineries that makes this area so special, these valleys are also memorable for their beauty. A visit to the Wine Country makes a pleasant excursion anytime of year. In summer the days are long and warm, perfect for bike rides, picnics, music festivals, concerts and art shows. As summer days give way to the cooler afternoons and crisp evenings of fall, the lush foliage on the thousands of acres of grapevines turn to red, gold and yellow—a colorful reminder that it is time for harvest. One can sense the energy of the crush as vintners work against the clock and weather to pick grapes at their prime. In winter, cool days are often washed by rain, but this is also an excellent time to visit since this is "off season" and the winery tours will be almost private as you travel from one winery to the next. Spring is glorious: mustard blossoms paint the valley yellow—contrasting dramatically with the dark bark of the vines laced with the delicate green of new leaves.

OUR RECOMMENDED PACING: The Napa and Sonoma wine regions can be squeezed into a day's journey from San Francisco. It requires only about an hour to drive from San Francisco to the southern boundaries of either the Napa or the Sonoma Valley. Running north and south, the Napa Valley spans a territory of approximately thirty-five miles and the Sonoma distances about seventeen miles. However, since the primary attraction in either valley happens to be its vineyards and wine tasting is offered at almost every one, it is most restful to investigate a few in an afternoon's time, sample their wines and then incorporate a nap into the day's schedule. Also, the prospect of returning to San Francisco and battling traffic at rush hour is not a welcome notion. Therefore, we recommend that you plan to leisurely spend one to two nights in the Napa Valley and one to two nights in the Sonoma Valley. You can also use either valley as a base from which to explore the wine region of both Napa and Sonoma. The actual distance between the valleys is only about ten to twelve miles.

WEATHER WISE: The Napa and Sonoma Valleys have a very similar climate. Summer days can be scorching hot and the valley's roads are often clogged with visitors. Autumn gives way to mild, sunny days, cooler afternoons and crisp evenings. From autumn to spring you can expect some rain although many days will be sunny. In winter temperatures are mild yet several degrees cooler than in the nearby San Francisco Bay Area.

This itinerary wends up the Napa Valley and down the Sonoma Valley, it is an introduction and a sampling of what the wine country has to offer. The featured wineries have been chosen for a variety of reasons such as their historical interest, the excellence of their wines, the appeal of their tour and their special ambiance.

From San Francisco, travel east on Highway 80 across the San Francisco-Oakland Bay Bridge. After crossing the bridge, stay in the left-hand lane and follow signs for Highway 80 in the direction of Sacramento. Approximately five miles after crossing the Carquinez Bridge watch for the Marine World Parkway (Highway 37) turnoff. Take the Parkway that takes you right past the exit to Marine World Africa U.S.A. A wonderful park and family attraction, if travelling with children you might want to allocate a day here. On an expanse of one hundred and sixty acres, there are numerous theaters that stage a multitude of shows to include both marine and African life: tigers, elephants, lions, chimpanzees, killer whales, dolphins, seals and sharks, to name a few. Admission to the park covers the cost of all shows and attractions. Shows are staggered throughout the day and it is feasible to see them all if desired. Food service is available throughout the park, but one can also pack a picnic and enjoy the expanse of tables set under trees adjacent to the children's playground. For additional information and their calendar, telephone: (707) 643-6722.

After Marine World Africa U.S.A. continue on the parkway for two miles and turn north on Highway 29 that travels in the direction of Napa. The road widens and the scenery improves dramatically as the road nears the base of the Napa Valley. When the road divides again, take the west (left) fork, signposted for Sonoma Highway 12 and Calistoga Highway 29, that cuts across the south edge of the valley, across the Napa River. (The east fork, Highway 121, goes to Napa and on to Lake Berryessa.) As you cross the bridge, glance north for a lovely, sweeping view of the valley from its widest point to where it narrows in the distance. Highway 29 curves north after the bridge and narrows to a two-lane (in some stretches four-lane) road that travels up the center of the valley from Napa in the south to Calistoga on its northern borders.

Just outside Napa (off Highway 121 and Trancas Street) another road, the Silverado Trail, also travels the length of the valley, hugging its eastern foothills. Highway 29 is the busier road, the address for many of the valley's larger wineries and all the towns. The Silverado Trail, the more scenic, less commercial route, twists and winds amongst smaller vineyards and often offers a welcome escape from the summer crowds and traffic. This itinerary suggests a route north through the Napa Valley, crossing the short distance back and forth between Highway 29 and the Silverado Trail, and then travels west to follow a route south through the Sonoma Wine Valley.

Stay on Highway 29 approximately a half mile past the northern outskirts of the town of Napa to Oak Knoll Avenue. Turn east on Oak Knoll, a beautiful drive bounded by almond trees and vineyards, and watch for a small signpost marking the entrance of Trefethen Vineyards. Surrounded by its own grapevines, Trefethen Vineyards is housed in the oldest wooden winery in the Napa Valley. Pumpkin in color with a brown roof, this handsome complex recently celebrated its one hundredth birthday and there was much reason to celebrate, as the Trefethen family fortunately rescued and lovingly restored the property. This wonderful old winery was designed by the same architect responsible for the larger and more renowned Inglenook and Beaulieu wineries. Trefethen Vineyards is a delightful, small winery, family-owned and operated, that has proved that size is in no way a factor in excellence. The Trefethens have converted a bulk winery to the production of fine estate-grown Chardonnay, Riesling, Cabernet Sauvignon, Pinot Noir and Eshcol. Trefethen wines are featured in some of the best restaurants. Old farming implements border the parking area and a brick walk encircles a handsome oak in front of the old winery where you can sample the wines. Tours are available each day at 10:30 a.m. and 2:30 p.m., but you must make an appointment, call: (707) 255-7700.

From the entrance of Trefethen Vineyards turn east on Oak Knoll Avenue that jogs north at Big Ranch Road and then continues east to where it ends at the intersection of the Silverado Trail where you turn north. From here the scenery seems only to get prettier as the valley narrows and hugs the eastern foothills. Tucked off this road there are numerous smaller vineyards that are open daily for tasting, but offer tours by appointment only: Clos Du Val, Stag's Leap Wine Cellars, Pine Ridge and Walt Disney's widow's winery—Silverado.

From the Silverado Trail, turn west at the well-marked Yountville Cross Road. When the road deadends at Yount Road, turn left in the direction of Yountville. The road winds round behind town to a stop sign that positions you directly opposite Vintage 1870, a wonderful complex of shops and restaurants housed in a quaint old brick winery. Even non-shoppers will enjoy a stroll through this marvelous old converted winery: the old brick, heavy beams and tiled and cobbled floors are dramatic against a meticulously groomed backdrop of green lawn and flowers. A variety of specialty shops make any purchase possible: toys, antiques, handmade sweaters, books, kitchenware, jewelry or art. An assortment of restaurants will appease most appetites should you desire a gourmet salad, pastries or simply a refreshing ice cream cone. You can also arrange for an early-morning balloon ride—the office for Adventures Aloft (P.O. Box 2500, Yountville 94599, (707) 255-8688), is located opposite Vintage 1870, next to the Vintage Cafe. Departures are at sunrise, the best possible time as the winds are gentle and the air is cool. The flights are expensive, but memorable.

Drive south from Yountville on California Drive, crossing under Highway 29 in the direction of the Veterans' Home. Just after passing under the freeway turn right onto the property of Domaine Chandon. When the proprietors of Möet & Chandon first came to the valley with the intention of making sparkling wine following the principles and rigid process of true French champagne, "methode champenoise," they contracted to use Trefethen Vineyards. Successful in their venture, their sparkling wine was well received and they recently moved to the present location and established their own winery called Domaine Chandon. Roses front the vineyards, a French tradition, copied both for its practicality as well as for its aesthetic value. The roses add a grace and beauty to the planted fields, but they are also susceptible to the same root diseases and insect problems. If the roses are blemished, vintners know to investigate the vines closely.

Although the winery is new, mature oak trees shade a lovely lawn and a series of terraced ponds with fountains. A wooden footbridge spans the creek-fed ponds to the stone winery tucked back into the hillside. Tours are offered daily on the hour between

11:00 a.m. and 5:00 p.m. The visitors' center is closed on Mondays and Tuesdays from November to April: for further information call: (707) 944-8844. The tours are hosted by courteous guides who are well informed about the aspects of "methode champenoise." Visitors see first the traditional storage of the wine in polished stainless steel tanks and then continue on to observe the additional steps involved in making champagne. In the cellar bottles of sparkling wine are aged and riddled (turned). In the bottling room you see the process of freezing then disgorging the sediment, corking, cleaning and labeling the bottles. After the tour visitors are invited back to the salon where Domaine Chandon's sparkling wines may be purchased by the glass and enjoyed with hors d'oeuvres. From the salon it is possible to view through a glass partition Domaine Chandon's elegant restaurant. A visit to Domaine Chandon shows French and Californian vintners, sharing expertise, working side by side.

From Domaine Chandon, return to Highway 29 heading north a few miles to the roadside town of Oakville. A few buildings comprise this town, the principal one being the original Oakville Grocery. If you plan to picnic, stop here for supplies and gourmet treats to accompany your wine-tasting purchases.

The Robert Mondavi Winery is easy to spot just past Oakville, off Highway 29, on the left as you travel north. This modern winery was styled after the Franciscan missions, with an open arched entry framing an idyllic view of vineyards. Reservations are advisable: (707) 963-9611. The one-hour tour is extensive, extremely informative and provides a good general introduction to the essence of wine making. By special arrangement, you can also make reservations for an in depth study, touring the fields and studying the grapes as well as the winery. After each tour guests are invited into the tasting room for wine tasting. The lovely lawn at back is the site of summer concerts and art shows.

A few miles farther north, just past Niebaum Lane on the left, is the entrance to the Inglenook Winery. From Highway 29 you catch only a glimpse of the dormer windows of the original ivy-covered stone cellar set amongst the vineyards. Inglenook, a Scottish term for "warm and cozy corner," is what attracted Gustave Niebaum to this wooded locale in the late 1870's. A Finnish sea captain, Gustave retired from shipping and trading to invest his fortune in wine making. Inglenook strives to maintain the standards and excellence of its wine as established by the founders. Inglenook is a handsome winery that enjoys a beautiful setting nestled against the western foothills. Dating back to the 19th-century, Inglenook is able to offer what the valley's new wineries cannot—character achieved with age and time. A highlight of Inglenook's tour is a walk through the original stone aging cellar containing some magnificent large German oak casks and a tour of Gustave Niebaum's tasting room, modeled after the Captain's cabin on his ship, finished with beautiful carved oak paneling and stained glass windows. Forty-five-minute tours start in the museum area at the entrance and include a movie and wine tasting. Reservations are not required, but for information call: (707) 967-3362.

Inglenook Winery

Wandering through the Wine Country

From Inglenook cross over Highway 29 to Rutherford Road, directly opposite. On the corner are a clustering of buildings that are Beaulieu Vineyards. Referred to as BV, Beaulieu is known for some excellent wine and now offers both a tour and wine tasting. For additional information call: (707) 967-5232.

Rutherford Road affords a scenic drive shaded by an archway of oak trees. Travel the short distance to its end, past the Louis Honig Winery, and then turn north on Conn Creek Road that then intersects with the Silverado Trail. Turn north on the Silverado Trail, but drive slowly as you want to take the first right turn onto Rutherford Hill Road that winds up past the Auberge du Soleil, to the Rutherford Hill Winery.

Although relatively new, the Rutherford Hill Winery is housed in a stunning building of weathered redwood in the shape of a chalet-barn, draped with Virginia creeper and wisteria and bounded by grass and flowers. The winery crowns a plateau and enjoys a spectacular valley view. Paths lead down the hillside to picnic tables set under olive trees where the views will tempt you to wile away an afternoon. Guides at Rutherford Hill are friendly and quite proud of (as well as knowledgeable about) the winery. Although wine making procedures are basically the same regardless of a winery's production, Rutherford Hill is a small winery and the guide's explanation of the step-by-step process seems easier to understand than the same explanation at a winery on a much grander scale. Visitors are encouraged to ask questions. Advance reservations are not needed, but for more information call: (707) 963-1871.

Rutherford Hill is the dream of a number of independent vintners who together purchased what was once the Souverain Winery (now located in the Sonoma Valley) in order to process and control the production of their limited quantities of grapes into wine. Labels depict which vineyard is responsible for any given bottle of wine. It is a centuries-old European tradition that great wines carry the names of the individual vineyards from which they are made. The owners also constructed the largest expanse of underground caves in the valley—these maintain a constant natural temperature of fifty-eight degrees that minimizes evaporation far more successfully than when temperatures are controlled by air conditioning. The tour of Rutherford Hill includes a visit to these caves that are impressive, but stark as a result of their newness and the recent vintages that they guard. The tour of Rutherford Hill both begins and ends in its dramatic reception and tasting hall. Rutherford is also the California capital for petanque, an ancient Mediterranean game of bowls, and in addition to its winery, picnic grounds and spectacular views also affords guests the opportunity to play on its petanque courts.

From Rutherford travelling north on Highway 29 it is just a few miles further onto St. Helena. Highway 29 becomes this lovely town's Main Street, lined with elegant stores, boutiques and restaurants. Detour east two blocks off Main Street via Adams Street to St. Helena's Library and Museum. The library has a very interesting section on wine and one wing of the museum is dedicated to Robert Louis Stevenson, the great Scotsman who settled with his new bride in an old miner's shack northeast of Calistoga. It was here that he wrote *Silverado Squatters*, a book romantically promoting the beauty of the Napa Valley. Stevenson buffs can also visit the Robert Louis Stevenson Park on Highway 29 between Calistoga and Middletown and also make an appointment to tour Schramsburg Vineyards, the winery Stevenson featured in his chronicles of the wine country.

Schramsberg Vineyards, which offers tours by appointment, (707) 942-4558, is tucked in the western foothills of the Napa Valley just off Highway 29 to the south of Calistoga. The production of sparkling wine dominates the several tunnels and cellar. Quantities are so limited that tasting is not possible, but as the proprietors remark, visitors to Schramsberg vineyards are usually already familiar with the excellence of their wines.

Before heading north again on Highway 29 from St. Helena or after exploring the charming shops of its main street, travel just a short distance south to V. Sattui Winery. Established in 1885 in San Francisco primarily as a bakery and then a winery, they relocated to the Napa Valley in 1973. Now wine is the premier interest of Vittorio Sattui, the founder's great-grandson. The thirty-two to thirty-five thousand cases of wine he produces each year are sold only at the winery. In a lovely garden setting this is an attractive winery where you can also purchase picnic supplies—they have over two hundred different kinds of cheese, salads, pates, breads and desserts. The winery has a wonderful picnic spot with tables set on the lawn beneath shady trees: (707) 963-7774.

As Highway 29 leaves the commercial district of St. Helena and enters a very exclusive residential district on its northern borders, watch carefully for the gated entry to Beringer Vineyards, set on a knoll, surrounded by beautifully landscaped grounds of mature trees, lawns and gardens. What was once the home of the founding Beringer family now houses a wine and gift shop. Reflecting its heritage and standing as a tribute to one of the valley's founding wineries, the dramatic stone and half-timbered building with a slate roof was one of two family homes built as a replica of the German home that Frederick and his brother Jacob left behind when they emigrated. The second and smaller home is currently under restoration. Half-hour tours are offered every day between 9.30 a.m. and 5.00 p.m. and you can make reservations in advance. Tours emphasize the historical aspect of the winery and include a memorable visit through the tunnels and caverns where the wine is aged in barrels. For information call: (707) 963-7115.

From Beringer head north another four miles and then turn right on Larkmead Lane. The Hanns Kornell Winery, a name synonymous with fine champagne, is located on Larkmead Lane. Hanns Kornell is devoted entirely to the production of traditional, bottle-fermented sparkling wines. Visitors are welcome and tours are informal and personalized to suit the group and the production activities of any particular day or hour. For information: (707) 942-0859. The tour is more informative than visual: an in-depth, detailed explanation is offered about the traditional methods of making sparkling wine.

A large sign on Highway 29 instructs you to turn just a few miles further at Dunaweal Lane to visit Sterling Vineyards. Reminiscent of a Moorish castle, Sterling Vineyards enjoys a crowning position on a hill idyllically set in the middle of the valley. From the winery you can savor panoramic views looking down through tall pines to a checkerboard of vineyards. Access to Sterling is possible only by small gondolas: for a fee of $6 (children under 16 free) you can ride the aerial tramway from the parking lot to the winery and back (first tram 10:00 a.m., last 4:30 p.m.). Arrows and detailed signs direct you on an informative, but impersonal, self-guided tour through the maze of rooms that comprise the winery. By appointment a special guided tour is offered at 11:00 a.m. and 2:00 p.m. Monday to Friday (707) 942-5151. At the end of the tour, a flight of steps leads up to a tasting room from which the views are a bit disappointing. One explanation offered as to why they didn't take advantage of the possible 360-degree views was that, if offered, no one would move on—and it is probably true! Although limited, the views are lovely, as is the wine. Another inviting feature about Sterling is the wonderful melodic sound of bells that ring out every quarter hour. These bells once hung in London's St. Dunstan's-in the-East Church.

The delightful town of Calistoga is just a few miles north from Sterling Vineyards at the intersection of Highway 29 and Highway 128. Bounded by rugged foothills and vineyards, Calistoga is an attractive town servicing local residents and tourists alike. Its main street, Lincoln Avenue, is lined on both sides by attractive shops and numerous restaurants. This charming town has been famous ever since Spanish explorers arrived in 1823 and observed Indians taking mud baths in steamy marshes. Sam Brannan, who purchased a square mile of land at the foot of Mount St. Helena, gave the town its name: he wanted the place to be the "Saratoga of California" and so called it Calistoga. He bought the land in the early 1860's and by 1866 was ready to open his resort of a few cottages and palm trees. The oldest surviving railroad depot in California, now serving as a quaint and historic shopping mall, received its first train load of passengers when they came to Calistoga for the much publicized opening of Sam Brannan's resort. For more than one hundred years, Calistoga has attracted visitors from all over the world, primarily for its hot springs and spas. People came in search of its glorious, healing waters long before the region became a popular destination for its wineries.

There are many spa facilities to choose from—at the eastern end of town look for the Calistoga Spa and Hot Springs (1006 Washington Street, Calistoga 94515, (707) 942-6269). Their facilities are newly renovated, expansive and modern and the attendants are professional and very nice. Offered are volcanic ash mud baths, mineral baths, steam baths, blanket wraps and massage. The entire package, "the works," takes almost two hours and their rates are very competitive.

If you are feeling adventurous, visit the Calistoga Gliders (1546 Lincoln Avenue, Calistoga 94515, (707) 942-5592) and arrange for a glider ride. You can also take a balloon flight with Once In A Lifetime (P.O. Box 795, Calistoga 94515, (707) 942-6541). A sunrise launch is arranged from a selection of wineries. This one-hour fantasy voyage includes a gourmet brunch.

If you have never seen a geyser, travel a few miles farther north from Calistoga on Highway 128 in the direction of Lakeport to Tubbs Lane. Turn right onto Tubbs Lane and in a half mile you see the entrance to the Old Faithful Geyser on the left. Anticipated at intervals of every fifty minutes, Old Faithful erupts with a spume of about four thousand gallons of water reaching more than sixty feet into the air. Old Faithful, one of only three such regularly erupting geysers in the world, is certainly an interesting phenomenon although the staging is a bit honky-tonk.

Leaving Calistoga take the Petrified Forest Road west in the direction of Santa Rosa forsaking the Napa Valley for the neighboring Sonoma Wine Valley. The road climbs and winds a scenic ten miles through forest and past pastures where cattle graze next to neighboring vineyards and orchards of apples and almonds. You may wish to stop at the rather commercial California Petrified Forest, a grove of redwoods that was petrified by ash from the volcanic eruption of Mount St. Helena over six million years ago. It is this same ash that is responsible for fertile wine valley soil.

On the residential outskirts of Santa Rosa Petrified Forest Road merges with Highway 12 and you turn south (left) toward Sonoma. This highway travels down the center of

Sonoma Valley, often referred to as the "Valley of the Moon," after Jack London's famous novel of the same name. London fell in love with Sonoma Valley's magnificent landscape—a wondrous mix of high hills, oak-covered knolls, open pastures, forests of oaks, madrones, fir and redwood trees, grassy fields and streams. The author chose the valley as his home—"a quiet place in the country to write and loaf in and get out of nature that something which we all need, only most of us don't know it."

Your first destination in this lovely valley, Château St. Jean, lies about seven miles south of Santa Rosa on the left, on Highway 12. An extremely pretty road winds up through the vineyards to the strikingly beautiful winery and main house surrounded by lush lawns. With the exception of its mock tower, Château St. Jean is Mediterranean French in its architecture; its red tile roofs and arched entries stunning against a backdrop of green hills. The estate is dedicated exclusively to the production of premium wines, but as a visitor you will feel that the winery's chief concern is making visitors feel welcome by outlining a very comprehensive self-guided tour of the wine making process. After the tour you cross the courtyard to the original "château" for tasting. Questions you have will be answered graciously. For information call: (707) 833-4134.

The next winery, Kenwood, is next door and completely different in character. Kenwood Vineyards occupies an attractive complex of old-wooden barns where wine is produced, stored and tasted. Tours of this small winery are offered by appointment on Wednesdays and tastings are offered daily between 10:00 a.m. and 4:30 p.m., tel: (707) 833-5891.

Nearby Glen Ellen, a quiet little country town set in a wooded valley, lies just a few miles south of Beltane Ranch, one of our favorite California bed and breakfasts. Travel the main road through Glen Ellen off Highway 12, following signs for Jack London State Park. Before you reach the park, take time to visit the Glen Ellen Winery, a family-run winery in the truest sense of the word—signs warn to watch for children at play. From babies to Goober, the family dog and "official reception committee," everyone at Glen Ellen is warm and friendly. If it's close to lunch time, take advantage of picnic tables set under redwood trees. The tasting room is quite a hike from the parking lot, so if someone in your party has difficulty with a hilly driveway, continue on to the handicapped area, or circle round to drop them off in the front. The Benziger family were wine importers in New York and moved here less than ten years ago to produce their own wines. They have concentrated on marketing their moderately priced wines to large outlets, consequently most Californians are familiar with their wine. Tours are offered daily, appointments are not necessary. For more information call: (707) 935-3000.

Nearby Jack London State Park, where Jack London is buried, is a lovely wooded park established as a tribute to the famous author who has had such an impact on the Sonoma Valley. This strikingly handsome man lived a life of rugged adventure and wrote passionately about life's struggles and how to survive them with integrity. In the sixteen years prior to his death at age forty, he wrote fifty novels that were immensely popular and are today considered classics. Two of his more renowned novels are *Call of the Wild* and *Sea Wolf*. This park offers a fitting tribute to Jack London, a courageous, dynamic man, full of life and concern for others. (Open all year, admission is $5 per vehicle, for information call: (707) 938-5216.)

In the park you can visit the ruins of Wolf House (London's dream house which mysteriously burned to the ground the night of its completion), Beauty Cottage (the cottage where London wrote much of his later work) and the House of Happy Walls (the home that Charmian London built after her husband's death). The House of Happy Walls is now an interesting museum that depicts London's life through numerous photographs, writings and furnishings that belonged to the author. From the museum walks lead to the other homes and the gravesite. From the park return to Arnold Drive and travel south (past the Sonoma State Home) to Madrone where you turn left, crossing over to Highway 12 that takes you into Sonoma.

Sonoma is a gem of a town. By simply exploring the boundaries of its main square you will glimpse some of California's most important periods in history. (A small admission price is charged to tour Sonoma's historic buildings.) On the square's northern edge sits the Sonoma Barracks, a two-story, adobe building that was the Mexican Provincial headquarters for the Northern Frontier under the command of General Vallejo. The adjacent wood-frame Toscano Hotel has been restored and on weekends guides provide interesting tours through the rooms. The nearby Mission San Francisco Solano De Sonoma, the last Franciscan mission built in California, was restored in the early 1900's. If you visit during the week you may see elementary-school children, dressed as missionaries with their simple cloaks and rope ties, experiencing history "hands on" as they work with crafts and tools from the days of the missionaries. In one hall of the mission is an unusually beautiful collection of watercolor paintings of many of California's missions. The long, low adobe building across the way, the Blue Wig Inn, originally built to house soldiers assigned to the mission, enjoyed a more colorful existence as a saloon and gambling room during the Gold Rush days.

In addition to the historic sites on Sonoma's plaza, there are numerous shops and boutiques to investigate. There are some wonderful specialty food stores where you can purchase picnic supplies. The Sonoma Cheese Factory on Spain Street is interesting to visit and easy to pop into between historic sites. The front of the shop has a deli and at the back, behind a glass partition, you can observe the making of cheese. On East Street, you can purchase delicious bread at the Sonoma French Bread shop and enjoy a tasty ice cream at the ice cream parlor.

Leaving the Square, go east on Napa Boulevard for two miles to Old Winery Road where you turn left to the Buena Vista Winery, the region's oldest winery. Nestled in a wooded glen, the old stone, ivy-covered buildings are very picturesque with arched caverns and old stone walls. Picnic tables are set under the trees (it is hard to find a spot in the summer). Wine tasting is offered in the old press house and a self-guided tour directs you through the old stone barn and three tunnels.

Mission San Francisco Solano Sonoma

General Vallejo, the Military Commander and Director of colonization of the Northern Frontier (until the Bear Flag Revolution established California as a free and independent republic) lived nearby with his wife and their twelve children.

Vallejo's Home, "Lachryma Montis" (translated to mean mountain tear, an adaptation of the Indian name given to a free-flowing spring that surrounds the property), is well signposted on the outskirts of town on Spain Street. In its day this lovely Victorian-style home was considered on of the most elegant and lavishly decorated homes in the area, and is still attractively furnished.

After you leave the Sonoma Valley, one more winery awaits you as you return to San Francisco. When Highway 12 dead ends at Highway 116, turn right onto Highway 116 (signposted Petaluma) and at the intersection of Highway 121 turn left in the direction of San Francisco. A short drive brings you to the Gloria Ferrer Winery, a fitting grand finale for this wine country itinerary. The Ferrer family hails from Catalonia in Spain and have only recently brought their expertise on Spanish sparkling wines to the Sonoma Valley. Consequently, the handsome winery with its stucco walls and tiled roof resembles a small Catalonian village. A wide road sweeps up to the winery through the vineyards. The very informative tours last half an hour and are available daily between 11:00 a.m. and 4:00 p.m. They start from the tasting room, a large, spacious room whose windows look out over the vineyards and valley. Most of the narrative is given in a room decorated with wine making instruments used a half a century ago in the Ferrer's winery in Spain. The riddling of the bottles to capture the sediment is explained, and then you go to the observation room to see the process of freezing then disgorging the sediment, corking, cleaning and labeling the bottles of sparkling wine. The tour then descends into a maze of interconnected wine storage tunnels. It is awesome to stand next to towering heights of stacked bottles. The tour concludes back in the tasting room. A fee is charged to sample the sparkling wine. For further information call: (707) 996-7256.

From the Gloria Ferrer winery it is about an hour's drive back to San Francisco by continuing along Highway 121 to Highway 37 and onto Highway 101 which takes you over the Golden Gate Bridge into San Francisco.

NOTE: We have tried to be as accurate as possible when giving information about touring wineries, but things change, so be certain to give each winery a call in advance to see whether or not they are open and whether you need an appointment for a tour or tasting.

Places to Stay

The location of the Albion River Inn is splendid, right on the bluff overlooking the handsome bay formed by the mouth of the Albion River as it flows into the ocean. Although this is a newly built hotel, the architecture creates the ambiance of a New England village: softly-hued clusters of cottages perch on the cliffs surrounded by a meadow where long grass waves in the wind. Gardens filled with brightly colored flowers line the walkways along the bluff and the quiet is broken only by the deep-throated call of the fog horn. Each of the bedrooms offers a sweeping view of the inlet where the fishing boats bob about in the ever-changing tides. All of the rooms are spacious, romantic and very private—many even have wood-burning fireplaces. The decor is most attractive and although not antique, reflects the hand of a professional decorator. There is an excellent restaurant adjacent to the inn with picture windows overlooking the sea—it is a good idea to request dinner reservations in advance. A hearty breakfast is offered each morning including fresh juices, seasonal fruits, made-to-order eggs, toast, home-fried potatoes, omelets, etc. Also coffee makers are set up in each room so guests can enjoy hot drinks whenever they want. *Directions:* From San Francisco drive north on Highway 101 to Cloverdale, west on Highway 128 to Highway 1 and north three miles to Albion. The Albion River Inn is on the northwest side of the Albion Bridge.

ALBION RIVER INN
Innkeepers: Flurry Healy & Peter Wells
3790 N. Highway One, P.O. Box 100
Albion, CA 95410
tel: (707) 937-1919
20 bedrooms with private bathroom
Double from $85 to $225
Open all year
Credit cards: MC VS
Children accepted

Amador City with its quaint old-west style houses was a bustle of activity during the Gold Rush days. Now it's a peaceful place (except for the logging trucks which rumble through town periodically), with its old wooden stores full of antique and craft shops, and the Imperial Hotel, looking as though it belongs in a cowboy movie. There is immediate charm as soon as you walk into this renovated western hotel where you wouldn't be surprised to see prospectors leaning at the bar. Beyond the bar lies a spacious, high ceilinged dining room, its red brick walls hung with fanciful Victorian art. Dining is casual, the menu is short: usually three appetizers, seven entrees, five or six desserts. Upstairs the six bedrooms are a delight—nothing fancy or frilly, but each well thought out and accompanied by a small, sparkling bathroom with tub or shower and heated towel bar. Room 6, decorated warmly in tans and navy, is a real winner with an elaborate art deco bed. The whimsical hand-painted headboard in Room 5 is echoed in the paintings of clothes on the closet in Room 3. Rooms 1 and 2 share the large balcony at the front of the hotel. There are two sets of adjoining rooms. Guests help themselves to early morning coffee and tea before going in for breakfast. *Directions:* Amador City straddles Highway 49, six miles north of Jackson. The Imperial Hotel is on your right at the bend in the main street.

IMPERIAL HOTEL
Innkeepers: Bruce Sherrill & Dale Martin
14202 Highway 49, P.O. Box 195
Amador City, CA 95601
tel: (209) 267-9172
6 bedrooms with private bathroom
Double from $75 to $90
Open all year
Credit cards: all major
Children accepted

A guest at our own inn recommended Cooper House with raves as a perfect retreat in the Gold Rush country. Built in 1911, Cooper House was home to Dr. George P. Cooper, accommodating both his family and patients of the gold mining community. Set above the heart of town, shaded by trees and enjoying lush green lawns and terraced gardens, Cooper House was and is still today considered one of the finest homes in town. Enter off the patio to the living room warmed by a large open fireplace. Just off the living room, the Cabernet room enjoys a little sitting area (a queen sleeper) an ensuite bedroom and a bathroom tucked 'round the corner. It is a nice setup if travelling with children. Across the hall from the Cabernet room, the Chardonnay suite is a cozy room with access to a private deck. Climb the stairs to the Zinfandel Suite that used to serve as Dr. Cooper's office and examining room. With its private entrance from the street, this suite also enjoys a private deck off the French doors and lots of sunshine. Innkeepers Tom and Kathy are very welcoming. Refreshments are offered in the afternoon and a full breakfast is served each morning. Although, the Cooper House does not have its own pool, the public pool is close by and Kathy can also direct you to the "Fireman's Hole"—a natural pool with a rope swing—perfect for children and a hot gold country afternoon. *Directions*: A small sign off Main Street directs you just a half block up Raspberry Street and then another sign takes you left on Church Street. The Cooper House is just on the left.

COOPER HOUSE
Innkeepers: Tom and Kathy Reese
1184 Church Street, P.O. Box 1388
Angels Camp, CA 95222
tel: (209) 736-2145, fax: (209) 736-9124
3 bedrooms with private bathroom
Double from $90
Open all year
Credit cards: all major
Children accepted

Aptos, just two hours south of San Francisco, is best known as a beach resort. Most tourists never realize that tucked into the coastal hills are beautiful redwood glens and adjacent to a 10,000 acre forest of redwoods, creeks and trails is Mangels House, an elegant, large, redwood home, built in the 1880's, painted white and wrapped in a two-tiered verandah. Once the holiday home of the wealthy Mangels family, whose fortune was in sugar beets; Mangels House now belongs to Jacqueline and Ron Fisher. You enter into a large living room dominated by a tall stone fireplace surrounded by two comfortable floral-patterned sofas and an easy chair. To the left is a formal dining room where a full breakfast is served each morning. The five individually decorated bedrooms vary considerably in size. Four rooms have a traditional ambiance while the other has an African motif, a reflection of the years the Fishers lived in Africa. One of the nicest aspects of Mangels House is that it is nestled in the woodlands, yet is only a five-minute drive to the beach. *Directions:* From Santa Cruz, drive six miles south on Highway 1, taking the Seacliff Beach-Aptos exit over the freeway (away from the bay). Turn right at the traffic light to Soquel Drive. Just before the Aptos Station Shopping Center turn left onto Aptos Creek Road (also entrance to State Park). The house is a half mile on your right.

MANGELS HOUSE
Innkeeper: Jacqueline Fisher
570 Aptos Creek Road
Aptos, CA 95001
tel: (408) 688-7982
5 bedrooms with private bathroom
Double from $98 to $125
Closed Christmas
Credit cards: all major
Children accepted over 12

The Lodge at Manuel Mill enjoys an idyllic setting at the end of what seemed at best a rough, dirt logging road. Although the lodge is open all year, I strongly recommend calling to see if the road is navigable after a rainstorm or snow. Secluded on forty-three acres of woods, the peaceful setting was once home to a Miwuk tribe and in 1850 was the site of a logging mill. The main building of the lodge is on the banks of the old mill pond, here you find badminton, volleyball, horse shoes, picnic tables and a row boat all ready for guests to use. A ski lodge feeling prevails in the warm and inviting living room with comfy sofas and armchairs clustered around a large open fireplace and a pair of old wooden skis hung on the wall. The smallest guestroom, whose cozy double bed dominates the decor, is tucked just off the living room. The other guestrooms open individually onto the expanse of back deck that overlooks the pond and enjoys the quiet of the setting broken only by the sound of rushing water. Rooms are intimate and each decorated to reflect the character of its namesake, from the uninhibited performer of Gold Rush days, Lottie Crabtree, to the masculine lair of the former lumberjack, Manuel Mill. The decor is Victorian with a clever flair for incorporating various knickknacks into the theme and arrangement. Old lace gloves drape gracefully over a leather suitcase, a collage of old buttons are framed and hung on the wall, breakfast tables set on the back deck are dressed with attractive grouping of leather bound books and fruit. *Call for directions.*

LODGE AT MANUEL MILL
Innkeepers: Michael and Lyn Gilman
White Pines Road, P.O. Box 998
Arnold, CA 95223
tel: (209) 795-2622
5 bedrooms with private bathroom
Double from $95 to $120
Open all year
Credit cards: MC VS
Children accepted

The lovely Ballard Inn is located in the Santa Ynez Valley, a lush region of rolling hills planted with vineyards or sectioned off with white picket fences. Set just off the road, the Ballard was built as an inn, but carries the appearance of a gracious sprawling residence. White picket fences enclose its narrow front garden and a wide porch winds round it. The dining room where bountiful breakfasts are served with an offering of two or three hot selections is located just off the entry to the right. To the left, another cozy room invites one to linger over a buffet of afternoon hors d'oeuvres, or venture on into the sitting room where large deep sofas steal you away for lazy conversations in front of an open fireplace. Guestrooms are located upstairs or in a neighboring wing just off the graveled driveway. Rooms are comfortable, attractively decorated, each with a small, functional private bathroom. Although, at first, rooms overlooking the front garden seem preferable to those overlooking the parking, for quiet, select a room at back as locals do head off to work and early morning traffic breaks the silence of the country morning. A final note: if you like horses, ask about the neighboring miniature horse farm. We visited in spring when every mother was matched with a miniature foal—adorable. *Directions:* Take Route 246 off Highway 101 in the direction of Solvang. Travel north on Alamo Pintado Road and then east on Baseline Road. The Ballard Inn is on the right.

THE BALLARD INN
Owners: Steve Hyslop & Larry Stone
Innkeeper: Kelly Robinson
2436 Baseline Avenue, Ballard, CA 93463
tel: (805) 688-7770, fax: (805) 688-9560
15 bedrooms with private bathroom
Double from $160 to $195
Closed Christmas
Credit cards: all major
Children accepted

The rustic yet deluxe Gold Mountain Manor was constructed in the late 1920's for Alexander Barret (a wealthy Hollywood investor) and his beautiful bride, Bessie. Setback on a lush green lawn shaded by towering pines, the mansion was a show place in its time: bird's eye maple floors, beamed ceilings, nine bedrooms, eight fireplaces, a wine cellar, chauffeur's quarters, etc. Today the mountain log cabin is so cozy and inviting that it is often used as a backdrop for magazine layouts—the central parlor whose walls are hung with prints has a dramatic stone fireplace fronted by inviting, well-worn chairs. The seven bedrooms each, have a different decor—original stencil patterns dress a number of the walls to blend with or set a theme. Although only three of the rooms have private baths, the Wildcat Room, small but cozy with velvet curtains, is the only room without a private fireplace. The Lucky Baldwin Room, handsomely decorated in plaids, has tartan robes laid out for guests' use. The Clark Gable Room commemorates the time this famous actor brought his love, Carole Lombard, for a romantic retreat: the fireplace is from his mountain cabin in Fawnskin. *Directions:* From Highway 10 exit on University in Redlands. Go north to Lugonia (Highway 38). Follow 38 into the mountains. Turn right at first stoplight (Greenway). Turn left at North Shore Drive. Go two blocks and turn right on Anita.

GOLD MOUNTAIN MANOR
Owners: Conny & John Ridgway
Innkeeper: Donna Doran
1117 Anita, P.O. Box 2027
Big Bear Lake, CA 92314
tel: (909) 585-6997
7 bedrooms, 3 with private bathroom
Double from $75 to $195
Open all year
Credit cards: MC VS
Children accepted over 12

The Post Ranch Inn is a stunning resort (a swimming pool, health spa, hiking trails, ocean-view restaurant and bar, library) built on ninety-eight acres overlooking the Big Sur coast. Great care has been taken to preserve the natural beauty and tranquillity of the prize site (homesteaded in the mid-1800's by William Post and his Indian wife, Anselma Onesimo). The reception building is just off Highway 1 and guards the private drive that winds up to the bluffs, the restaurant and accommodation. Cars are discreetly left near the reception area and guests are transported to their rooms by van. One can select from coastal cottages snuggled into the hillside high above the ocean with roofs of sod and panoramic water views or the most unusual tree-house-like units, the Butterfly houses, perched on stilts that look through the trees to the distant mountains. Each room is named for one of Big Sur's early settlers and is appropriately designed with wood siding inside and out, handsome slate in the bathrooms and accents of deep-sea-blue fabrics. All of the rooms have fireplaces, jacuzzi tubs and mini-bars. Although extremely expensive, there are few places in California where one can enjoy accommodation perched above the ocean. *Directions:* Located thirty miles south of Carmel, in Big Sur, on the west side of the Highway 1.

POST RANCH INN
Owner: Michael Freed
Innkeeper: Jim Pawling
Highway 1, P.O. Box 219
Big Sur, CA 93920
tel: (408) 667-2200, fax: (408) 667-2824
30 bedrooms with private bathroom
Double from $255 to $495
Open all year
Credit cards: all major
Inappropriate for children

Ventana, surrounded by two hundred forty acres of meadows and forests, is nestled in Big Sur, a gorgeous stretch of coast where the hills plunge down to meet the crashing sea. In contrast to the coastline, there is nothing rugged about Ventana. It pretends to be somewhat rustic, but in reality, behind the weathered wooden facade of the cottages, lies a most sophisticated, deluxe resort where guests are pampered and provided with every luxury. The Ventana has grown in stages, so each cluster of natural wood buildings has its own patina of age. The exteriors are not outstanding, but, inside, each guest room is spacious and decorator-perfect. The decor varies (depending upon which section you are in) but each guest room has the same country ambiance with natural wood paneling, luxurious fabrics and wicker chairs. Most rooms have a large terrace with a latticed wood screen—some have private hot tubs. All have a pretty view either of the hills and forest or to the sea on the far horizon. There are two lounges where wine and cheese are served in the afternoon and breakfast (a scrumptious buffet of home-baked pastries and fruit) is set out each morning. Guests can either take a tray to their room, or eat on one of the tables in the lounge or outside on the terrace. There are also two 75-foot swimming pools with adjacent hot tubs. *Directions:* Twenty-eight miles south of Carmel on Highway 1.

VENTANA
Innkeeper: Robert Bussinger
Highway 1
Big Sur, CA 93920
tel: (408) 667-2331, fax (408) 667-2287
60 bedrooms with private bathroom
Double from $180 to $360
Suite from $320 to $790
Open all year
Credit cards: all major
Inappropriate for children

Accommodations within walking distance to Calistoga's shops and restaurants are offered at the prettily elegant Christopher's Inn. The talents of Christopher Layton, a San Francisco architect and landscape designer are ever present in this country inn. What was once three buildings are now one and the gardens are lovely. Finished in a cozy English country style, each of the guestrooms is decorated individually and completely with *Laura Ashley* linens, window and wall coverings, down to the padded clothes' hangars in the closet areas. They seemed as fresh and pretty as band boxes. Unfortunately, at the time of my visit I was unable to see all of the rooms, the ones I was able to see were on the small side. However, although small, they all have nice private baths, large windows and their own private porch or garden patio areas complete with matching seating, shielded from walkways and the parking areas. Five of the rooms offer the warmth and romance of fireplaces. Details such as the carefully tended landscape, fresh flowers and antiques make this a special place to stay. A country basket is delivered mornings with a bounty of delicious treats: fresh coffee, juice, croissants or Danish, fresh fruit with yogurt or warm baked cobbler. The staff at Christopher's are cheery and helpful. *Directions*: The inn is located in Calistoga, seven miles north of St. Helena. The inn's parking lot is five hundred yards past the tractors, on the right, close to the intersection of Foothill Boulevard and Lincoln.

CHRISTOPHER'S INN
Innkeepers: Adele & Christopher Layton
1010 Foothill Boulevard
Calistoga, CA 94515
tel: (707) 942-5755
10 bedrooms with private bathroom
Double from $117 to $184
Open all year
Credit cards: all major
Children accepted

With the Hanns Kornell Winery as its neighbor, the Larkmead Country Inn is tucked a short distance off the St. Helena Highway on Larkmead Lane. Set behind a fieldstone fence and gates, this lovely two-story, white clapboard home was built by one of the first wine producing families in the Napa Valley. Its broad porches shaded by magnificent sycamores, magnolias and cypress trees provide a lovely place to settle after a day of wine tasting. The entrance to the inn is at back and up a flight of stairs to the second floor. Owned and managed by Gene and Joan Garbarino, the inn is beautifully furnished with antiques, lovely paintings, prints and Persian carpets. Guests are encouraged to enjoy the warm ambiance of the central living room with a large fireplace, bay window and upstairs porch. The four guest rooms are named after wines of the Napa Valley and appropriately look out over the surrounding vineyards. Chardonnay and Chablis are twin-bedded rooms while Chenin Blanc and Beaujolais are furnished with queen beds. Each room is attractively furnished, is air-conditioned and has a private bath or shower. Chablis and Beaujolais enjoy the privacy of an enclosed porch. *Directions*: Located four and a half miles north of St. Helena off Highway 29 on Larkmead Lane. Look for the home on the right just before the Hanns Kornell Winery—there is no sign advertising the inn.

LARKMEAD COUNTRY INN
Innkeepers: Joan & Gene Garbarino
1103 Larkmead Lane
Calistoga, CA 94515
tel: (707) 942-5360
4 bedrooms with private bathroom
Double from $100 to $125
Closed December & January
Credit cards: none accepted
Children accepted over 14

Meadowlark Country House is located at the northernmost end of the Napa Valley, buffered from any road noise by a long drive and twenty acres of grounds that contain a large swimming pool, a pasture grazed by magnificent Arabian horses and wood-land walks that wind beneath cherry trees. The two-story home appears new, but was originally built in 1886. Kurt Stevens, the owner, decorated his inn combining English antiques with contemporary furniture. Inside, light wood floors contrast beautifully with country-pine antiques and handsome fabrics. The atmosphere (one of sophisticated elegance) and the hospitality both reflect Kurt's European background. This is a country house where guests can relax and make themselves "at home." The spacious living room with its large French windows, the country-French dining room and large verandah are all for guests' use. Kurt sets guests at ease and wants them to enjoy the inn as if it were their home in the country. Meadowlark opened in the spring of 1988 and its guest register reflects numerous repeat visitors. One guest who reserved a room confusing the inn with the super deluxe Meadowood Resort, claims it is the "best mistake she ever made!" *Directions:* Take Foothill Boulevard north from Calistoga to Petrified Forest Road. The road will be posted with signs to San Francisco and Santa Rosa. Meadowlark is on the left just a few hundred yards off Petrified Forest Road.

MEADOWLARK COUNTRY HOUSE
Innkeeper: Kurt Stevens
601 Petrified Forest Road
Calistoga, CA 94515
tel: (707) 942-5651
4 bedrooms with private bathroom
Double from $110 to $125
Open all year
Credit cards: MC VS
Children accepted over 12

Tucked on a wooded hillside on the west side of the Napa Valley, the contemporary-designed Quail Mountain Bed & Breakfast brings the forest into the home. The approach is a narrow paved road that winds up through madrona, douglas fir, oak, dogwood, manzanita and redwood trees. The setting is secluded, tranquil and beautiful: twenty-six acres with vineyard and two running streams shared with deer, raccoons, squirrels and numerous species of birds and quail. In warm months guests gather in the sunroom where wicker chairs and white wrought-iron furniture are set on slate floors and floor-to-ceiling windows look out onto the expanse of greenery. The inn's three guestrooms, located down one wing of the inn, are quite small—basically large enough to accommodate the king-size bed decked with goose down pillows, comforters and hand made quilts. Each has a private bathroom tucked into a small nook. Stepping stones lead down the side of the house to a beautifully landscaped pool enveloped by redwoods and blue spruce. The inn's garden and fruit orchard provide the morning fare: baked apples, gingered pears, pumpkin pancakes. *Directions:* North on Highway 29 from St. Helena, take the first road on the left after passing Dunaweal Lane and Stonegate Winery. About a quarter of a mile on the right is the turnoff to Quail Mountain Bed & Breakfast.

QUAIL MOUNTAIN BED & BREAKFAST
Innkeepers: Alma & Don Swiers
4455 North Saint Helena Highway
Calistoga, CA 94515
tel: (707) 942-0316
3 bedrooms with private bathroom
Double from $100 to $110; Suite $125
Open all year
Credit cards: MC VS
Inappropriate for children.

Although located on the Silverado Trail, one of the two main arteries through the Napa Valley, Scarlett's Country Inn, tucked in a pocket canyon, is blissfully hidden from the road. The inn consists of two buildings: the original turn-of-the century farmhouse with two suites, and behind it, a newer ranch house with one guest room, dining room and kitchen. Ask to stay in the original farmhouse which is charming, like a doll house with just two suites, each with its private entrance. The Gamay Suite has a bathroom on the first floor and upstairs a small parlor plus a bedroom tucked under the eaves. The Camellia Suite on the first floor is a real prize with a living room with sofa bed, wood-burning fireplace and a wet bar, plus a separate bedroom. In front of the house the lawn is shaded by a large tree from which hangs an old-fashioned rope swing. In the rear garden is a beautiful swimming pool, tranquilly set amongst the trees. In addition there is an aviary with colorful finches and two plump hens (Blondie and Blackie). Although small, Scarlett's Country Inn offers many niceties often lacking in much fanciers hotels: daily fresh flowers in each of the rooms, turn down service at night, and complimentary wine upon check in. *Directions:* Located just about mid-way between Calistoga and St. Helena on the Silverado Trail. Watch carefully for the address number (3918) indicating the small lane leading east from the main road to the inn.

SCARLETT'S COUNTRY INN
Innkeeper: Scarlett Dwyer
3918 Silverado Trail, North
Calistoga, CA 94515
tel: (707) 942-6669, fax: (916) 992-1336
3 bedrooms with private bathroom
Double from $95 to $150
Open all year
Credit cards: none accepted
Children accepted

The Silver Rose Inn, situated on an oak-studded knoll just to the east of Calistoga, is cleverly named for its position at the junction of the Silverado Trail and Rosedale Road. Flagstone steps lead up to the front door of this relatively new two-story building of wood and shingle. From the entrance one looks down into the large Gathering Room with its huge stone fireplace and vaulted ceilings and up to the railed walkway that leads to the nine guest rooms whose names denote their individual themes: the Oriental Suite enjoys a large private balcony and jacuzzi tub; Bears in Burgundy abounds with teddy bears; Peach Delight is frilly and romantic; Country Blue is restful in shades of dusty blue; Turn of the Century is decorated with pieces of old lace, period dolls and has a clawfoot tub. Four new "theme" rooms have been added as of May, 1993. Although time has yet to soften and warm the "newness," the inn has two impressive features: its setting and its gracious owners. Silver Rose Inn terraces up from a magnificently landscaped pool carved out of the natural rock hillside, and looks out over vineyards, open fields and surrounding hillsides. *Directions:* From downtown Calistoga travel east on Lincoln avenue and take the Brannon Street cutoff to the Silverado Trail. Take a short jog south on the Silverado Trail and then the first, almost immediate, left on Rosedale Road. The entrance to the Silver Rose Inn is just on the right.

SILVER ROSE INN
Innkeepers: Sally and J-Paul Dumont
351 Rosedale Road
Calistoga, CA 94515
tel: (707) 942-9581, fax: (707) 942-0841
9 bedrooms with private bathroom
Double from $115 to $195
Suite from $160 to $185
Open all year
Credit cards: all major
Inappropriate for children

If a comfortable, homey atmosphere is what pleases you, then the Zinfandel House is just that place. From the moment you're cheerily greeted over the front deck railing of this brown, wood-sided, contemporary home by innkeeper, Bette Starke, a sense of warm hospitality pervades your stay. A wonderful view overlooking vineyards and mountains awaits from atop the deck, as the inn is perched high on the west side of the valley. Two of the bedrooms are cozily decorated and share a bath, the largest room with its own bath, shares the view with a reading room and comfortable living room. All three have goose down pillows, comforters and handmade quilts. The Starkes, long-time residents of the valley, offer their knowledge on food, wine and the area. They'll gladly make dinner reservations at the many very good restaurants this valley has to offer. Their guest book is a delightful collection of comments and memories—Bette takes polaroids of everyone who stays with them and they become part of her extended family! Located a short distance above Highway 29, half way between the towns of St. Helena and Calistoga, this inn makes a great spot to base your wine country adventures. *Directions:* On Highway 29, four miles outside St. Helena and about two hundred yards past Larkmead Lane on the right, slow down, and look for a group of mailboxes, opposite these, you turn left up Summit Road, bear left around some old farm buildings and go up slowly three tenths of a mile from the highway to the inn's marked driveway on your left.

ZINFANDEL HOUSE
Innkeepers: Bette & George Starke
1253 Summit Drive
Calistoga, CA 94515
tel: (707) 942-0733, fax:(707) 942-4618
3 bedrooms, 2 with private bathroom
Double from $83 to $111
Open all year
Credit cards: none accepted
Inappropriate for children

As an alternative to the cute and frilly bed and breakfasts, near Cambria's shops and galleries, the Blue Whale offers guests more privacy and the opportunity to stroll for miles along Moonstone Beach. The front room and parlor enjoy views across the road to the beach and expansive ocean through six large picture windows. It is here that guests are served a delicious breakfast, and wine, cheese and cookies are set out in an afternoon. Stretching out behind the main building are the newly constructed guestrooms, each opening at an angle onto a border of front garden that buffers the rooms from the parallel parking. Country in their decor, the rooms are attractive in their light pine furnishings, chintz and floral fabrics and canopy beds. Each of the spacious bedrooms has television, telephone, a refrigerator, and a tiled modern bathroom. Karleen and Bob Hathcock, your charming hosts, extend a warm welcome and offer gracious service. Motels and hotels line the beach frontage and without a doubt The Blue Whale is the best of the bunch. *Directions:* Turn west at the exit sign for Moonstone Beach Drive off Highway 1, north on Moonstone Beach Drive past the hotels that line this coastal frontage, to the Blue Whale.

THE BLUE WHALE
Owner: Fred Ushijima
Innkeepers: Karleen & Bob Hathcock
6736 Moonstone Beach Drive
Cambria, CA 93428
tel: (805) 927-4647
6 bedrooms with private bathroom
Double from $135 to $170
Open all year
Credit cards: MC VS
Inappropriate for young children

The Olallieberry Inn, built in 1873 in the Greek revival style, features on the National Register of Historic Buildings. This darling, simple country clapboard cottage on the main street of town, is furnished with pieces representative of the 1800's. The home has been a bed and breakfast for a good many years. The present owners, Carol Ann and Peter Irsfeld, personally manage their inn and give guests a warm welcome. A guest book is left in every room and each is filled with telling praises. The inn has six bedrooms, three clustered upstairs and three downstairs. They are all with private bath, but not all bathrooms are en suite—if a bathroom is located down the hall from a room, a small blackboard directs you to its location. The rooms are intimate in size and the bedroom decor is very romantic, fussy Victorian, with lots of lace and feminine touches. The country kitchen (the "gathering room") looks out onto the greenery of the back yard with a rather ornate fountain, lawn and the Santa Rosa Creek. An elegant full breakfast is served (including, of course, Olallieberry jam). Each evening complimentary wine and appetizers are served in the intimate front parlor. Carol Ann and Peter take pride in pampering and spoiling their guests, striving to give the personal touch. *Directions:* The Olallieberry Inn is on Cambria's Main Street just a few blocks south of East Village.

OLALLIEBERRY INN
Innkeepers: Carol Ann & Peter Irsfeld
2476 Main Street
Cambria, CA 93428
tel: (805) 927-3222
6 bedrooms with private bathroom
Double from $85 to $125
Open all year
Credit cards: MC VS
Inappropriate for young children

The Inn at Depot Hill, located just two blocks up the hill from the beach and picturesque village of Capitola-by-the-Sea, dates back to 1901 when it was built as a Southern Pacific railroad station. The imaginative decor reflects the theme of first class train travel at the turn-of-the-century: the bedrooms, not overly spacious, are lovingly decorated and named after different parts of the world—as if a guest were taking a railway journey and stopping at different destinations. Each bedroom is meticulous in decor—"decorator perfect" down to the tiniest detail. Suzie Lankes (whose grandfather was an architect for the Southern Pacific Railroad) has added many of her own caring touches such as real linen sheets, lacy pillowcases and sumptuous feather beds. Plus there are a wealth of other amenities: writing desks, tastefully cupboarded televisions and VCRs, fireplaces, bathrobes, hair dryers, luxurious marble bathrooms, some jacuzzi tubs on private outdoor patios, even mini-televisions in all of the bathrooms. An elegant breakfast is served each morning either in the dining room, in the romantic walled garden, or brought to your room. Complimentary early evening wine and hors d'oeuvres are served from the dining room buffet as well as late evening desserts and port. *Directions:* South on Highway 1 from Santa Cruz. Take the Park Avenue exit, turn right and go one mile. Turn left onto Monterey, then immediately left into the inn's driveway.

THE INN AT DEPOT HILL
Owners: Suzie Lankes & Dan Floyd
250 Monterey Avenue
Capitola, CA 95010
tel: (408) 462-3376, fax: (408) 462-3697
8 bedrooms with private bathroom
Double from $155 to $250
Open all year
Credit cards: all major
Children accepted

The Cobblestone Inn is a remarkable conversion of a rather ordinary motel into a country inn with great appeal: the central parking courtyard has been paved and enhanced with trees, flowers and creepers, a brick patio has been set with tables and chairs and the inn has been attractively decorated and furnished in an appealing English-country style. The Cobblestone Inn is part of a group of small hotels that pride themselves on having perfected the art of personalized innkeeping. This one is certainly no exception. The staff are young, enthusiastic and attentive and you feel thoroughly spoiled by all the little extras: flowers, fruit, balloons announcing special occasions, a handwritten note welcoming you by name, your bed turned down at night and a newspaper at your door in the morning. Besides their delightful decor, bedrooms have every amenity: good reading lights, refrigerator, phone, television and fireplace. Beverages and snacks are always available. Hearty hors d'oeuvres arrive in the evening. A full buffet breakfast is served and you can take it outside to the patio to enjoy the sunshine of a Carmel morning. With all this comfort and attention it is not surprising that reservations need to be made well in advance. *Directions:* From Highway 1 take the Ocean Avenue exit, then turn left on Junipero. The Cobblestone is on your right on the corner of 8th Street.

COBBLESTONE INN
Innkeeper: Ray Farnsworth
Corner of Junipero & 8th St., P.O. Box 3185
Carmel, CA 93921
tel: (408) 625-5222, fax: (408) 625-0478
24 bedrooms with private bathroom
Double from $95 to $175
Open all year
Credit cards: all major
Children accepted

In a quiet district of Carmel within easy walking distance of Ocean Avenue (the principal shopping street) stands The Happy Landing, a group of bright pink color washed cottages, accented by vivid teal blue paint work. The cottages are clustered around beautiful gardens banked high with colorful flowers. Pots and baskets of flowers fill every nook and cranny. This picture-perfect garden contains an array of whimsical garden statuary, such as a gnome fishing in the pond, a frog fountain and several large metal birds. Arched cottage doors lead into the bedrooms where high cathedral ceilings give a spacious feeling. The rooms appear a bit dated, though pleasantly furnished; some have fireplaces and sitting rooms and all have spotless older-style bathrooms. Everything throughout the inn is immaculately tended. A fun touch: when you open your curtains in the morning it is the signal that you would like your breakfast tray brought to you. Many guests enjoy breakfast in the pretty garden amongst the flowers. Guests are welcome to use the distinctive, large, cathedral- ceilinged reception/common room where teas and coffee are provided in the afternoon. *Directions:* Take the Ocean Avenue exit from Highway 1 to Monte Verde where you turn right. The Happy Landing is on your right between 5th and 6th Streets.

THE HAPPY LANDING
Owner: Dick Stewart
Innkeeper: Robert Ballard
Monte Verde, P.O. Box 2619
Carmel, CA 93921
tel: (408) 624-7917
7 bedrooms with private bathroom
Double from $90 to $110, Suite: $145
Open all year
Credit cards: MC VS
Children accepted over 12

With the Carmel Mission as its neighbor, the Mission Ranch is located on a sprawling twenty-two acres of pasture stretching towards the distant ocean. The ranch offers a wide range of accommodation in terms of setting, views and, price. The least expensive rooms are found in the old barn and although attractive, offer no view. The six cozy bedrooms in the farmhouse are a little more expensive, have hand made quilts dressing each bed, and enjoy the use of the ornate Victorian living room with its heavy oak furniture and grand piano. The old bunkhouse is a rustic retreat with wooden floors and western style furnishings in the living room and bedroom, and a wrap around porch that enjoys views out to the meadow. Our favorite units are the three triplex cottages and the fourplex near the tennis court. These rooms all enjoy views of the meadow, fireplace, private deck or balcony, and bathrooms equipped with whirlpool tubs. Romantics will enjoy The Loft tucked under the eaves of the haybarn, and warmed by a pot bellied stove. There are six tennis courts, workout room, and The Restaurant at Mission Ranch which is open for casual dining in the evenings and serves as the inn's breakfast room in the mornings. When we stayed the staff was efficient but did not exude the warmth of welcome frequently found at family run hotels. *Directions:* From Highway 1 turn west onto Rio Road, then left at the Mission (Lausuen Road), and wind round the Mission to the ranch.

MISSION RANCH
Owner: Clint Eastwood
Innkeeper: John Purcell
26270 Delores
Carmel, CA 93923
tel: (408) 624-6436, fax: (408) 626-4163
31 bedrooms with private bathroom
Double from $95 to $225
Open all year
Credit cards: all major
Children accepted

Just a block or two off of Ocean Avenue, the principal shopping district of Carmel and just a block or two up from the beautiful blue waters and white sand of its glorious beach is the charming San Antonio House. Set back from the road, the San Antonio House is nestled amongst its own little garden areas with ivy covered walls. Enjoy a lush front lawn shaded by trees, walk under a lovely trellis to another almost secret garden at back. The San Antonio House has the feel of a cottage set in the Cotswolds. Each of the four guestrooms enjoy their own private entrance and wood-burning fireplace. Although not spacious, the rooms are cozy and intimate, a delightful retreat on a foggy coastside day. The Patio room opens onto the front garden with its own private stone patio secluded behind its border of colorful flowers; the Dollhouse is reached by a little stairway, is decorated with lace, tapestry, cuddly bears, a dollhouse and has a cozy little day bed tucked under the eaves in a separate alcove; the Treetops is located above the carriage house, the most spacious, it is secluded and overlooks the gardens, and the delightful Garden Room is country cozy and the sitting area in front of its fireplace is an inviting spot to linger away an afternoon. A bountiful continental breakfast is served on a tray to be enjoyed in the privacy of your room or in the garden. *Directions:* Ocean Avenue west off Highway 1, turn south on San Antonio. San Antonio House is in the first block on the east side.

SAN ANTONIO HOUSE
Innkeeper: Sarah Anne Lee
San Antonio between Ocean & 7th
P.O. Box 3683, Carmel, CA 93921
tel: (408) 624-4334
4 bedrooms with private bathroom
Double from $120 to $165
Open all year
Credit cards: MC VS
Children accepted over 12

With the ocean three blocks away, Sea View Inn is within easy walking distance of the much photographed Carmel beach and it may just be possible to catch the tiniest glimpse of the ocean through the trees from the third floor of the inn. This large Victorian house looks as though it were once a large home, when in fact it has always been an inn. Cream-colored board and batten wainscoting accented by a plate rail displaying antiques and interesting bric-a-brac sets the welcoming mood for the living room and adjacent parlor—both rooms are warmed by cozy fireplaces. Games, books and magazines add a comfortable, lived-in feel. The largest bedrooms are found on the second floor. Room 6 is most attractive in shades of white on white complemented by pine furniture. The adjacent room 7 has stark white walls and window blinds with a dramatic Oriental-style four-poster bed draped with blue and white Chinese motif fabric. The four tiny bedrooms on the third floor provide the snuggest of accommodation tucked under the steeply slanting attic ceilings. Each is lavishly decorated in a mellow English floral print gathered into canopies and covering huge bed pillows. *Directions:* Take the Ocean Avenue exit from Highway 1 to Camino Real where you turn left—Sea View Inn is just after 11th Street on the left hand side.

SEA VIEW INN
Owners: Diane & Marshall Hydorn
Innkeeper: Margo Belt
P.O. Box 4138
Camino Real between 11th & 12th Streets.
Carmel, CA 93921
tel: (408) 624-8778
8 bedrooms, 6 with private bathroom
Double from $85 to $115
Open all year
Credit cards: MC VS
Children accepted over 12

Carmel's quaint gingerbread architecture, profusion of colorful flowers and tall, shady trees are all happily combined at the Vagabond's House Inn. Set around a flagstone courtyard shaded by a giant oak tree and surrounded by fuchsias, azaleas, camellias and rhododendrons, the inn is made up of a group of attached storybook English cottages, brick and half-timbered topped by a thick shake roof, making this one of Carmel's most appealing-looking inns. Most of the guest rooms open directly onto the courtyard with its fountain and profusion of flowers including colorful fuchsias cascading from hanging boxes set in the oak tree. Except for one bedroom (which is a favorite with returning guests), all have been totally refurbished and are very inviting with pretty coordinating fabrics on the comforters, cushions, and window coverings. There are at least two antique clocks in every bedroom, plus, many have their own fireplace and cozy sitting nook. In the morning you phone reception to let them know when you would like a breakfast tray brought to your room. When you check in, be sure not to miss the antique toy collection in the lounge—especially the fabulous lead soldier display in the cabinet. *Directions:* Take the Ocean Avenue exit from Highway 1, turn right on Dolores Street and go a few blocks to 4th Street. The Vagabond's House Inn is on the corner of 4th Street and Dolores.

VAGABOND'S HOUSE INN
Owner: Dennis LeVett
Innkeeper: Honey Spence
Dolores & 4th Street, P.O. Box 2747
Carmel, CA 93921
tel: (408) 624-7738, fax: (408) 626-1234
11 bedrooms with private bathroom
Double from $86 to $148, Suite from $224
Open all year
Credit cards: all major
Children accepted over 12

We tend to stay away from hotels in our recommendations, and yet every once in a while we happen on a hotel, be it large or small, where the service is exceptional and welcoming and we find we want to share it with our readers. This is a lovely, romantic retreat and the fact that it is family owned and operated is evident in the quality and caring of the service. Set high on the hillside above the perhaps, more renowned, Highlands Inn, the Tickle Pink is a two story pink motel-like building that hugs the hillside and looks out through the greenery of Cypress trees to the distant rugged ocean. Rooms are attractively decorated with light pine furnishings in warm colors of beiges,, creams, and pinks. Most guestrooms have their own private deck and handsome stone fireplace; all enjoy a TV with VCR (movies available for rental), terry robes, coffee service. Included in the room rate is a lovely afternoon buffet of wine complimented with an assortment of cheeses and fruit and an appealing continental breakfast either served in your room or on the patio off the lounge. Ocean views vary depending on the location within the inn, but the staff is extremely helpful in describing the differences in accommodation and patient in assisting you with a selection over the phone. *Directions:* The Tickle Pink is located four miles south of Rio Road in Carmel just off Highway 1. Highland Drive is marked by a sign for both the Highlands Inn and the Tickle Pink.

TICKLE PINK INN
Owners: The Gurries Family
Innkeeper: Mark Watson
155 Highland Drive
Carmel Highlands, CA 93923
tel: (408) 624-1244, fax:(408) 626-9516
34 bedrooms with private bathroom
Double from $139 to $259
Open all year
Credit cards: all major
Children accepted

Threading into the hills east of Carmel is the beautiful Carmel Valley where, unlike Carmel, which tends to be foggy, almost every day is blessed with sunshine. Here, tucked into its own 330-acre oasis, is Stonepine, built by the Crockers, an early-California dynasty of great wealth. Anticipation of the very special treat awaiting builds as impressive, wrought-iron gates magically open, allowing you to enter. The road crosses a small bridge then winds through the trees, ending in the courtyard of a beautiful home, Italian in feel with a muted pink facade accented with red tile roof, shuttered windows and fancy grille-work. Inside, a quiet elegance emanates from every niche and corner. No expense is spared in the splendid furnishings which give no hint that this is a commercial operation. You definitely feel like a guest in a private mansion as you roam from library to sitting room to dining room, each decorated to perfection. The dining room, handsomely lined in mellow antique paneling, is set exquisitely for dinner each night with fine crystal and china. Upstairs are eight beautiful bedrooms—four more are in the guest house. Although there is a swimming pool and a tennis court, Stonepine was built as a ranch, and horses are the main attraction. Stonepine is very expensive and exclusive. *Directions:* Signposted on right after leaving Carmel Valley Village going east on G16.

STONEPINE
Owner: Gordon Hentschel
Director: Daniel Barduzzi
150 E. Carmel Valley Road
Carmel Valley, CA 93924
tel: (408) 659-2245, fax: (408) 659-5160
10 bedrooms, 4 suites, with private bathroom
Double from $225, Suite from $375
Open all year
Credit cards: all major
Children accepted over 12

Cassel is a town of a few houses, an old-fashioned general store and an inn (Clearwater House) set upon the banks of Hat Creek California's famous trout water. Catering specifically to fly-fishermen you enter through the front porch, tackle room—full of waders, boots, rods and vests into the living room with fish prints hung on the wall, an old fishing basket decorating a side table and a library of books about fly fishing. Comfy sofas are drawn around the fire, oriental rugs cover the wood floor and guests dine together at the long polished cherrywood table. The bedrooms are very plainly decorated, twin or king-sized beds with flowery spreads and country curtains, each with a small basic bathroom. Created by Dick Galland, a former wilderness guide, the inn is run on a day to day basis by Lynn Bedell who offers a sincerely warm welcome and ensure that guests are well fed. Cookies and drinks are always available. Fishing guides and two to five day schools are available for beginning, intermediate or advanced fly fishers. For non-anglers there are driving tours and hiking in nearby Lassen National Park, and spectacular waterfalls around Burney. *Directions:* From Redding take Highway 299 east through Burney and continue two miles beyond the intersection of the 299 and 89 where you turn right for the four mile drive to Cassel. Cross the creek and the inn is on your right.

CLEARWATER HOUSE
Innkeepers: Dick Galland & Lynn Bedell
21568 Cassel Road
Cassel, CA 96016
tel: (916) 335-5500
7 bedrooms with private bathroom
Double from $260, includes all meals
Open last Saturday in April to November 15th
Credit cards: MC VS
Children accepted

The Garden House Inn, a most appealing white, three-story house, brightly trimmed with green, is conveniently situated just a two-minute walk to Avalon's waterfront. As soon as you enter, you immediately realize that the attractiveness is more than skin deep—all the rooms are bright and pretty and show the loving attention to detail of the owners, the Olsen family, who are no strangers to Catalina—they have owned a second home here since the 1930s. The idea to open a small hotel was son Jon's, but the success of the operation is definitely a family affair. Jon's sister, Cathy, is also involved in making the Garden House Inn very special. But don't get the idea that this is a homespun operation: it is definitely a sophisticated, professionally run establishment. It is the kind of inn conducive to making friends with other guests. When the weather is nippy, guests congregate about a corner fireplace in the lounge, but, when the sun is out, the favorite spot is the garden terrace set with tables and umbrellas. Upstairs the bedrooms vary in size and decor: all are sunny and pretty and show the clever hand of a professional decorator. In the evening wine and hors d'oeuvres are complimentary and in the morning a delicious cold buffet is served. *Directions:* Boats from Long Beach, San Pedro, and Newport Beach. Helicopters from Long Beach and San Pedro

GARDEN HOUSE INN
Innkeepers: Jon & Cathy Olsen
125 Claressa
Avalon, Catalina Island, CA 90704
tel: (213) 510-0356
9 bedrooms with private bathroom
Double from $125 to $250
Open all year
Credit cards: all major
Children accepted over 16

Staying at the Inn on Mt. Ada is like stepping into a fairy tale—suddenly you are "King of the Mountain." This is not too far from reality, since the inn is the beautiful Wrigley family mansion (chewing gum, you know), their vacation "cottage" built high on the hill overlooking Avalon harbor. If you arrive by ferry at Catalina Island, you cannot miss the house: the mansion appears like a white wedding cake to your left above the harbor. The inn is expensive, but money seems almost immaterial, because, once through the door, you have bought a dream. You are truly like a pampered guest in a millionaire's home, with hardly a hint of commercialism (until you pay the bill) to put a damper to the illusion. The lounges and dining room have been redecorated with soft, pretty colors and traditional furniture and fabrics appropriate to the era when the house was built. Upstairs are six individually decorated bedrooms, the grandest having a fireplace, sitting area and a terrace with breathtaking views of the harbor. Rates include all the extras such as complimentary use of your own golf cart, a full scrumptious breakfast, a deli-style lunch and traditional Country Inn dinner; plus coffee, tea, soft drinks, fruit juice and freshly baked cookies always available in the den and sun porch. *Directions*: Boats from Long Beach, San Pedro, and Newport Beach. Helicopters from Long Beach and San Pedro.

INN ON MT ADA
Innkeepers: Marlene McAdam & Susie Griffin
1 Wrigley Road
Avalon, Catalina, CA 90704
tel: (213) 510-2030
6 bedrooms with private bathroom
Double from $230 to $590
All meals included in rates
Closed Christmas
Credit cards: MC VS
Children accepted over 14

Ye Olde Shelford House, a stately, white Victorian farmhouse dating back to the 1880s, is located just to the east of Cloverdale, perched on a small knoll overlooking fields of grapes. A large porch, complete with an old-fashioned swing, wraps around the front of the home. Downstairs the parlor is very formal, decorated with fussy Victorian furniture. Upstairs there are two fresh and pretty bedrooms which share a large bathroom. A downstairs bedroom has a private bathroom. On all of the beds there are beautiful quilts—every one of them lovingly sewn by Ina Sauder. Behind the main home is an annex where three more guest rooms are built above the carriage house. These rooms each have a private bathroom and share a parlor. The bedroom in front has a real country view out over the pool to the horse corral and fields of grapes. In the corral you will probably spot Brandy, the horse who pulls an old-fashioned, turn-of-the-century surrey. Upon prior arrangement (and of course at extra charge), Al will hitch up the surrey and take guests on wine tours with a picnic lunch, to some of the surrounding vineyards. When you return from wine touring, the pool is most inviting on a hot day. *Directions:* Take the main street through the town of Cloverdale, Highway 101, and turn east on First Street to River Road. After going over the bridge, you see the inn on your right.

YE OLDE SHELFORD HOUSE
Innkeepers: Ina & Al Sauder
29955 River Road
Cloverdale, CA 95425
tel: (707) 894-5956
6 bedrooms with private bathroom
Double from $85 to $110
Closed January
Credit cards: all major
Children accepted

The Coloma Country Inn, a handsome early-American farmhouse, was built in 1852, four years after gold was discovered at Sutter's Mill which is located just down the street. Today Coloma is a sleepy little village where the scant remains of the heady Gold Rush days are separated by wide green lawns which give it the air of being a well-kept park sloping up from the American River. The Coloma Country Inn sits in the middle of the park, its wrap-around porch inviting guests to relax and sip a glass of wine while soaking in the beauty of the surrounding tranquil countryside. Inside the decor is perfectly lovely, simple, very appealing American country style, though some rooms do have some Victorian pieces. Each bed is accented by a lovely antique quilt from Cindi's large collection. Some rooms feature a balcony or brick patio with a rose garden. An 1898 carriage house features two new suites, each with its own flowering courtyard and kitchenette. Behind the inn is an attractive pond with a little boat moored at the dock. The surrounding gold country is a great attraction to visitors to these parts, but, if you are looking for alternate means of transportation, Alan, a commercial, hot air balloon pilot, can arrange to take you aloft. If you are game for further excitement he can arrange one-or two-day raft trips on the nearby river. *Directions:* Take Highway 50 from Sacramento to Placerville, then exit on Highway 49 heading north for the eight mile drive to Coloma.

COLOMA COUNTRY INN
Innkeepers: Cindi & Alan Ehrgott
345 High Street, P.O. Box 502
Coloma, CA 95613
tel: (916) 622-6919
7 bedrooms, 5 with private bathroom
Double from $95 to $135
Suite from $125 to $145
Open all year
Credit cards: none accepted
Children accepted

Columbia is a state-preserved gold-rush town whose shops and stores have been re-created to show life in the heyday of the California Gold Rush. On Main Street is the exquisitely restored City Hotel. Prior to 1874 the building was a gold assay office, the state company headquarters, an opera house and a newspaper office. Now it is owned by the State of California and partially staffed by students from Columbia College's hotel management program (consequently the staff, dressed in their period costumes, are exceedingly young and wonderfully friendly). The excellent restaurant and the conviviality of the adjacent What Cheer Bar provide an especially pleasant way to spend an evening. The high-ceilinged bedrooms have Victorian or early-American furniture. The very nicest rooms open directly onto the parlor, Rooms 1 and 2 having the added attraction of balconies overlooking Main Street. All the bedrooms have private en-suite toilets and washbasin. It is not a problem to have showers down the hallway when slippers, robes and little wicker baskets to carry soap, shampoo and towels are provided. A bountiful Continental breakfast is served on the buffet in the dining room. *Directions:* From the San Francisco area take Highway 580 for sixty miles, then Highway 120 east to Sonora and Highway 49 north from Sonora for the four mile drive to Columbia.

CITY HOTEL
Owner: California State Parks System
Manager: Tom Bender
Main Street
Columbia State Historic Park, CA 95310
tel: (209) 532-1479, fax:(209) 532-7027
10 bedrooms with half baths
Showers down the hall
Double from $70 to $95
Closed one week in January
Credit cards: all major
Children accepted

The Fallon Hotel is owned and operated in the same way as the nearby City Hotel in this gem of a gold-rush town. The hotel opened in 1986 after experiencing a $4,000,000 refurbishment from the State of California. The bedrooms are perfect reflections of the opulent 1880s, with patterned ceilings, colorful, ornate wallpaper and grand antique furniture. Front rooms have shaded balconies. All have en-suite pull-chain toilets and ornate washbasins. Like the nearby City Hotel, showers are down the hall and slippers, bathrobes and baskets of toiletries are handily provided. One downstairs room has wider doors for wheelchair access. A simple buffet-style Continental breakfast is served in the adjoining ice cream parlor. In the Fallon Hotel building is the Fallon Theater, offering a year-round schedule of contemporary dramas, musicals and melodramas. When making reservations at either the City or Fallon Hotels ask about their excellent value-for-money theater and dinner packages. *Directions:* From the San Francisco area take Highway 580 for sixty miles, then Highway. 120 east to Sonora and Highway 49 north from Sonora for the four mile drive to Columbia which is off the main highway.

FALLON HOTEL
Owner: California State Parks System
Manager: Tom Bender
Washington Street
Columbia State Historic Park, CA 95310
tel: (209) 532-1470, fax:(209) 532-7027
13 bedrooms with half baths
Showers down the hall
Double from $55 to $95
Open all year
Credit cards: all major
Children accepted

The Blue Lantern Inn, perched on a bluff, offering unparalleled views of the fascinating harbor of Dana Point and on the blue Pacific, is an outstanding inn on southern California's Riviera. The new construction is designed in a Cape Code theme—a most appealing building whose many gables, towers and jutting roof lines create a whimsical look. The facade is painted a soft gray made even prettier by its crisp white trim. Inside the color scheme reflects the sea with the use of hues of periwinkle blue, soft lavender, and sea foam green. Each of the twenty-nine guest rooms is individually decorated—some with light pine furniture, some with wicker, others dark mahogany. The furnishings are mostly reproductions of excellent quality with a traditional ambiance. All of the rooms have a gas log fireplace and spacious bathroom with jacuzzi tub. Many of the rooms capture magnificent views of the sea. Breakfast is served each morning in the lounge, a cheerful room where sunlight streams through the wall of windows. Off the reception area is the library where tea is served in the afternoon. There is also a conference room available plus a well-equipped exercise room. The Blue Lantern is more of a sophisticated small hotel than a cozy bed and breakfast, but the management is superb and the warmth of welcome cannot be surpassed. *Directions:* From the Pacific Coast Highway 1, turn west on Street of the Blue Lantern and go one block.

BLUE LANTERN INN
Innkeeper: Tom Taylor
34343 Street of the Blue Lantern
Dana Point, CA 92629
tel: (714) 661-1304, fax: (714) 496-1483
29 bedrooms with private bathroom
Double from $135 to $350
Open all year
Credit cards: all major
Children accepted

The Ritz-Carlton Laguna Niguel is truly a gem—without a doubt, one of the finest beach resorts in California. As such (even though larger than most hotels in this guide) we want to share its merits with our readers. There is a magic to the management of the Ritz-Carlton group of hotels. They instill the warmth and charm of a small inn into a large hotel. All the help—from the bell hop to the maid who turns down your bed—seem to take genuine pride in making your stay very special. In addition to the fabulous service, the hotel is a show place of refined elegance. A wide entrance hall leads to a nautical-style bar where wood paneling and book shelves create a cozy niche to settle for afternoon tea or a refreshing drink. To the left of the bar, the lounge stretches out, highlighting a continuous row of arched windows, accented by thick louvered shutters, that frame a panorama of the ocean. The color scheme throughout repeats the colors of the sea: pastel peaches, creamy whites, beiges and light turquoise. Accents of fine antiques, outstanding oil paintings, enormous displays of fresh flowers, and large potted-palms add to the feeling of utter luxury. In addition to the two miles of beach stretching below the hotel, there are two swimming pools, four tennis courts, and an adjacent 18-hole golf course. *Directions*: From highway 5, take the Crown Valley parkway exit west to the Pacific Coast Highway, then south one mile, and turn right on Ritz Carlton Drive.

THE RITZ-CARLTON LAGUNA NIGUEL
Manager: John Dravinski
33533 Ritz-Carlton Drive
Dana Point, CA 92629
tel: (714) 240-2000, fax: (714) 240-0829
393 bedrooms with private bathroom
Double from $199 to $450, Suite from $485
Open all year
Credit cards: all major
Children accepted

Deep within Lassen National Park lies Drakesbad Guest Ranch set in an idyllic high mountain valley. A broad sweep of grassy meadow cut by a tumbling river gives way to towering pines that rise to rocky peaks. There's no electricity at Drakesbad—the warm glow of a kerosene lamp lights your cozy paneled bedroom. Furnishings are simple: polished pine log chairs and beds topped by quilts, simple country curtains and a pine dresser and bedside table. Our favorite rooms are in the little cabins that nestle at the very edge of the meadow with their smart modern bathrooms and sliding doors that open to a tiny deck where you can sit and watch the deer grazing at twilight. Other cabins nestle in the pines. Rooms upstairs in the main lodge have half baths. Evenings are for books, games and conviviality by the fireplace in the lodge, conversation around the campfire, or star gazing from the soothing warmth of the swimming pool that is fed by the natural warmth of a hot spring. Days are for walks, horseback riding and swimming. A bell is rung to announce meals which are served in the rustic pine dining room whose tables are topped with flowery mats and napkins. It's a family place full of people who came as children who return year after year with children and grandchildren—some who remember when guests slept in tents on the meadow. *Directions:* Turn left at the fire station in Chester and follow Warner Valley Road to the ranch. The last 4 miles are dirt road.

DRAKESBAD GUEST RANCH
Innkeepers: Billie & Ed Fiebiger
end of Warner Valley Road
Lassen National Park, Chester, CA 96020
Winter tel: (916) 529-1512, fax: (916) 529-4511
Summer tel: Drakesbad 2 via 916 Susanville
19 bedrooms with private bathroom
Double from $164 includes all meals
Open first Fri. in June to first Sun. in October
Credit cards: MC VS
Children accepted

Tucked, seemingly miles away into the countryside, Brookside Farm is actually only a thirty-five minute drive from the outskirts of San Diego. Edd and Sally Guishard have done a remarkable job of converting an ordinary complex of farm buildings into an inviting inn. The location and mood set the them of may of the rooms: the Bird's Nest tucked under the eaves has lovely bird stenciling on the walls, while Captain Small's room has a red and blue quilt and blue checked chairs. Two new rooms, The Carpenter's Shop and La Casita, have been added in the barn. The original well house is now the Hunter's Cabin and has a rustic decor, wood-burning stove, planked floors and overlooks the creek through a wall of paned windows and screened porch. Edd is responsible for the inn's stained glass windows as well as being a wonderful chef. On weekends he prepares an inviting four-course dinner, inviting guests to share in the preparation (he owned several restaurants in the San Diego area before moving here). On Monday nights, a complimentary supper is served to guests. The setting of the inn is lovely: you can play badminton on the lawn, laze away the hours on the patio or relax in the spa under the grape arbor. *Directions:* From San Diego take Highway 94 east to Dulzura, go one and a half miles past the cafe and turn right on Marron Valley Road.

BROOKSIDE FARM B & B INN
Innkeepers: Edd & Sally Guishard
1373 Marron Valley Road
Dulzura, CA 92017
tel: (619) 468-3043
9 bedrooms, 7 with private bathroom
Double from $65 to $85
Open all year
Credit cards: MC VS
Inappropriate for children

The Griffin House, a pretty little clapboard house, painted gray with white trim and white picket fence, dates back to the late 1800's when it served as the local doctor's office and pharmacy. Later, behind the doctor's office, five cottages were added to house some of the lumber men coming to the growing town of Elk. Today, the owner Leslie Lawson, lives in the main house and has renovated the cottages for guests. The garden cottages are pleasant, but truly outstanding are the three doll-house-like cottages on the edge of the bluff. In fact, these three separate little houses offer the most sensational views anywhere on the California coast. Each of these cottages, named after one of the early settlers of Elk, has a wood-burning stove, a sitting area, a wall of window overlooking the coast and a private redwood deck with chairs and table. These tiny cottages are simple in decor, nothing contrived or quaintly cute, just old fashioned comfort. But, I promise you, these cottages offer a vista so breathtaking that you will be back again. And again. Leslie, the very gracious, warm-hearted owner is a natural at innkeeping—which she finds a breeze by comparison to her previous job as Dean of Students at the University of California at Santa Barbara where she "mothered" 18,000 students. Her new endeavor is a pub where guests can enjoy light meals and good cheer. *Directions:* Off Highway 1, at the center of Elk.

GRIFFIN HOUSE
Innkeeper: Leslie Griffin-Lawson
5910 South Highway 1
P.O. Box 172
Elk, CA 95432
tel: (707) 877-3422
7 cottages with private bathroom
Double from $80 to $135
Credit cards: MC VS
Children accepted

The Harbor House has a fantastic location—on one of the prettiest bluffs along the Mendocino coast. There is even a little path, with benches along the way, winding down the cliff to a secluded private beach. The home was built in 1916 as a guest house for the Goodyear Redwood Lumber Company, so it is no wonder to find everything inside and outside built of redwood. The inn is extremely appealing, reflecting the ambiance of a beautiful, elegant country lodge. You enter into a charming redwood-paneled living room dominated by a large fireplace, also made of redwood. An Oriental carpet, comfortable sofas, beamed ceiling, soft lighting and a piano tucked in the corner add to the inviting warmth. Doors lead from the lounge to the verandah-like dining room, stretching the length of the building, with picture windows looking out to the sea. A broad wooden staircase leads upstairs to comfortably furnished, homey bedrooms. Other guest rooms are in adjacent cottages. All the bedrooms have sea views, and all, but one, have wood-burning fireplace. Included in the room rate are both dinner and breakfast—and the food is terrific: home-baked breads, freshly ground coffee, garden vegetables and, of course, wonderful fish. *Directions:* Take Highway 101 north from San Francisco to Cloverdale, then Highway 128 west to the ocean and Highway 1 south for five miles to Elk.

HARBOR HOUSE
Innkeepers: Helen & Dean Turner
5600 South Highway One
Elk, CA 95432
tel: (707) 877-3203
10 bedrooms with private bathroom
Double from $165 to $245
Includes breakfast & dinner
Open all year
Credit cards: none accepted
Children accepted over 12

Without hesitation I can say that no inn featured in our California guide has a more sensational setting than the Sandpiper House Inn, superbly positioned on a bluff overlooking the most beautiful section of the Mendocino coast. The front of the gray shingled house, enclosed with a white picket fence, is most inviting. But just wait. It is not until you come inside and look out the windows to the ocean that you realize what a prize you have discovered. Behind the house, a beautifully tended green lawn embraced by an English garden, stretches out to the edge of the bluff below which the waves crash against awesome rock formations. Benches are strategically placed to capture the glory. A path leads down the steep incline with a half-way resting point before continuing on down to the private beach. Because of the setting the house would be a winner if it were just a shell within, but happily, the interior does justice to the setting. The decor is unpretentiously lovely with a homelike ambiance and excellent taste. Three of the bedrooms capture the view, the fourth overlooks the meadows and has a fireplace. My very favorite, one I will always remember, is the Clifton room with a large bay window where two white wicker chairs are strategically placed to capture the sweeping view. To add perfection, the owners are as warm and gracious as their home they share with guests. *Directions:* Located on Highway 1 at the north end of the village.

SANDPIPER HOUSE INN
Innkeepers: Claire & Richard Melrose
5520 South Highway One, P.O. Box 49
Elk, CA 95432
tel: (707) 877-3587
4 bedrooms with private bathroom
Double from $110 to $165
Open all year
Credit cards: MC VS
Children accepted over 12

The Carter House Country Inn is not old, but it is certainly appears so, because it is an exact copy of an early Victorian home built in Eureka. The inn is the dream of Mark Carter who grew up in Eureka with her many Victorian homes. He built the inn using the original plans for a Victorian house designed by the architect who built the Carson Mansion (a Victorian showplace in Eureka). His inn now consists of three settings: The Cottage, the Inn and a gourmet restaurant. Mark and his wife, Christi, personally manage the entire operation. Christi, an excellent chef, has gained national recognition for outstanding dinners as well as breakfasts. The small Victorian parlor, where guests are served wine and hors d'oeuvres at 6 p.m. and nightcaps at bedtime, looks as if it were straight out of the 19th century. The bedrooms are comfortable, each with an antique ambiance. Best yet, there are down comforters, fluffy pillows and cozy flannel robes to make guests really feel "at home." The very attractive guest rooms are decorated with antique and reproduction light pine furniture. *Directions:* Take Highway 101 north to Eureka. The highway turns into Fifth Street. From Fifth Street, turn left on L Street and go two blocks.

THE CARTER HOUSE
Innkeepers: Mark & Christi Carter
1033 Third Street
Eureka, CA 95501
tel: (707) 445-1390, fax: (707) 444-8062
7 bedrooms, 3 with private bathroom
Double from $95 to $185
Suite from $185 to $300
Open all year
Credit cards: all major
Children accepted over 12

Ferndale is a jewel—a wonderfully preserved Victorian town five miles from the northern California coast. Happily, for those who want to immerse themselves in the nostalgia of days-gone-by, accommodations are available at The Gingerbread Mansion, an inn oozing with Victorian ambiance. Within this restored fantasy of turrets and gables lies a small hotel of great sophistication: the bath water is instantly hot, the towels lush, the beds comfortable, reading lamps properly placed, beds turned down each night, chocolates on the pillow, bathrobes tucked in the wardrobe. Many of the bedrooms are very elaborate; several have extra fancy bathrooms. Our favorites, however, were the less extravagantly furnished guest rooms, which also happen to be less expensive. Like the house, the beautiful garden is meticulously groomed. The flower beds abound with color and the formal hedges are trimmed to perfection. However, all is not stiffly formal: bits of whimsy such as "his and hers" clawfoot tubs in two of the bedrooms and bicycles painted to match the inn, insert a bit of lightheartedness. *Directions:* Ferndale is approximately two hundred fifty miles north of San Francisco. Coming from San Francisco on Highway 101, take the Fernbridge/Ferndale exit. Follow the signs to Ferndale. When you reach Main Street, turn left at the Bank of America and go one block.

THE GINGERBREAD MANSION
Innkeeper: Ken Torbert
400 Berding Street
Ferndale, CA 95536
tel: (707) 786-4000
9 bedrooms with private bathroom
Double from $95 to $205
Open all year
Credit cards: MC VS
Children accepted over 10

The Noyo River Lodge has a superb location on the hillside overlooking Ft Bragg's harbor, definitely one of the most colorful fishing harbors along the coast of California. Rooms are available in two sections of the hotel—either in the newly built annex featuring six spacious suites, each with a private balcony and each offering all the latest modern amenities, or in the more appealing, original old family home which now has two gorgeous suites, each with private sunroom and fireplace, and five lovely upstairs bedrooms. These bedrooms in the main house just ooze with character. Although not decorator perfect, they are refreshingly "real" in their decor: old-fashioned, comfortable rooms which make you feel you are really stepping back to the last century. Ask for room Number 1. This is just a gem, a spacious corner room with a king-sized bed and an enormous bathroom tucked under the eaves sporting a wonderful claw-footed tub. But the best part of Room 1 is the view. From the windows you look down through the trees to the picturesque Noyo River where the colorful boats dock, protected from the sea. Breakfast is served either in the dining room, or when weather permits, outside on the deck overlooking the harbor. *Directions:* From Highway 1, just north of the bridge spanning the Noyo River, take North Harbor Drive which loops down to the fishing harbor. Before reaching the harbor, jog left when you see the sign.

NOYO RIVER LODGE
Innkeeper: Ellie Sinsel
500 Casa del Noyo Drive
Fort Bragg, CA 95437
tel: (707) 964-8045, fax: (707) 964-5354
16 bedrooms with private bathroom
Double from $80 to $120
Suite from $130 to $150
Open all year
Credit cards: all major
Children accepted

You would think you were in England instead of northern California when you first see the large, Tudor-style Benbow Inn. The English theme continues as you step inside the lounge with its large antique fireplace flanked by comfortable sofas, antique chests, paintings, needlepoint, cherrywood wainscoting, two grandfather clocks, potted green plants and a splendid Oriental carpet. At tea time complimentary English tea and scones are served along with mulled wine when the days are nippy. The dining room too, is very English: a beautiful, sunny room with beamed ceiling and dark oak Windsor chairs. Both the reception hall and the dining room open out to a pretty courtyard overlooking the river. The traditionally decorated bedrooms vary in size—all the way from small rooms to spacious suites with fireplaces, wet bars and private jacuzzis. There are bedrooms located both in the main hotel and in an annex which also opens onto the courtyard. The one disadvantage of the Benbow Inn is its proximity to the freeway, but loyal guests do not seem to mind. A wonderful feature here is the very special Christmas celebration—events including Christmas movies, caroling and dancing are planned each day, and there is a very festive English Christmas dinner. *Directions:* Drive north on Highway 101. Just south of Garberville, take the Benbow exit. The hotel is on west side of the freeway.

BENBOW INN
Innkeeper: Patsy Watts
445 Lake Benbow Drive
Garberville, CA 95440
tel: (707) 923-2124
55 bedrooms with private bathroom
Double from $88 to $250
Closed January 2 to mid-April
Credit cards: MC VS
Children accepted

Georgetown's unusually wide, tree-lined streets faced by wood-frame buildings give character and charm to this town perched high on a hill nine miles above the South Fork of the American River. The American River Inn was once a boarding house for gold miners who came to make their fortune, but they certainly did not have today's luxuries of a spa and swimming pool. The main house is a picture-perfect Victorian whose interior beautifully complements the lovely exterior. Inside the spacious, individually decorated bedrooms are furnished with antiques appropriate to the period and the bathrooms have clawfoot tubs and pull-chain toilets. A nifty-gifty shop occupies a small front room. A full breakfast is served in the dining room or on the patio and guests have the use of a comfortable parlor. Across the lawn and past the swimming pool and spa is the Queen Ann House which is perfect for seminars, retreats, or wedding parties. A more recent addition to the complex are the Woodside Mine Suites in a very 20th-century building where the addition of country-cute decor cannot overcome aluminum windows and 1950's architecture. The inn is happy to make arrangements for white water rafting, kayaking, bicycling or hot air ballooning. *Directions:* From Sacramento take Highway 50 or 80 to Auburn or Placerville, then Highway 49 to 193 which brings you into Georgetown. The American River Inn is on Main Street at Orleans.

AMERICAN RIVER INN
Innkeepers: Maria & Will Collin
Main at Orleans Street, P.O. Box 43
Georgetown, CA 95634
tel: (916) 333-4499, fax: (916) 333-9253
17 bedrooms, 8 suites, 18 with private bathroom
Double from $85 to $98
Suite from $108 to $118
Open all year
Credit cards: all major
Children accepted over 8

Mary Jane and Jerry Campbell have perfected innkeeping in the decade and a half that they have opened their home to overnight guests. Time has served not to weather but rather enrich their enthusiasm and warmth of welcome. The Campbell Ranch Inn is a contemporary home whose appeal are its hosts and its absolutely spectacular location. Set on the hillside with a backdrop of fir and pine trees, views from the inn stretch out across its lovely garden and swimming pool to the miles and miles of vineyards that carpet the surrounding countryside and rolling hills. It is a beautiful setting, very quiet and very soothing—the perfect escape. If you could survive on a bountiful breakfast and the wonderful homemade pie offered each evening as dessert, you might never choose to venture back down the Campbell's drive. The idyllic setting encourages you to relax, read by the pool or perhaps muster up energy for a game of tennis. With the exception of one cottage, the guestrooms (all with king-sized beds) are actual bedrooms in the Campbell home. They are furnished as they were for their family and are nondescript in their decor. The cottage affords more privacy and has a sitting room with a fireplace and vine covered deck with million dollar views in addition to a bedroom and bathroom. The cottage is just adjacent to where Jerry keeps his pigeons and model trains. *Directions:* On Highway 101, eighty miles north of San Francisco, take the Canyon Road exit at Geyserville and travel west one and six tenths of a mile.

CAMPBELL RANCH INN
Innkeepers: Mary Jane & Jerry Campbell
1475 Canyon Road
Geyserville, CA 95441
tel: (707) 857-3476
5 bedrooms with private bathroom
Double from $100 to $165
Open all year
Credit cards: MC VS
Inappropriate for children

It is hard not to notice Beltane Ranch, a pale yellow board and batten house encircled on both stories by broad verandahs, set on the hillside off the Valley of the Moon Road. Rosemary, the owner, will probably be in the cozy country kitchen when you arrive, but if she is away from home she will write you a welcoming note on the chalkboard hung by the back door. The house has no internal staircase, so each room has a private entrance off the verandah—which was probably a very handy thing when this was the weekend retreat of a San Francisco madam. Incidentally, this also explains the rather southern architecture of the house as "madam" hailed from Louisiana. The bedrooms, decorated in family antiques, have a very comfortable ambiance. Chairs and hammocks are placed on the verandah outside each room and offer a wonderful spot to settle and enjoy peaceful countryside views beyond Rosemary's well-tended garden. Beltane has been in the family for fifty-five years and grows a well known Chardonnay as well as other varieties of wines. For sports enthusiasts, there is a tennis court and walking trails. Beltane Ranch remains a personal favorite. *Directions:* From Sonoma take Highway 12 towards Santa Rosa: Beltane Ranch is on your right shortly after passing the turnoff to Glen Ellen.

BELTANE RANCH
Innkeeper: Rosemary Wood
11775 Highway 12 (Sonoma Highway)
P.O. Box 395
Glen Ellen, CA 95442
tel: (707) 996-6501
4 bedrooms with private bathroom
Double from $95 to $120
Open all year
Credit cards: none accepted
Children accepted over 4

Grass Valley has continued to prosper since the heady Gold Rush days when Cornish miners arrived from England seeking their fortunes in gold. Although the town cannot compete for charm with adjacent Nevada City, it certainly has a first-class hostelry in Murphy's Inn—this small inn, its broad verandah decorated with topiary ivy baskets, was once the mansion of North Star Mine owner Edward Colman. It has been lovingly restored and refurbished. Bedrooms in the main house range from Theodosia's Suite with its king-size brass bed draped in lace sitting before the fireplace, to a small upstairs bedroom that shares a bath. One room just off the kitchen has a delightful pot-belly stove and sunny skylights. The entire inn is furnished in Victorian finery. The Donation Day House, just across the street has two suites, one with a full kitchen, which could accommodate guests with children. Tom and Sue encourage guests to make themselves at home and stocks the refrigerator with juices, sodas and goodies. They also prepare a hearty breakfast while chatting with guests. The "swim spa" on the back verandah is heated like a spa in the winter and used as a small pool in the summer. *Directions:* From the San Francisco area take Highway 80 to 49 north to Grass Valley, exit on Colfax, then go left on South Auburn and left on Neal.

MURPHY'S INN
Owners: Sue & Tom Meyers
Innkeeper: Linda Beam
318 Neal Street
Grass Valley, CA 95945
tel & fax: (916) 273-6873
8 bedrooms with private bathroom
Double from $75 to $100
Suite from $125 to $145
Open all year
Credit cards: all major
Children accepted over 10

Groveland is a quaint Gold Rush town just a half hour from the west entrance to Yosemite. Highway 120 becomes Groveland's one main street as it transects the charming town. It is a great place to break the drive and stop for either breakfast or lunch at the corner PJ's Cafe (Parker and Nan Johnson proprietors, telephone: (209) 962-7501) or should you choose to overnight and just take a day trip into the park, the Groveland Hotel offers very comfortable and attractive accommodation. Fronting main street, the Groveland Hotel, is actually two buildings that date from 1849 and 1914, joined by a wrap around verandah. One building dates from the Gold Rush and the other was built as a boarding house to accommodate the rowdy men who worked the massive Hetch Hetchy water project. No two rooms are alike and yet each is pleasing in its decor, decorated with a blend of antiques and attractive fabrics. Although opening onto the street, the front upstairs rooms enjoy the lovely bay windows and on the basement-like level there are two rooms, one with a queen the other twin beds that are limited in terms of window and therefore no views, but they are a steal at $85 per night. A continental breakfast is included in the room rate, and the restaurant also offers a full breakfast, lunch and dinner menu. *Directions:* Groveland is a two hour drive from Sacramento along the historic stretch of Highway 120.

THE GROVELAND HOTEL
Innkeepers: Peggy Mosley, Mary Wollitz
18767 Main Street, P.O. Box 481
Groveland, CA 95321
tel: (209) 962-4000, fax: (209) 962-6674
17 bedrooms with private bathroom
Double from $85 to $170
Open all year
Credit cards: all major
Children accepted

Many of the hotels in this guide have been converted from buildings previously used for other purposes. Not so with the Old Milano Hotel: it has been taking guests since the first day the doors opened in 1905. Although built upon a bluff overlooking the ocean in what appears to be quite an isolated location, at the turn of the century the hotel was the center of activity, serving overnight stagecoach guests, lumber barons and travellers on their way up the coast by train. Today, the old hotel has been beautifully restored reflecting its original Victorian elegance. The large dining room and wine parlor, with a massive stone fireplace, are especially attractive. From Wednesday through Sunday gourmet dinners are served (be sure to make reservations in advance). None of the six guest rooms upstairs has a private bath, but all are attractively decorated with Victorian antiques and most have outstanding views of the ocean. On the first floor is a lavish suite (with a memorable view) where the original owners, the Lucchinetti family, lived. A room is tucked into a cottage in the rear garden and another into an old-fashioned train caboose set amongst the trees. Although it has many attributes, the hotel's most outstanding feature is its perfect location on a lawn which sweeps down to a bluff overlooking the ocean. *Directions:* The Old Milano Hotel is on the Coastal Highway just north of Gualala.

OLD MILANO HOTEL
Innkeeper: Leslie Linscheid
38300 Highway One
Gualala, CA 95445
tel: (707) 884-3256
9 bedrooms, 3 with private bathroom
Double from $80 to $ 115
Suite from $145 to $180
Open all year
Credit cards: all major
Inappropriate for children

Until it was converted to a small inn, Applewood was a private residence. The present owners, Jim Caron and Darryl Notter, have transformed it into a well- tended, European-style inn— not trendy, just quietly elegant. The atmosphere is that of a country lodge, with a large stone fireplace opening on two sides, warming both the living room and a cheerful glassed-in sun porch. Just off the living room is a dining room with an enormous crystal chandelier hanging above a central table surrounded by individual small tables. In addition to breakfast, with a reservation, Applewood offers their guests dinner featuring fresh Sonoma County produce, much of it grown in the hotel's own gardens. Dining room windows look over a wooded area and a lovely swimming pool on the terrace. The immaculate bedrooms are all individual in their decor, just as if you were staying in a private home. Their price reflects the size and location, although each has a TV, direct-dial phone, and comfortable queen bed decked with down comforter and pillows. The furnishings are elegant, slightly formal, but still showing the homey touch of the owners. In fact, Darryl designed and his mother (Mary) hand-sewed the covers on the comforters, the draperies and even the slip-covers on the chairs. Plans are underway for additional guest rooms which might be available by the time you make your plans. *Directions:* On Highway 116, a half a mile south of the bridge as you leave Guerneville.

APPLEWOOD
Innkeepers: Jim Caron & Darryl Notter
13555 Highway 116
(Pocket Canyon), Guerneville CA 95446
tel: (707) 869-9093
10 bedrooms with private bathroom
Double from $125 to $225
Open all year
Credit cards: all major
Inappropriate for children

There is an old Victorian house on Half Moon Bay's historic Main Street, restored with labor and love, that became an inviting bed and breakfast. The pink 1890's house has gingerbread trim painted in colors of salmon and cream. A parking area in front is bordered by gardens and a white picket fence. An enormous palm tree, which must be very old, dominates the front yard. You enter into an old fashioned, Victorian front parlor. The guest rooms, some on the first floor and others upstairs, are individually decorated with antiques. Some have the added bonus of a fireplace and some have double size whirlpool tubs. One of the most pleasant features of the inn is its garden. The name "Old Thyme Inn" is a play on words—a former owner (who had a love of plants and a real green thumb) designed a fragrant herb garden featuring many varieties of thyme at the side of the house. Guests are welcome to browse and perhaps the inn will even provide a cutting if they want to start their own garden. *Directions:* Take Highway 1 south from San Francisco to Half Moon Bay (thirty miles). Turn left at the first stop light onto Main Street. Drive through town and watch for the Old Thyme Inn on the left.

OLD THYME INN
Innkeepers: George & Marcia Dempsey
779 Main Street
Half Moon Bay, CA 94019
tel: (415) 726-1616
7 bedrooms with private bathroom
Double from $75 to $150
Suite from $165 to $220
Open all year
Credit cards: all major
Children accepted

The Zaballa House, built in the mid-1800s, has the honor of being Half Moon Bay's oldest building. Its original owner, Estanislao Zaballa, was quite the man about town. He owned much property including the general merchandise store, several stables, and a saloon on Main Street. His home on Main Street where he lived with his wife and five children, is the only building remaining. Today it has been beautifully restored into one of Half Moon Bay's cutest-looking bed and breakfasts: a soft gray-blue clapboard house with white trim and white picket fence. Downstairs there is a small parlor as you enter and a guest dining area off the central hallway. Some of the guest rooms are located on the first floor, others are up the staircase on the second level. All are individually decorated with their own personality. My favorite bedroom is a bright and cheerful corner room on the first floor, overlooking the garden. This room is in the oldest section of the house and has white wainscoting half way up the walls, prettily accented above by dark blue floral wallpaper. A bountiful breakfast is served each morning and for other meals, there are many restaurants as well as tempting shops just steps away on Main Street. *Directions:* Take Highway 1 south from San Francisco to Half Moon Bay (thirty miles). Turn left at the first stop light onto Main Street. As you drive into town, the Zaballa House is just past the bridge on the right side of the road.

ZABALLA HOUSE BED & BREAKFAST
Innkeeper: Simon Lowings
324 Main Street
Half Moon Bay, CA 94019
tel: (415) 726-9123
9 bedrooms with private bathroom
Double from $65 to $150
Open all year
Credit cards: all major
Children accepted

For those who love to be lulled to sleep by the rhythmic sound of crashing waves, the Cypress Inn might be just your cup of tea. It is positioned directly across the road from the five-mile-long, sandy stretch of Miramar Beach. The design of the Cypress Inn is not "old world," nor is it meant to be. Rather, it is a contemporary building with a tan-colored weathered-wood facade with turquoise trim. Giving credence to the inn's name, a wind-swept cypress tree towers by the entrance. Inside a Mexican Indian folk art theme prevails. As you enter, there is a snug sitting area to your left with wicker chairs and sofa grouped around a fireplace. Terra cotta floors lead to the bedrooms. More intimate in size than spacious, all of the guestrooms are very similar in decor except each has its own color scheme (most of the walls are painted in very bright colors—if you prefer softer tones, ask for one of the less vibrantly painted rooms). Each of the rooms has a gas-log fireplace, built in bed with reading lamps, cactus plants, wicker chairs, a writing desk, and louvered doors opening onto private balconies—each overlooking the ocean. The Cypress Inn is a managed property. *Directions:* Take Highway 1 south from San Francisco. Turn right on Medio Avenue (one and a half miles beyond the stop light at Pillar Point Harbor). Cypress Inn is at the end of the street on the left.

CYPRESS INN
Owners: Suzie Lankes & Dan Floyd
407 Mirada Road
Miramar Beach
Half Moon Bay, CA 94019
tel: (415) 726-6002, fax: (415) 712-0380
8 bedrooms with private bathroom
Double from $150 to $275
Open all year
Credit cards: all major
Children accepted

On the hillside across from the Simi Winery, the Belle de Jour Inn is set in its own quiet world. A complex of old farm cottages built in 1873, buffered from the busy main road by a long drive shaded by pine trees and bordered by lush lawn, backing onto a hillside planted with vines, this inn offers an inviting countryside retreat. The complex has four cottages of guest rooms and a single-story farmhouse that is Tom and Brenda's home. Once the grain and tack room, the Caretaker's Suite has a pine four poster, king-size canopy bed topped with Battenberg lace and French doors that open onto a trellised deck. The Terrace Room is charming, with a fireplace and a whirlpool tub for two viewing terrace and vineyards. The Morning Hill Room is cozy with a wood stove and a shuttered window seat. The Atelier (the only room without a vineyard view) is large and lovely. A full country breakfast is served in the owners' kitchen or on the front porch. For a memorable wine tasting experience, Tom will take you in his 1925 vintage auto along the backroads of the wine country. Return for a gourmet picnic lunch at the inn and perhaps a refreshing afternoon dip in the cleverly cut-down wine cask, complete with rubber ducky. *Directions:* North on Highway 101. Exit at Dry Creek Road and go east to Healdsburg Avenue. Turn left at the lights and go north for one mile. The entrance is directly across from Simi Winery.

BELLE DE JOUR INN
Innkeepers: Brenda & Tom Hearn
16276 Healdsburg Avenue
Healdsburg, CA 95448
tel: (707) 431-9777, fax: (707) 431-7412
4 bedrooms with private bathroom
Double from $115 to $185
Closed Thanksgiving & Christmas
Credit cards: MC VS
Inappropriate for children

Healdsburg's main square is a green park bordered by shops and restaurants. If you want to stay in this charming town the Healdsburg Inn on the Plaza overlooks the main square. The entrance is through an awning-covered door into a freshly painted, high-ceilinged reception that doubles as an art gallery. A dramatic, long flight of stairs winds up to a central salon where a jigsaw puzzle is left for each successive guest to work a bit on. Off the salon are nine bedrooms decorated in a very Victorian decor, a few of which overlook the old plaza through bay windows, some have fireplaces. An enclosed rooftop room has white tables and chairs, lots of greenery and colorful Oriental carpets. There are two breakfast servings: cereal, toast, jam and beverages are available for early risers and later, at 9:00 a.m., a hot egg dish plus fresh fruit platter and juice are served. Plan on arriving around 4:00 p.m. to enjoy vegetable dip, cheese and crackers, ice tea and lemonade. Complimentary wine and fresh buttered popcorn are served at 5:30 p.m. Plus, when you return from dinner, a delicious orange liquor and dark chocolates await you. Friday and Saturday night rates are higher and include a spectacular morning brunch. The Inn on the Plaza is a very friendly, welcoming hotel and Genny or her daughter Dyanne are usually there to greet you. *Directions:* The inn is on the south side of Healdsburg's main plaza.

HEALDSBURG INN ON THE PLAZA
Innkeeper: Genny Jenkins
110 Matheson
Healdsburg, CA 95448
tel: (707) 433-6991
10 bedrooms, 9 with private bathroom
Double from $75 to $160
Open all year
Credit cards: MC VS
Children accepted

The Madrona Manor is a very special small hotel. Crowning a small hill in the country, yet just minutes from Healdsburg; the spectacular building is a fantasy gingerbread mansion whose grounds are glorious—eight acres of manicured gardens. The rooms in the manor are attractive—most with fireplaces, all filled with authentic Victorian antiques. On warm days the lovely pool nestled in the garden is a welcome distraction. Breakfasts are lovely and the restaurant offers gourmet dinners—Todd Muir is a fabulous chef who has been featured in *Gourmet*. But the greatest asset of the hotel are the owners, Carol and John Muir. They bought the property in 1981 and spent two years of love and labor converting it into a commercially successful, sophisticated little hotel. Carol and John really care and it shows in every detail from the well-trained staff to the guest rooms where, although the beds might be antique, the mattresses are firm and the linens of the finest quality. The entire family is involved in the operation. Son, Todd, is the renowned chef, son, Mark, worked on the renovations, son-in-law, John Fitzgerald, was the landscape architect, son Rob is a partner in the business. *Directions:* Driving north on Highway 101, take the Central Healdsburg exit, turn left at the intersection and go under the freeway. You will be on Westside Road.

MADRONA MANOR
Innkeepers: Carol & John Muir
1001 Westside Road
Healdsburg, CA 95448
tel: (707) 433-4231, fax: (707) 433-0703
21 bedrooms with private bathroom
Double from $135 to $185
Suite from $185 to $225
Open all year
Credit cards: MC VS
Children accepted

Idyllwild is a mile-high village of some three thousand residents, and with its magnificent hiking trails affords a wonderful weekend getaway from the city of Los Angeles. The Fern Valley Inn is a rustic country inn of eleven log cabins nestled in the pines. Each cottage is furnished with antiques, handmade quilts and equipped with a refrigerator, television and fireplace or log stove. Themes vary from a western motif to The School Room with its old school prints, a drawing slate and printed rules for teachers. Rooms are supplied with coffee, tea and a basket of nut breads as breakfast fare. Suzie Vening and Kris Logan personally manage the inn and care for their guests. The grounds are immaculately kept—swept pathways wind amongst the cottages, leading to the heated pool, rose garden and parlor. The parlor with its porch is a welcoming place for guests to congregate and enjoy a glass of sherry, Scrabble and puzzles are always left out. *Directions:* Take Highway 10 west from Los Angeles to Banning and Highway 243 to Idyllwild. Turn left on North Circle, right on South Circle, then left on Fern Valley Road.

FERN VALLEY INN
Innkeepers: Suzie Vening & Kris Logan
25240 Fern Valley Road, P.O. Box 116
Idyllwild, CA 92549
tel: (909) 659-2205, fax: (909) 659-2071
11 bedrooms with private bathroom
Double from $65 to $95
Open all year
Credit cards: MC VS
Inappropriate for children

The Strawberry Creek Inn, a lovely dark-shingled building with etched glass windows, sits back off the main road on the final approach to town. It is owner managed, with Jim Goff and Diana Dugan the lovely hosts: Jim's domain is the expansive gardens, while Diana's personal warmth is reflected in the decor—she is responsible for every nook and inviting touch. In the shingled main house the parlor is set with a large comfy sofa, tables and chairs before the fireplace and its bookshelves are brimming with novels and games. Diana has selected coordinating wallpapers, borders and trims in colors of warm beige and greens. Off the parlor in a cheerful, enclosed sun porch, long trestle tables accommodate guests with a bountiful feast—German, French toast with bratwurst, fruit, juice, coffee or tea is just one example for breakfast. The bedrooms are located both in the main house and in a newer back wing that wraps around a sunny courtyard. Each room is decked with country handmade quilts or crocheted spreads. Rooms in the main house, four upstairs and one down, are charming, and give the feeling of being "back home." The courtyard rooms were built with private fireplaces, baths and skylights and equipped with a small refrigerator and queen beds. A cottage on the creek offers king bed, whirlpool tub, two baths, fireplace, kitchen, glassed in porch and roomy back deck. *Directions:* Approaching town from the south, on Highway 243 the inn is on the right past South Circle Drive.

STRAWBERRY CREEK INN
Innkeepers: Diana Dugan & Jim Goff
26370 Highway 243, P.O. Box 1818
Idyllwild, CA 92349
tel: (714) 659-3202
9 bedrooms with private bathroom
Double from $80 to $95, Cottage: $125
Closed Thanksgiving & Christmas
Credit cards: MC VS
Children accepted

The Blackthorne Inn is the whimsical creation of Susan and Bill Wigert. They have built a Hansel and Gretel house tucked among the tree tops, loaded with peaked roofs, dormer windows, funny little turrets, bay windows and an octagonal tower. You wind up through the trees to the main entry level which is wrapped by an enormous wooden deck, emphasizing the tree house look. The living room is very spacious, dominated by a floor-to-ceiling stone fireplace. Skylights, a stained glass window, a Chinese carpet, wood-paneled walls, baskets of flowers and walls of windows looking out into the trees make the room most appealing. The guest rooms, located on various levels, are attractively decorated, not in any particular period or style, but with a pretty, fresh, country look. The favorite choice of many guests is the Eagle's Nest, located in the octagonal tower, where walls of glass give the impression one is sleeping under the stars—camping at its best. Each of the other guest rooms has its own personality. The Overlook has stained glass windows, The Lupine Room has a private entrance, The Studio has a separate sitting room and The Hideaway (one of our favorites) has a bay window looking out into the trees. *Directions:* From Highway 101 take Sir Francis Drake Boulevard to Olema. Turn right, go for about two miles, then left toward Inverness. Go a little over one mile and turn left on Vallejo Avenue (at the Knave of Hearts Bakery).

BLACKTHORNE INN
Innkeeper: Susan Wigert
266 Vallejo Avenue, P.O. Box 712
Inverness, CA 94937
tel: (415) 663-8621, fax: (415) 663-1805
5 bedrooms, 3 with private bathroom
Double from $105 to $195
Closed Christmas
Credit cards: MC VS
Children accepted over 14

Built as a hunting lodge by the Empire Club in 1917, this dark shingled building highlighted with a white trim porch hung with greenery is a wonderful escape in the woods just up from the bay. Previously a restaurant only, under the artistically brilliant direction of its new owner, Manka's now offers intimate accommodation and a restaurant (open Thursday through Sunday) whose menu is in keeping with the theme of a hunting lodge—much of the food is grilled over an open fire. Four guestrooms are found up a narrow flight of stairs above the restaurant. They occupy the four corners of the lodge and open onto a hallway hung with antlers and old paintings that creaks round the stairwell. Two of the rooms enjoy an expanse of deck that looks out through the trees to the bay. Four rooms are located in an rambling annex at the back of the wooded property. All the guestrooms are cozy in size, the two cabins are the most spacious. Some rooms have a fireplace. We love the wonderful four-poster beds made from rough hewn Oregon fir, enhanced by warm flannel checks and plaids, and draped with heavy throw blankets. Manka's charm is its appealing, comfortable, rustic ambiance—a homey hideaway inviting you to nestle in with a good book and romantic company. *Directions:* Manka's is at the intersection of Argyle and Callendar Street.

MANKA'S INVERNESS LODGE
Innkeeper: Margaret Grade
30 Callendar Street, P.O. Box 1110
Inverness, CA 94937
tel: (415) 669-1034, fax: (415) 663-8308
8 bedrooms, 2 cabins, with private bathroom
Double from $95 to $160
Open all year
Credit cards: MC VS
Children accepted

Ten Inverness Way is a most attractive-looking inn—a cozy, redwood-shingled building fronted by a carefree, happy English garden. Originally built in 1904 as a family home, it was bought in 1980 by Mary Davies who converted it into an inn—Mary is the very proficient manager. A flagstone path leads from the road up a slope, through the flower beds to the front door. Inside, a staircase takes you to the second level and opens to the living room which has an informal ambiance with a large stone fireplace, redwood walls, Oriental carpets, comfortable furnishings and a few antique accents. The room is not elegant nor decorator perfect, but is very inviting. This is where Mary says guests relax and make themselves at home—playing games or snuggling up on the sofa with a good book. As the tensions of city life recede, guests strike up conversations with fellow visitors. The four small bedrooms are simply decorated, but fresh and immaculately clean, with handmade quilts on the beds adding a special touch. A suite has been added, complete with French doors leading to its own garden, and kitchen. In the morning Mary serves a delicious full breakfast in the sunny breakfast room, opening through French doors off the living room. After breakfast, Point Reyes National Seashore is just waiting to be explored. *Directions:* Drive into Inverness on the main road, Sir Francis Drake Boulevard, and watch for the sign pointing to your left to Ten Inverness Way.

TEN INVERNESS WAY
Innkeeper: Mary Davies
Ten Inverness Way, P.O. Box 63
Inverness, CA 94937
tel: (415) 669-1648
5 bedrooms with private bathroom
Double from $110 to $130; Suite from $150
Open all year
Credit cards: MC VS
Children accepted

Antiquing is an especially popular pastime with Jeannine and Vic's guests who use The Wedgewood Inn as a base for forays to antique stores in Jackson, Amador City and Sutter Creek. The Beltz' are avid collectors and had this large Victorian home purposely built as an inn and filled it with their antiques, knickknacks and family mementos. The bedrooms are packed with delightful country by-gones: spinning wheels, photos, albums, dolls, toys, clothes, and *absolutely* everything has a story behind it. The *piece de resistance* room is the Carriage House suite, located in a separate cottage. Here you can curl up in a rocker before the wood-burning stove, leaf through photo albums, admire the delicate stitchery in old needlework and play with the toys. Stop to admire Henry, the 1921 Model T Ford in the adjoining garage showroom. An especially nice room is the Victorian Rose with its woodburning stove and large bathroom. Terraced gardens feature a gazebo, fountains and room for croquet, hammocks and horseshoes. At 9 a.m. Jeannine rings the breakfast bell and the open dining room door reveals a table laid with silver and china for a breakfast feast. For dinner, guests usually drive the nine miles to Sutter Creek where there are several restaurants. *Directions:* Take Highway 88 east from Jackson for six miles, turn right on Irishtown/Clinton roads, and immediately right on Clinton road. After six tenths of a mile, turn left on Narcissus. After a quarter of a mile, the inn's gates are on the left.

THE WEDGEWOOD INN
Innkeepers: Jeannine & Vic Beltz
11941 Narcissus Road
Jackson CA 95642
tel: (209) 296-4300
6 bedrooms with private bathroom
Double from $85 to $115
Suite from $130 to $170
Open all year
Credit cards: MC VS
Children accepted over 12

Jamestown, with its high wooden sidewalks and wooden store fronts with broad balconies hanging to the street, wears an air of yesteryear—you expect to see old-time cowboys emerging from the saloon and a stagecoach rumbling down its main street. It seems that every Gold Rush town had a hotel similar to this one, but today few can boast of a city hotel that has received the careful restoration that the Jamestown Hotel has. The outside looks much as it did in its heyday, a simple brick false-front building whose second-story balcony forms a roof above the sidewalk. The lobby, cocktail lounge (where drinks are available in a cozy fireside setting in the evening and breakfast is served in the morning) and dining room occupy the ground floor. The restaurant abounds with the same old-world ambiance as the rest of the hotel and prides itself on serving excellent food. On summer days meals are served on the patio. The bedrooms are quaintly Victorian, neat as new pins. Some are two smaller rooms made into a sitting room and bedroom combination. All have attractive, spotless bathrooms and are named for famous personalities, being decorated with that person in mind—Black Bart, Joaquin Murietta, Lotta Crabtree, Jenny Lind, Buffalo Bill. *Directions:* From the San Francisco area take Highway 580 for sixty miles, then Highway 120 east to Jamestown which is just before Sonora.

JAMESTOWN HOTEL
Innkeepers: Michael & Marcia Walsh
P.O. Box 539, 18159 Main Street
Jamestown, CA 95327
tel: (209) 984-3902, fax: (209) 984-4149
8 bedrooms with private bathroom
Double from $80 to $110
Open all year
Credit cards: all major
Children accepted over 7

Julian was founded by ex-confederate soldiers when gold was discovered here in 1869. Albert Robinson, a freed slave and an excellent baker, was befriended by a confederate colonel who financed a restaurant and bakery, which later became a hotel. Albert's business was surprisingly well received in this predominantly confederate town. The Julian Hotel, the sole survivor of this town's several Victorian hotels, is the oldest continuously operating hotel in southern California and has had only four owners in its ninety-odd years of operation. Guests today are offered quaint rooms that appear much as they would have in the Gold Rush days. The owners, Steve and Gig Ballinger, have taken great pride in their project to authenticate as best as possible a decor in keeping with the history and character of the inn. With a selection of stylized Victorian wallpapers, patterned carpets and antique furnishings, they have masterfully and attractively achieved their goal. There are eighteen bedrooms, each named for an individual associated with the inn, varying in size as well as decor. Fans cool the rooms in the summer months. The Parlor, where a hearty breakfast and evening tea are served, as well as a lovely native stone terrace patio set with redwood tables and surrounded by gardens are available for guests' use. *Directions:* From San Diego, travel thirty-five miles east on Highway 8, then twenty-two miles north on Highway 79.

JULIAN HOTEL
Innkeepers: Gig & Steve Ballinger
2032 Main Street, P.O. Box 1856
Julian, CA 92036
tel: (619) 765-0201
18 bedrooms, 5 with private bathroom
Double from $64 to $94
Suite from $110 to $145
Open all year
Credit cards: all major
Children accepted

Located in a residential area south of the old Gold Rush town of Julian, is a miniature southern mansion, painted white and with four stately columns accenting the front of the house. The style especially appealed to Alan whose family, many years ago, used to own a plantation. The tranquil setting appealed to Mary, the large wooded lot is perfect for weddings—bridal party planning is her specialty. Inside, the home is simple, but very pleasant. The living room opens onto a sunlit dining room with a wall of windows, looking out to a sloping forest of trees. The dining room is where Mary hosts small bridal receptions and also where each morning guests are served a full, home made breakfast on family china and silver. Downstairs there is one bedroom (the only room with private bath), wallpapered in muted shades of tan and dusty pink and with a handsome Louis XVI antique bed. This is the French Quarter Room where feather masks and Mardi Gras memorabilia set the New Orleans theme. Upstairs three bedrooms are nicely decorated in pastel blues and pinks, two share an immaculate bathroom down the hall; the other is the honeymoon suite with a private bath. My favorite room is the upstairs East Room with a white wrought iron bed and Laura Ashley fabrics. *Directions:* From Julian head south on Highway 78. Turn left on Pine Hills Road. Turn right at second street which is Blue Jay Drive. (Total driving distance from Julian about four miles).

THE JULIAN WHITE HOUSE
Innkeepers: Mary & Alan Marvin
3014 Blue Jay Drive, P.O. Box 824
Julian, CA 92036
tel: (619) 765-1764
3 bedrooms, 1 with private bathroom
Double from $90 to $100; Suite from $107
Open all year
Credit cards: none accepted
Inappropriate for children

From the street The Bed & Breakfast Inn at La Jolla is a nondescript building with a pale peach stucco wash, but behind its facade is a surprising oasis of luxury. The inn is located a few blocks from the heart of La Jolla's elegant shopping district as well as its lovely beach and directly across the street from public tennis courts. The owners describe their decor as "elegant cottage style": beautiful furnishings, lovely fabrics, handsome prints and splendid antiques have been carefully selected to suit the mood of each room. From the Bird Rock, the smallest and least expensive room, charmingly decorated in Laura Ashley blue and white pinstripes and dainty flowered prints, to the spacious and elegant Holiday room with its canopied four-poster bed, dramatic fireplace and color scheme of white on white with beige accents, each room is unique and inviting. Fresh fruit, sherry and flowers are placed in each guest room. Ten rooms are located in the historic house and six in the annex. On sunny days pass through the arched doorway and laze in the back yard at tables set on a brick patio bordered by grass and flowers. Breakfast is served either in the dining area, on the patio, the sun deck or in your bedroom. *Directions:* From San Diego take Route 5 and exit right on La Jolla Village Drive. Turn left on Torrey Pines Road, proceed two and a half miles to Prospect Place. Turn right, drive nine blocks, then turn left on Draper Avenue.

THE BED & BREAKFAST INN AT LA JOLLA
Innkeeper: Pierrette Timmerman
7753 Draper Avenue
La Jolla, CA 92037
tel: (619) 456-2066, fax: (619) 453-4487
16 bedrooms, 15 with private bathroom
Double from $85 to $225
Open all year
Credit cards: MC, VS
Children accepted over 12

Doing justice to La Jolla is the romantic La Valencia Hotel: subtle-pink adobe-like walls, thick Spanish tiled roof and a characterful tower domed with blue and gold mosaics set the stage for this special hotel. There is a captivating, old world charm from the moment you stroll under the colonnade, alongside the palm-shaded garden restaurant, and through the front door. The hotel dates back to the 1920's: thankfully the essence and dream of the original hotel have been faithfully preserved—and even bettered. The reception parlor opens onto a dramatic long parlor whose soft-buff-colored walls, wrought-iron chandeliers, subdued lighting, blue and yellow tiled planter, luscious displays of fresh flowers and painted ceiling are dramatized at the end of the room by a wall of glass that frames the sea. All of the guest rooms are individually decorated in a traditional style of furnishings and fabrics. The most expensive rooms are those with a view of the ocean, but even the less expensive rooms (such as those next to the garden) are lovely. One of my favorites (room 813 overlooking the front street) is especially spacious and has the added bonus of a kitchenette. On one of the lower terraces there is a lovely pool enhanced by perfectly tended gardens and nearby a "secret gate" allows guests to stroll from the hotel grounds down the road to La Jolla's beautiful little coves. *Directions:* Exit Highway 5 north at Ardath Road (5 south at La Jolla Village), travel to Torrey Pines Road and right on Prospect Street.

LA VALENCIA HOTEL
Innkeeper: Patrick Halcenwicz
1132 Prospect Street
La Jolla, CA 92037
tel: (619) 454-0771, fax: (619) 456-3921
100 bedrooms with private bathroom
Double from $145 to $295 (without breakfast)
Suite from $325 to $600 (without breakfast)
Open all year
Credit cards: all major
Children accepted

Eiler's Inn, although on a busy highway, has been carefully designed so that none of the guest rooms face the traffic, but front onto a central courtyard where, instead of car noises, the only sound is that of the gurgling fountain. This inner brick-paved patio, filled with colorfully blooming plants and potted greenery, is the heart of the inn where guests gather in the evening for wine and cheeses and again in the morning for a wonderful buffet breakfast. If the weather is chilly, guests congregate around the blazing fire in the front lounge. Frequently, one of the owners, Henk or Annette Wirtz, is present. They were guests themselves at Eiler's Inn many years ago when on holiday from Germany, then, when the inn came on the market, they bought it and returned to stay. Their warmth and hospitality are what really make the inn special. A feeling of camaraderie is somehow established amongst the guests—a mood of warmth and informal friendliness. The bedrooms each differ in decor: my favorites were room 209 with flowered wallpaper and an antique wooden headboard and room 204 with a wine-colored print wallpaper contrasting nicely against a white headboard and wicker chairs. The rooms are pleasant, but not outstanding in decor. However, guests seem happy with both the hotel and its proximity to the beach—just a two-minute walk down the hill. *Directions:* On the coastal Highway 1, just south of the town center.

EILER'S INN
Owners: Annette & Henk Wirtz
Innkeeper: Jonna Iversen
741 South Coast Highway
Laguna Beach, CA 92651
tel: (714) 494-3004, fax:(714) 497-2215
12 bedrooms with private bathroom
Double from $100 to $130
Suite from $175
Open all year
Credit cards: all major
Children accepted

It was quite a change in careers when Lee left her job at Capital Records and moved with her husband, Johan, from Pacific Palisades to Lake Arrowhead. They bought a Cape Cod style home tucked in the trees in a residential area above the lake. Happily Johan, who was born in Holland, is a talented craftsman and through his major renovations, followed by Lee's creative decorating, what was once a simple little cottage has been transformed into an appealing bed and breakfast. You cannot miss the house. A wonderful old-fashioned buggy sits front, leading the way to the soft blue house, with white trim and a cheerful front door painted bright red. You enter into a small living room which leads into the dining room and beyond to the prettiest room downstairs, a sun room wrapped in windows with comfy sofa and chairs slip-covered in a cheerful English floral print. French doors open onto a large deck, the perfect spot to relax and enjoy a view through the trees to the lake. Upstairs are three guestrooms. My favorite is the *Brougham Room*, charmingly decorated in pastels and whites and with a window seat from which to enjoy the view through the trees to the lake. Lee's warmth of welcome makes all guests want to return. *Directions:* From the Rim Forest Road, take Highway 173 signposted to Lake Arrowhead. Turn right at the stoplight when you reach the village. Continue for about two miles and turn right on Emerald Drive.

THE CARRIAGE HOUSE
Innkeepers: Lee & Johan Karstens
472 Emerald Drive
Lake Arrowhead, CA 92352
tel: (714) 336-1400
3 bedrooms with private bathroom
Double from $95 to $120
Open all year
Credit cards: all major
Children accepted over 12

The Château du Lac, perched on the hillside above the crystal blue water of Lake Arrowhead, is a very sophisticated bed and breakfast owned by Jody and Oscar Wilson who left the Los Angeles area a few years ago. They were lucky to find a home serenely set amongst the trees overlooking Lake Arrowhead. It was perfect: large enough to provide six guest rooms, yet small enough to maintain a homelike ambiance. Although of new construction, the effect is a pleasing adaptation of a Victorian style with pretty light brown wood facade accented by crisp white trim and accents of French-blue shingles. But there is none of the Victorian gloom inside. The spacious living areas all opening on to another. The "prize" is the stunning dining room with French windows opening to a romantic deck that stretches around the house and provides a beautiful vista through the trees to the lake. The furnishings in the individually decorated bedrooms are mostly new, but achieve a French country look. All of the bedrooms have private bath except for two on a lower level which share a bath. Jody is a gourmet cook and was a professional caterer in Los Angeles, so guests are certainly well-tended in the food department. *Directions*: From the Rim Forest Road take road 173 signposted to Lake Arrowhead. When you reach the village, turn right at the first stop light and continue for about three miles. Turn right at Hospital Road. The Château du Lac is the first house on your right.

CHÂTEAU DU LAC
Innkeepers: Jody & Oscar Wilson
911 Hospital Road
Lake Arrowhead, CA 92352
tel: (909) 337-6488, fax: (909) 337-6746
6 bedrooms, 4 with private bathroom
Double from $95 to $130
Suite from $175 to $250
Closed Christmas
Credit cards: all major
Children accepted over 14

Although Eagle's Landing is a bed and breakfast, it is run so professionally that guests have the feeling that they are indeed in a miniature hotel. There are four guest rooms with private bath and, although each varies in decor, they all maintain a comfy-homey ambiance and are all meticulously kept—everything "neat as a pin." One of the bedrooms, the Lake View Suite, is enormous, with its own fireplace and a spacious private deck with a view of the lake. However, my favorite room is the cozy Woods Room, tucked amongst the trees with its own little terrace and entrance. The living room has a large fireplace in the corner and a splendid long wooden trestle table, big enough for all the guests to gather and share their day's adventures. Just off the dining room is a cozy nook where guests can enjoy breakfast. Speaking of breakfast, Dorothy prides herself on treating her guests to a special brunch on Sunday mornings, a hearty start for exploring the lake which is located a short walk from the hotel. However, since this is a private lake, public access is available only in the town of Arrowhead (about a five-minute drive away). *Directions:* Turn north from Highway 18 following signs for Blue Jay. Before you reach the lake, the road splits. Turn left on North Bay and watch for Cedarwood on your left—Eagle's Landing is on the corner of North Bay and Cedarwood.

EAGLE'S LANDING
Innkeepers: Dorothy & Jack Stone
27406 Cedarwood, Lake Arrowhead, CA
P.O. Box 1510, Blue Jay, CA 92317
tel: (714) 336-2642
4 bedrooms with private bathroom
Double from $95 to $185
Open all year
Credit cards: all major
Children accepted over 16

The Saddleback Inn is tucked into its own wooded oasis just a short stroll from Lake Arrowhead Village. Although the inn dates back almost seventy years when it was built in the style of an English tavern by two sisters from the Midwest, there is nothing "dated" about this small inn. Its present owners have completely renovated every nook and cranny, creating a slick, very sophisticated hotel. Luckily they have kept the old-world look with the use of a few antiques plus many reproductions in the decor. The reception area is located in the main lodge which exudes a Victorian mood in its cozy bar and dining room. The original staircase leads off the lobby to ten guest rooms, some quite small but all attractive. Scattered throughout the three and a half acres are small cottages connected by pathways which house the remaining guest rooms. All of the rooms are decorated with Laura Ashley fabrics and wallpapers, and most have a jacuzzi tub in the bathroom—a wonderful respite after a day of hiking or sightseeing. The Saddleback Inn appears more "slick" than "homey," but behind its commercial facade is the warmth the manager, Liza Colton, who creates the ambiance of a small inn. This hotel is an especially suitable choice when travelling with children, as a pretty beach is within walking distance. *Directions:* From Highway 173 take the Lake Arrowhead turnoff. Drive two miles. The hotel is on the left at the entrance to Lake Arrowhead Village.

SADDLEBACK INN
Innkeeper: Liza Colton
300 S. State Highway 173, P.O. Box 1890
Lake Arrowhead, CA 92352
tel: (714) 336-3571, fax: (909) 337-4277
10 rooms, 24 cottages, with private bathroom
Double from $110 to $155 (without breakfast)
Suite from $160 to $325 (without breakfast)
Open all year
Credit cards: all major
Children accepted

Lakeport, located on the banks of Clear Lake, is usually thought of as a playground for water enthusiasts. However, tucked in among the weekend cottages, there are many old Victorian homes. One of these, whose history dates back to the time of the Civil War, is the Forbestown Inn, a pretty clapboard house, with an old fashioned front porch heavily draped with wisteria. Upon entering, a hallway leads to a cozy living room with a cheerful dining area to one side with a wall of windows opening to one of the nicest features of the house—a lovely back garden with a towering redwood tree shading a generously-sized hot tub and swimming pool. There are two guest rooms downstairs which share a very spacious bathroom with a clawfoot tub. Upstairs are two more guest rooms tucked under the eaves. These are a bit smaller than the rooms downstairs, but they share a lounge area at the top of the stairs which makes them more commodious. My favorite is the upstairs guest room, nicely decorated with color coordinating fabric and wall paper in soft blues and peach tones and with its own private bathroom. Nancy and Jack have converted the adjacent carriage house into their own private quarters so are always close at hand to cater to their guests' every need. Jack is a gourmet cook and treats guests to a bountiful breakfast each morning. *Directions:* Located one block west of Main Street, between 8th and 9th.

FORBESTOWN INN
Innkeepers: Nancy & Jack Dunne
825 Forbes Street
Lakeport (Clearlake), CA 95453
tel: (707) 263-7858, fax: (707) 263-7878
4 bedrooms, 1 with private bathroom
Double from $85 to $120
Open all year
Credit cards: all major
Children accepted over 12

Glendeven is a charming New England-style farmhouse, built in 1867 by Isaiah Stevens for his bride, Rebecca. Today, this beautiful clapboard home, elegant in its simplicity, is owned by Jan (a native of Holland) and his wife Janet who purchased the property in 1977 and created one of the most delightful inns on the Mendocino Coast. From the beginning Jan and Janet have poured their love and work into Glendeven, adding improvements over the years. Not only are they a hardworking couple, but both are very talented designers whose eye for proportion, style and color are apparent in every detail. In addition to the beautifully decorated guest rooms in the main farm house (painted a creamy tan and trimmed with crisp white), there are equally inviting rooms in the Stevenscroft. Also, the 1800s Haybarn which has been converted into an elegant two-bedroom suite, and is actually more like an entire house. Most of the accommodations have fireplaces. The first floor of the barn houses *The Gallery*, featuring contemporary fine art and crafts as well as furniture designs in cherry and walnut. The inn, located across the street from the ocean, nestles on a two-acre parcel of land which has been transformed into a beautifully tended garden. Whether it is the parklike grounds or the rooms, everything is immaculate and shows the professionalism and caring of the deVries and their gracious staff. *Directions*: Located on the east side of the Highway 1, south of Mendocino.

GLENDEVEN
Innkeepers: Janet & Jan deVries
8221 North Highway One
Little River, CA 95456
tel: (707) 937-0083, fax:(707) 937-6108
6 bedrooms, 4 suites; with private bathroom
Double from $90 to $160
Suite from $185 to $200
Open all year
Credit cards: MC VS
Children accepted

The Salisbury House is conveniently located just off the Santa Monica Freeway (Highway 10), making easy access to Los Angeles' freeway network. Although the neighborhood, called Arlington Heights, is somewhat bland, it is better than most in the area, and West 20th Street (where the Salisbury House is located) is one of the more attractive streets. Here many of the homes have a good deal of architectural charm, and among these, Salisbury House is one of the nicest. The house, built in 1909, is square, with an interesting gabled roof line and several bay windows. Stained and leaded glass windows add to the old-world ambiance. Inside, the decor is very pleasant: beamed ceilings, wood paneling and lots of windows set a nice background for attractive, country-style furnishings. In the separate dining room one large table is set where guests enjoy a full hot breakfast. There are five bedrooms: because they were occupied I was not able to see them all, but those I did see were prettily decorated. I especially liked the Green Room, newly redone with rose-patterned wallpaper and a four-poster bed. It shares a bathroom but seems a good buy at $75 per night. On the top floor, cozily tucked under the eaves, is the Attic Suite, a spacious suite with a king-sized brass bed and an antique clawfoot tub. *Directions:* Take the Santa Monica Freeway east. Turn off at Western Avenue. Go north over the freeway and turn left on 20th (it is the first street).

SALISBURY HOUSE
Innkeepers: Sue & Jay German
2273 West 20th Street
Los Angeles, CA 90018
tel: (213) 737-7817
5 bedrooms, 3 with private bathroom
Double from $75 to $100
Closed Christmas
Credit cards: all major
Children accepted over 10

Hotels where the family are truly on the premises with "hands on" management seems to guarantee a superior quality of service. Such is the case at Barnabey's where four generations of the Post family participate. The stuccoed pink exterior with turquoise trim, green awnings, and tiled roof set a Mediterranean theme. Yet once inside, the mood leans heavily to the Victorian. The parlor-like reception area has wallpapered walls, wood paneling, ornate china displayed in cabinets, fancy drapes and lace curtains. The individually decorated guest rooms all continue the old-world look with Victorian-style wallpapers and antique headboards. I preferred some of the standard rooms with large windows facing the street (such as room 330) rather than some of the deluxe rooms overlooking the inner courtyard (which seemed a bit dark). There is a swimming pool just off the courtyard in a glass enclosed greenhouse. Guests are treated to a full breakfast that is served until 9:30 a.m.. Breakfast is not the only meal available: Barnabey's Restaurant offers several pretty dining rooms. A free shuttle service takes guests to or from the Los Angeles airport or to the delightful small town of Manhattan Beach to browse through the shops, eat at quaint restaurants, or enjoy the fabulous wide beach. *Directions*: Three miles south of the Los Angeles Airport. From Highway 405, take the Rosecrans exit and go west to Sepulveda. The hotel is on the southwest corner of Rosecrans and Sepulveda.

BARNABEY'S HOTEL
Innkeepers: Barnaby & Post Family
3501 Sepulveda Boulevard
Manhattan Beach, CA 90266
tel: (310) 545-8466, fax: (310) 545-8621
126 bedrooms with private bathroom
Double from $144 to $159
Open all year
Credit cards: all major
Children accepted

The McCloud Guest House has a wonderful setting—in its own pretty little park, surrounded by green lawn and trees, while in the distance is Mount Shasta, northern California's 14,162-foot giant. The inn is not pretentious, but most attractive in its simplicity. Built entirely of wood, the square building is wrapped with a spacious verandah whose supporting columns reach up to a steeply pitched roof from which little dormer windows peek out into the trees. Built in 1907, the inn was originally the home of J. H. Queal, the president of the McCloud River Lumber Company. After extensive renovations, it re-opened as a restaurant on the ground level with five bedrooms upstairs. As you enter the foyer, the massive stone fireplace and wood-paneled walls set the country lodge feeling. Upstairs the guests have their own private parlor highlighted with an ornate pool table from the Hearst collection. The original master bedroom is decorated with flowered wallpaper in soft shades of mauve and pink set off by white wicker chairs. Each of the other guest rooms has its own color scheme. Most have antique white iron beds, but one has a four-poster bed which looks quite handsome against a dark plaid wallpaper. *Directions:* Drive north on Highway 5, then east on Highway 89 for twelve miles to McCloud. Before the village turn left on Colombero Drive.

McCLOUD GUEST HOUSE
Owners: Dennis & Pat Abreu
Innkeepers: Bill & Patti Leigh
606 West Colombero Drive
P.O. Box 1510, McCloud, CA 96057
tel: (916) 964-3160
5 bedrooms with private bathroom
Double from $75 to $95
Open all year
Credit cards: MC VS
Inappropriate for children

The Blue Heron Inn is not the typical Mendocino Victorian, but a simple, New England-style house, painted white with blue trim. A white picket fence encloses the garden to each side, completing the cottage look. On the first floor there is a small restaurant (The Chocolate Mousse Cafe) and upstairs are two modestly priced, attractively decorated bedrooms sharing a bath. One of the bedrooms is called the Bay Room, a charming corner room with queen bed which has a sweeping view of the ocean on one side and village rooftops on the other. The other bedroom is the Sunset Room: a cozy, double-bedded, dormer room, which although tiny, is especially appealing, with a French writing table tucked beneath the window, puffy comforter on the bed, a wicker sofa, and a beautiful ocean view. In an attached cottage, reached by its own private entrance, is a third bedroom, the Garden Room, which has a queen-sized bed, its own private bathroom, a corner Franklin stove, ocean-view private deck, and French doors opening out to the garden. Although the Garden Room is more spacious, I prefer the country decor of the simple rooms in the main house which are a very good value. In the morning a Continental breakfast with croissants or coffee cake and fresh squeezed orange juice is served. *Directions:* Follow Highway 1 north into Mendocino. Turn left at Jackson Street, follow Jackson Street to Kasten Street and turn right.

BLUE HERON INN
Innkeeper: Linda Friedman
390 Kasten Street
Mendocino, CA 95460
tel: (707) 937-4323
3 bedrooms, 1 with private bathroom
Double from $64 to $90
Open all year
Credit cards: none accepted
Inappropriate for children

The Headlands Inn is an especially friendly, most attractive small inn located within walking distance of all the pretty shops and fun little restaurants in Mendocino. This New England-style home, dating from 1868, is a three-story, squarish building with a bay window in front and gables peeking out from the steep roof. A picket fence encloses the front yard which is usually abloom with flowers in a cheerful English garden. When you enter the small parlor, either Sharon or David will probably be there to greet you: both are extremely gracious and intent on making your stay a happy one. Steps lead to the upper two floors where four of the bedrooms are located—the fifth is in a detached cottage. There are wood-burning fireplaces in four of the bedrooms, and an old-fashioned wood-burning parlor stove in the other. Each of these antique-filled guest rooms is exceptionally attractive—none of the heavy Victorian feeling, just light, airy and pretty. My favorite room was Bessie Strauss, a spacious room with a private sitting nook and a large bay window with a view over the garden to the bay. But, whatever room you are in, a bountiful full breakfast is brought to you on a tray decorated with fresh flowers from the garden—Sharon is an exceptional cook and breakfast at the Headlands is a special treat. *Directions:* From San Francisco drive north on Highway 101, just past Cloverdale, turn left on Highway 128 west to Highway 1, and north to Mendocino.

THE HEADLANDS INN
Innkeepers: Sharon & David Hyman
Howard & Albion Streets, P.O. Box 132
Mendocino, CA 95460
tel: (707) 937-4431
5 bedrooms with private bathroom
Double from $103 to $172
Open all year
Credit cards: none accepted
Children accepted

The Joshua Grindle Inn, located just a short walk from the center of Mendocino, is surrounded by a two-acre plot of land. A white picket fence encloses the front yard and a walkway leads up to the inn, a most attractive, white clapboard farmhouse which, although architecturally simple, has hints of the Victorian era in the fancy woodwork on the verandah. In the 1879 farmhouse is the guest lounge, a sedate room with old paintings and portraits on the walls, a fireplace, white lace curtains, a trunk for a coffee table and an antique pump organ tucked in the corner. The light, airy guest rooms have a New England country ambiance enhanced by the owner's early-American antiques and some have their own fireplace. Of the five guest rooms in the main building two overlook the town of Mendocino and the distant ocean. A natural wood cottage just behind the house contains two additional bedrooms. The favorite rooms of many guests are those tucked romantically into the weathered-with-age Watertower in the rear garden; especially attractive is Watertower II, a sunny, cozy room on the second floor where the ocean can be glimpsed through the trees. All of the bedrooms are spotlessly maintained, immaculately decorated, have well lighted comfortably arranged sitting areas and private bathrooms. *Directions:* Drive north on Highway 1 through Mendocino and turn left on Little Lake Road.

JOSHUA GRINDLE INN
Innkeepers: Arlene & Jim Moorehead
44800 Little Lake Road
P.O. Box 647, Mendocino, CA 95460
tel: (707) 937-4143
10 bedrooms with private bathroom
Double from $95 to $140
Open all year
Credit cards: all major
Children accepted over 10

Most of our selections for Mendocino feature the coastal splendor, but although not next to the ocean, the Mendocino Farmhouse has its own special qualities. It is located at the end of a narrow lane which weaves through a beautiful redwood glen, crosses a small creek and then opens into a lovely meadow. There, amidst beds of flowers, next to a little duck pond and surrounded by a white picket fence, you will find an appealing tan farmhouse with white trim. Although it appears to be quite old, in reality the inn was newly constructed in 1976. Inside the decor is fresh and pretty, with antique accents giving it an eclectic style. The breakfast tables capture the sunshine in a many-windowed niche overlooking the flower garden, or dining outside under redwoods is an option in good weather. A large family kitchen is located off the living room. Upstairs there are three bedrooms, each sparkling clean and with its own bathroom. The latest additions are suites in the converted barn overlooking the garden, each with a sitting area and a large wood-burning fireplace. One suite is more rustic in mood, with cedar paneling, antlers over the fireplace and wicker furniture. The other suite has a bit of a Scandinavian look, with whitewashed pine walls. *Directions:* Just south of Mendocino, turn right off Highway 1 on Comptche-Ukiah Road. Go one and a half miles and turn left on Olson Lane—the Mendocino Farmhouse is at the end of the road.

MENDOCINO FARMHOUSE
Innkeepers: Margie & Bud Kamb
Olson Lane, P.O. Box 247
Mendocino, CA 95460
tel: (707) 937-0241, fax:(707) 937-1086
5 bedrooms with private bathroom
Double from $85 to $105
Open all year
Credit cards: MC VS
Children accepted

At first glance The Stanford Inn by the Sea appears to be more like a motel than a country inn, but this is definitely untrue. Joan and Jeff Stanford have done a marvelous job in creating a cozy, sophisticated little hotel within an attractive, but not unusual, two-story, natural wood building. The inn is located across the road from the ocean at the crest of a grassy meadow where a few llamas graze in the blowing grass. The building is cleverly constructed so that every room has a view, either from a private deck or patio. Each guest room has been transformed into a cozy yet elegant little hideaway, with country antiques, many four-poster beds, color television, telephones, bouquets of flowers and either a wood-burning fireplace or stove—with plenty of wood to keep you warm on nippy nights. Everything is fresh and pretty and immaculately clean. The entire operation seems extremely professional and yet has a very personal touch. Each room has a complimentary carafe of wine which is kept replenished. A wonderful bonus is the glass enclosed sauna and "greenhouse" pool where guests can enjoy a swim even on blustery days. Renovations are constantly being introduced: the latest plans are for a dining room and new suites. *Directions:* A quarter of a mile south of the village of Mendocino at the intersection of Highway 1 and Comptche-Ukiah Road.

THE STANFORD INN BY THE SEA
Innkeepers: Joan & Jeff Stanford
Highway 1 and Comptche-Ukiah Road
Mendocino, CA 95460
tel: (707) 937-5615, fax: (707) 937-0305
25 bedrooms with private bathroom
Double from $165 to $185
Suite from $195 to $250
Open all year
Credit cards: all major
Children accepted

Gene and Ann Swett converted their family home into what continues to be one of the very nicest country inns in California. Their home is a most attractive Tudor-style house shaded by giant oak trees in an acre of wooded gardens full of colorful begonias, fuchsias, rhododendrons and lush ferns in a quiet Monterey suburb. Everything is beautifully tended, giving the grounds a park like appearance. The inside of the house is an oasis of gentility and tranquillity where everything is done with the comfort of the guest in mind. Most of the bedrooms in the main house, cottage and carriage house have fireplaces, all are beautifully decorated and thoughtfully appointed. The library stands out as a particularly memorable bedroom with its book-lined walls, cozy fireplace and private balcony overlooking the garden. A refrigerator is kept stocked with complimentary beverages, and juices and hot beverages are always available. In an evening the Swetts join their guests for wine and cheese in the living room. They are especially gracious hosts, adding great warmth and professionalism to their little inn. Breakfast is served at the long oak table in the dining room or brought to your room on a tray. This is certainly the place for a romantic getaway. *Directions:* Travelling south on Highway 1 take the Soledad/Munras exit, cross Munras Avenue, then go right on Pacific Street: Martin Street is on your left in a little over half a mile.

OLD MONTEREY INN
Innkeepers: Ann & Gene Swett
500 Martin Street
Monterey, CA 93940
tel: (408) 375-8284
10 bedrooms with private bathroom
Double from $160 to $220
Open all year
Credit cards: MC VS
Inappropriate for children

As an alternative to a bed and breakfast we recommend the Spindrift Inn as a lovely hotel with a great location overlooking the Monterey Bay. Just down the street from the fabulous Monterey Bay Aquarium its rooms either overlook the bustle of Cannery Row or the serenity of the bay. We stayed in a front room overlooking Cannery Row and were pleasantly surprised to find that the deep set windows and heavy drapes blocked out the noise of the late night revelers. Guestrooms on the bay side enjoy wonderful water views and corner rooms are spacious and enjoy a lovely window seat. The Spindrift Inn offers forty-one bedrooms, each handsomely decorated with rich country fabrics, all with wood-burning fireplaces, beds topped with feather down comforters and bathrooms finished in marble and brass. The feeling is European and the amenities are first class. A continental breakfast of Danish or croissants and a selection of fruit is served on a silver tray to the room and in the evening a buffet of wine and cheese is offered in the front lobby. Service is cordial. There is almost always someone at the front desk in the lobby to assist with information or reservations, but shifts change regularly. This is a hotel, efficient, attractive, comfortable with a premier location. *Directions:* Take the Pacific Grove, Del Monte exit off Highway 1. Follow signs to Cannery Row and the Aquarium. The Spindrift is located right on Cannery Row.

SPINDRIFT INN
Innkeeper: Helen Callahan
652 Cannery Row
Monterey, CA 93940
tel: (408) 646-8900, fax: (408) 646-5342
41 bedrooms with private bathroom
Double from $149 to $389
Open all year
Credit cards: all major
Children accepted

Karen (Brown) Herbert and her husband, Rick, have built their own romantic English-manor-style hideaway, Seal Cove Inn. Located just half an hour's drive south of San Francisco, the inn is bordered by towering, wind-swept cypress trees and looks out over fields of wild flowers and acres of park-land to the ocean. You enter through a spacious entrance hall into an elegantly comfortable living room with a large fireplace centered between French doors. Adjoining the living room is a dining room, and next to that, a small conference room—all with park and ocean views. Antiques are used throughout: grandfather clocks, cradles filled with flowers, handsome tables, antique beds, side boards, trunks, etc. Each of the large bedrooms has a wood-burning fireplace, comfortable reading chairs, television, VCR, hot towel rack, and a refrigerator stocked with complimentary soft drinks and wine. Best yet, each of the bedrooms has a view of the ocean and doors opening either to a private balcony or onto the terrace. From the inn you can walk to a secluded stretch of beach or stroll through the forest along a path that traces the ocean bluffs. Karen has already had the pleasure of welcoming many guests to Seal Cove Inn who are also readers of her travel guides. *Directions:* From San Francisco take Highway 1 south to Moss Beach (about twenty miles). Turn west on Cypress (at the Moss Beach Distillery sign). Seal Cove Inn is one block off the road on the right.

SEAL COVE INN
Innkeepers: Karen & Rick Herbert
221 Cypress Avenue
Moss Beach, CA 94038
tel: (415) 728-7325, fax: (415) 728-4116
10 bedrooms with private bathroom
Double from $165 to $250
Closed Christmas
Credit cards: all major
Children accepted

The Pelican Inn, nestled among pine trees, jasmine and honeysuckle, is a wonderful re-creation of a cozy English tavern with a few attractive guest rooms tucked upstairs. Your host, Barry Stock (from Devon), has a delightful British accent that adds to the impression that you must be in England. Wide wood-planked floors, an appealing small bar (with dart board), low beamed ceilings, a giant fireplace with priest hole (secret hiding place), a cozy little guest lounge and a dining room with trestle tables complete the first floor scene. Besides the large indoor dining room, there is also a trellised patio where guests can have snacks or dine (in the evenings the candle-lit tables are set with linens). Lunch features such English treats as succulent bangers and mash and fish n'chips; dinner includes prime rib, rack of lamb, etc. Upstairs there are seven cozy bedrooms where the English motif is carried out with heavily draped half-tester beds, Oriental carpets, a decanter of sherry and fresh flowers. The location of the Pelican Inn is fabulous: only a few minutes' drive from the giant redwood grove at Muir Woods and a short walk to the ocean. Note: reservations needed six months in advance for weekends. *Directions:* From Highway 101 take the Stinson Beach/Highway 1 turnoff. At the Arco station, go left for five miles on Highway 1 to Muir Beach. Pelican Inn is on the left.

PELICAN INN
Innkeeper: Barry Stock
10 Pacific Way
Muir Beach, CA 94965-9729
tel: (415) 383-6000
7 bedrooms with private bathroom
Double from $145 to $160
Closed Christmas
Credit cards: MC VS
Children accepted

As the gold boom passed, Murphys was left to sleep under its locust and elm trees until tourists discovered its beauty and slower pace of life. A few old stone buildings survive, one of which contains the Old Timers' Museum filled with pioneer and Gold Rush regalia. The Dunbar House, 1880, is a handsome inn with a wrap-around porch where guests can sit and sip gold-country wine or enjoy a refreshing glass of lemonade. Bob and Barbara's pride in their small inn is apparent—they have lavished their time and attention on making it extremely comfortable. Each of the four cozy guest rooms has a fireplace and a small refrigerator with ice and a complimentary bottle of wine. The Sequoia room has a queen-size bed and a clawfoot tub set before a wood stove. The Cedar room, just off the downstairs parlor, is a suite offering a luxurious jacuzzi. Upstairs are two additional pretty bedrooms. Each room also provides a TV with VCR hidden away in an amoire. While you are out at dinner your bed will be turned down and chocolates placed on your pillow. Breakfast, served in the dining room by the fire, in the century old garden, or in the privacy of your room, includes juice spritzer, fresh fruit, muffins, turnovers, an egg dish and a hot beverage. An appetizer buffet is offered in the afternoon. *Directions:* From San Francisco take Highway 580 to Highway 99 north to Highway 4 east, drive through Angels Camp towards Arnold. Murphys is nine miles east of Angels Camp.

DUNBAR HOUSE, 1880
Innkeepers: Barbara & Bob Costa
271 Jones Street, P.O. Box 1375
Murphys, CA 95247
tel: (209) 728-2897, fax: (209) 728-1451
4 bedrooms with private bathroom
Double from $105
Suite from $145
Open all year
Credit cards: MC VS
Children accepted over 10

Nestled just off the road with six hundred acres of vineyards as its backdrop, Oak Knoll Inn offers a very picturesque and tranquil setting. The entry and front sitting room are housed in the original farmhouse that once sat in the middle of the vineyards. An additional building was then added on to each side to house guestrooms. Breakfast is a feast served on winter mornings in front of the fireplace, or on warm mornings on the deck when you can often watch the graceful hot-air-balloons as they drift silently over the vineyards and down the valley in the early morning sunshine. The four guestrooms all open onto the deck. The guestrooms are luxurious in their size, magnified by the high vaulted ceilings and the two end rooms enjoy the bonus of one arched side window that towers to the height of the ceiling. The rooms are all similar in appointments and in their contemporary decor. Each enjoys a king-sized brass bed, a sitting area before a fireplace, and thick stone walls that insulate from summer heat and winter cold. The bathrooms are modern, but surprisingly small by comparison to the spacious rooms. What the Oak Knoll Inn offers most is its spectacular setting. You can sit poolside with a glass of wine and enjoy the quiet and beauty of a backdrop of vineyards and the gorgeous hills of the Napa Valley. *Directions:* North on Highway 29 through Napa, left on Oak Knoll Avenue, which has a left-right-zig-zag cross Big Ranch Road.

OAK KNOLL INN
Innkeepers: Barbara Passino & John Kuhlmann
2200 E. Oak Knoll Avenue
Napa, CA 94558
tel: (707) 255-2200
4 bedrooms with private bathroom
Double from $175 to $250
Closed Christmas Eve
Credit cards: MC VS
Inappropriate for children

La Residence is an inn that has grown around the Mansion, a beautiful Gothic revival home built in the 1870s as a farmhouse to accommodate the large family of Harry Parker, a riverboat pilot from New Orleans. In later years additions more Victorian in style changed the appearance of the home. Nine rooms are housed in the original mansion and are dramatic in their decor which blends well with the grand feeling of the home. Rooms vary from cozy, top-floor rooms tucked under slanted ceilings to spacious and elegant accommodations with fireplaces on the first floor. The eleven rooms in the newly constructed Cabernet Hall, shingled and built in the style of a French barn, are beautifully designed and commodious, each enjoying a private bath, fireplace and French doors that open onto a private patio or balcony. These bedrooms are handsomely decorated with pine antiques imported from France and England and Laura Ashley prints. Breakfast is served in the Cabernet Hall's lovely dining room with tables set before a blazing fire. Between the Mansion and the Cabernet Hall are a heated swimming pool and jacuzzi spa. The excellence of the inn reflects the expertise and talents contributed by the partners who share in the management. *Directions:* Take Highway 29 through Napa. Take the first right turn after the Salvador intersection onto a frontage road (no name) which winds back south to the inn.

LA RESIDENCE
Innkeepers: David Jackson & Craig Claussen
4066 St. Helena Highway
Napa, CA 94558
tel: (707) 253-0337, fax: (707) 253-0382
20 bedrooms, 18 with private bathroom
Double from $90 to $155
Suite from $170 to $190
Closed Christmas Eve
Credit cards: all major
Children accepted

When gold was discovered, Nevada City became an affluent boom town. It remains prosperous-looking, its beautifully restored downtown area full of tempting restaurants and inviting shops. Just beyond Broad Street's shopping district, enclosed within a mature garden of long rolling lawns and tidy bushes, sits Grandmere's Inn, a stately colonial revival home built for Aaron Sargant, a U.S. Congressman and his suffragette wife, Ellen. Ellen's friend, Susan B. Anthony, often stayed here and Aaron authored the bill that eventually gave women the right to vote. Now Grandmere's is the loveliest of country inns decorated with flair; with gray as the dominant background color, although each of the rooms has a very different personality, the Master Suite is a luxurious ground floor unit with a separate living room and bedroom. Mama's and Papa's is a large upstairs bedroom with a sitting area. Gertie's, a downstairs suite, has a private garden entry. The parlor and dining room are beautifully decorated in country style. In the morning the aroma of coffee fills the air and at 9:00 am the sideboard is loaded with sliced fruits, breakfast casseroles, muffins and croissants. Portions are so bountiful that there is no need to worry about lunch. *Directions:* From San Francisco take Highway 80 to Highway 49 north twenty-nine miles to Nevada City, exit at Broad Street, turn left up Broad Street.

GRANDMERE'S
Innkeepers: Geri & Doug Boka
449 Broad Street
Nevada City, CA 95959
tel: (916) 265-4660
7 bedrooms with private bathroom
Double from $100 to $125
Suite from $135 to $150
Open all year
Credit cards: MC VS
Children accepted in the downstairs suite

It was fun to discover The Doryman's Inn, a sophisticated, elaborately decorated small hotel next to the Newport Beach Pier. In fact it sits just across the street, next to the old wooden wharf, where the fishermen still go to sea every day (as they have for one hundred years) in their brightly painted dories and return to sell their catch from the back of the boats. For beach buffs, the sand stretches for miles to the entrance to Balboa Harbor. The hotel entry is quite discreet: just a tiny hall where an elevator takes you up to the reception area—the inn is located above the 21 Ocean Front Restaurant, a dining establishment famous for its seafood. When you step off the elevator you are immersed in the romantic ambiance of the Victorian era with elaborate paneling, reproduction gas lamps, dark wallpaper and busy floral carpeting. The bedrooms open off the long hallway which is lit with skylights and graced by baskets of hanging ferns. Each of the bedrooms is elaborately decorated with splendid antique beds, fireplaces, and Italian-marble sunken bathtubs. No expense was spared—and it shows. In the morning a light breakfast of fresh pastries, seasonal fruits, yogurts and assorted cheeses is served buffet-style in the small dining room or out on the patio. *Directions:* Take Highway 5 west to 55 south toward Newport Beach, follow the signs to the Newport Pier: the hotel is across the street.

DORYMAN'S INN
Innkeeper: Michael D. Palitz
2102 West Ocean Front
Newport Beach, CA 92663
tel: (714) 675-7300, fax: (714) 675-7300
10 bedrooms with private bathroom
Double from $135 to $225
Suite from $185 to $275
Open all year
Credit cards: all major
Children accepted over 5

Heavy iron gates magically swing open allowing you to enter a world far removed from the neon signs that line the main street of Oakhurst, a town just to the south of Yosemite National Park. You enter through the château's heavy doors, across a cool, flagged limestone foyer and step down into a stunning living room opening onto a circular tower room where a grand piano sits center stage beneath a whimsically frescoed ceiling. Doors open to reveal a sunny breakfast room and a tiny chapel. A spiraling stone staircase leads up to the individually decorated bedrooms named for herbs and flowers: Saffron has an enormous ebony bed and black marble fireplace, Lavender is sunny in bright blues and yellows, and Elderberry is cool in blue and white. Each of the splendid bedrooms has a wood-burning fireplace (placed at just the right height that you can see it from the bed), goose down duvet, hidden CD player, luxurious bathroom with a deep soaking tub (many large enough for two), the finest toiletries, thick towels, and the softest of robes. In the evening, just walk across the garden, by the swimming pool, to the Elderberry House Restaurant (closed Tuesday in winter) where the château's owner, Erna Kubin-Clanin, presents a spectacular fixed price ($53) six-course dinner. *Directions:* From the center of Oakhurst take Highway 41 toward Fresno. As the road climbs the hill, turn right at the medical complex and in through the wrought iron gates.

CHÂTEAU DU SUREAU
Owner: Erna Kubin-Clanin
Innkeeper: Kathryn Kincannon
48688 Victoria Lane, P.O. Box 577
Oakhurst CA 93644
tel: (209) 683-6860, fax: (209) 683-0800
9 bedrooms with private bathroom
Double from $250 to $350, 10% service chg.
Open all year
Credit cards: MC VS
Inappropriate for children

Occidental is a dear country town nestled between the rugged Sonoma coast and the vineyards of the Russian River valley. A quiet Victorian town, the one main street of Occidental is appealing in its contrast with the more bohemian Russian River towns and resorts to the north. The Heart's Desire Inn at Occidental is just a block or two up from main street, dates from 1867 and was refurbished as an inn in 1988. The "Gallery at the Inn" occupies the first level of the building off the driveway and features local artists. One level up, entered off the porch is the reception and just off the entry is the intimate restaurant (opened both to the public and residents of the inn) whose few tables are set in front of the lovely woodburning fireplace. Mornings, the restaurant becomes the breakfast room and a bounty of croissants and fresh fruit precede such tempting delights as cinnamon-apple waffles. Beautiful fir floors are exposed throughout the public and eight guestrooms of the inn. The rooms are very small but fresh and pretty in their decor. Lovely pine beds, armoires and chests of drawers have been selected for the furnishings and white linen dresses the down comforters atop the comfortable beds. This is a managed property. *Directions:* Located ninety minutes north of San Francisco, travel Highway 101 north to the Highway 12 exit, direction of Sebastopol. In Sebastopol take the Bodega Highway 5, miles west to Bodega Bay to the Bohemian Highway and on to Occidental.

HEART'S DESIRE INN AT OCCIDENTAL
Owners: Howard & Justina Selinger
Innkeeper: Meg Sorensen
3657 Church Street
Occidental, CA 95465
tel: (707) 874-1047, fax: (707) 874-1078
8 bedrooms with private bathroom
Double from $102.60 to $212.50
Open all year
Credit cards: all major
Inappropriate for children

Sandwiched between the busier resorts of Monterey and Carmel, Pacific Grove has managed to avoid much of their more touristy ambiance and retains the air of being an inviting Victorian summer retreat. And the Gosby House is a perfect place to retreat to, with certainly a lot more fun and frolic than in days gone by when it was the summer home of a stern Methodist family. While the decor is decidedly Victorian in flavor, it has been done with such whimsy and fun that all formal stuffiness has been dispelled: a glass-fronted cabinet in the dining room is filled with antique dolls and teddy bears are rakishly posed on each bed. The bedrooms are scattered upstairs and down, some have garden entrances and several occupy an adjacent clapboard house tucked behind the pretty garden. Over half the bedrooms have fireplaces and all but two have luxuriously appointed bathrooms. Each room is appealingly decorated in soft colors and many benefit from the romantic touch of antique beds. Before you venture out for dinner, enjoy hors d'oeuvres, wine and sherry in the living room. When you return, your bed will be turned down and a rose and chocolates placed on your pillow—such a sweet way to end the day. *Directions:* Take Highway 1 to Highway 68 west to Pacific Grove. Continue on Forest Avenue to Lighthouse Avenue, turn left and go three blocks to the inn.

GOSBY HOUSE
Owners: Sally & Roger Post
Innkeeper: Jillian Brewer
643 Lighthouse Avenue
Pacific Grove, CA 93950
tel: (408) 375-1287, fax: (415) 655-9621
22 bedrooms, 20 with private bathroom
Double from $85 to $140
Open all year
Credit cards: all major
Children accepted in annex rooms

The Green Gables Inn is sensationally positioned overlooking Monterey Bay. This romantic, half-timbered, Queen Anne-style mansion with many interesting dormers is as inviting inside as out. The living room and dining room have comfortable arrangements of sofas and chairs placed to maximize your enjoyment of the view. Upstairs many of the bedrooms, set under steeply slanting beamed ceilings with romantic diamond-paned casement windows, offer ocean views. While the Garret room does not have an ocean view, it is the coziest of hideaways. All but one of the upstairs bedrooms share a bathroom. The ground floor suite has a sitting room and fireplace. The more modern rooms in the adjacent carriage house all have fireplaces, sitting areas and private bathrooms. While a guest at The Green Gables Inn you will certainly not perish from hunger or thirst—beverages are available all day, goodies readily available in the cookie jar, and wine and hors d'oeuvres appear in the evening. Breakfast, too, is no disappointment: a hearty buffet of fruit, homemade breads and a hot egg dish. *Directions:* From Highway 1 take the Pacific Grove—Del Monte exit. As you go through the tunnel Del Monte becomes Lighthouse Avenue which you follow into Pacific Grove. Go right one block and you are on Ocean View Boulevard and the inn is on the corner at Fifth Street.

THE GREEN GABLES INN
Owners: Sally & Roger Post
Innkeeper: Shirley Butts
104 Fifth Street
Pacific Grove, CA 93950
tel: (408) 375-2095
11 bedrooms, 7 with private bathroom
Double from $100 to $140; Suite from $160
Open all year
Credit cards: all major
Children accepted

The Casa Cody, a moderately-priced hotel in the heart of Palm Springs, although quite simple, stands out like a gem from its neighbors. The one-story inn has two U-shaped garden courtyards, each with its own swimming pool. There is a nostalgic, old-fashioned comfort to this pink-stuccoed building with turquoise trim. Once owned by Wild Bill Cody's niece, the Casa Cody (the second oldest, still functioning hotel in Palm Springs) had fallen into a state of hopeless-looking disrepair until bought by Therese Hayes (who is French) and Frank Tysen (who is Dutch). After hard work, lots of imagination, and much love, the hotel once again blossomed into an appealing small hotel with a nice choice of accommodations—ranging from a standard double to a spacious two-bedroom, two-bath suite. Many of the rooms have the added bonus of kitchenettes and fireplaces. The interior decor exudes a fresh, clean "Santa Fe" look with a pastel color scheme and handmade furniture. This friendly, comfortable inn is a remarkable value, especially the reasonably-priced studio units such as 2, 3 and 4 that have both fireplaces and well-equipped kitchens. However, my very favorite is the 1920's doll-house-like, one bedroom cottage (with kitchen) tucked in under the trees in the corner of the property. *Directions:* Drive south through Palm Springs on Palm Canyon Drive. Turn right on Tahquitz-McCallum Road for two blocks, then left on Cahuilla Road.

CASA CODY
Owners: Therese Hayes & Frank Tysen
Innkeepers: Therese Hayes & Elissa Goforth
175 South Cahuilla Road
Palm Springs, CA 92262
tel: (619) 320-9346, fax: (619) 325-8610
19 rooms, 18 with private bathroom
Double from $65 to $105, Suite to $160
Open all year
Credit cards: all major
Children accepted mid-week

As you enter the large wrought iron gates of the Ingleside Inn, you have the impression of being the guest on a private estate. This is not surprising, since the Ingleside Inn was once the home of the Humphrey Birge family, manufacturers of the Pierce Arrow automobile. Although the hotel is located in the heart of Palm Springs it is an oasis of tranquillity. The park like grounds are surrounded by a high adobe wall and the San Jacinto Mountains rise steeply behind the hotel, forming a dramatic backdrop. A pretty pool and gazebo highlight the front lawn of the hotel. Some of the guest rooms open off an inner courtyard, while others are nestled in nearby cottages. Each room is individually decorated and features antiques, and all have whirlpool tubs and refrigerators stocked with complimentary light snacks: many have wood-burning fireplaces. Breakfast is served either on the verandah, poolside, or on your private patio. The owner of Ingleside Inn, Melvyn Haber, also owns one of the famous restaurants in Palm Springs, appropriately called "Melvyn's," which is located next to the lobby. In the evening the restaurant traffic intrudes somewhat upon the solitude, but it is wonderfully convenient to have such an excellent restaurant so close at hand. *Directions:* Drive through Palm Springs south on Palm Canyon Drive and turn right on Ramon Road.

INGLESIDE INN
Innkeeper: Melvyn Haber
200 West Ramon Road
Palm Springs, CA 92264
tel: (619) 325-0046, fax: (619) 325-0710
29 bedrooms with private bathroom
Double from $95 to $275
Suite from $135 to $575
Open all year
Credit cards: all major
Children accepted over 16

Most of the new comers to Palm Springs are slick, trendy resorts, trying to outdo each other in money spent on glitzy glamour. However, the magic of the desert can best be captured on balmy, star-lit nights from the bougainvillea-shrouded patios of intimate hotels with the laid-back style and grace of yesterday. A rare example of such perfection is the Korakia Pensione, a Moorish-style villa built in 1924 by Scottish artist Gordon Coutts, just three blocks from the heart of the Palm Springs. The derelict building had immediate appeal to Doug Smith who spent four years on a tiny Greek Island running a bar and restaurant, catering to the rich and famous yacht-set. Doug (an architect specializing in restoring historic buildings) saw the great potential of the Korakia, which reminded him of the sun drenched houses of the Mediterranean. After several years of love and labor, his dream of a jewel of a small hotel has materialized. With a backdrop of the San Jacinto Mountains, this little inn has the flavor of Europe mingled with the romance of the Greek Islands: white-washed walls, Oriental carpets, handmade furniture, lovely natural fabrics, antiques, Moroccan fountains, fragrant fruit trees, and a pool surrounded by gardens create a stunning ambiance. Best of all, the undercurrent of what makes this hotel so special is the faultless taste and charm of Doug. There are only nine bedrooms—each is an absolute dream. *Directions:* Turn west off Palm Canyon on Areanas, go three blocks, turn south on Patencio Road.

KORAKIA PENSIONE
Innkeeper: Doug Smith
257 South Patencia Road
Palm Springs, CA 92262
tel: (619) 864-6411
9 bedrooms with private bathroom
Double from $89 to $155
Open all year
Credit cards: only to hold room
Children accepted

The Villa Royale is a romantic desert oasis. From the moment you enter this charming small hotel, you step into a magical world reflecting the essence of Spain: softly splashing fountains, walls draped in bougainvillea, decorative mosaic tile work, secluded little nooks, columned arcades, overhanging tiled roofs and meandering paths. The guest rooms too are very special. Not only do many have their own wood-burning fireplaces and private spas, but each accommodation represents a country, so you can choose your room to complement your mood, with such options in decor as Irish, English, Moorish, Swiss, Italian, German, Spanish, Dutch or Greek. There are three and a half acres of walled oasis in which the rooms are cleverly arranged for maximum privacy around secluded interior courtyards. The main courtyard has a swimming pool with a nearby terrace where tables are set for lunch or snacks. In the evening, dinner is served outside or in a romantic dining room, reminiscent of the French countryside. The Villa Royale is a short distance from the center of town—a bit too far to walk, but bicycles are conveniently at hand for guests to use for shopping or sightseeing excursions. *Directions:* Drive south through Palm Springs on Palm Canyon Drive and just a couple of blocks after the road makes a bend to the left and becomes East Palm Canyon Drive, turn left on Indian Trail.

VILLA ROYALE
Innkeeper: Robert Lee
1620 Indian Trail
Palm Springs, CA 92264
tel: (619) 327-2314, fax: (619) 322-4151
33 bedrooms with private bathroom
Double from $75 to $225
Open all year
Credit cards: all major
Inappropriate for children

Palo Alto, home to famous Stanford University, is an attractive town filled with art galleries, gift shops, smart boutiques and fun restaurants. Just one block from the town's main street (University Avenue), Susan and Maxwell have converted a beautiful old Victorian into a most attractive, well-run inn. The guest rooms are located both in the main house and in the carriage house located in the back garden. All of the guest rooms are individually decorated with great charm and taste. The beds, most four-poster or canopy-style, are fine quality antique reproductions with excellent mattresses. Susan personally chose the furniture and fabrics throughout the inn and planned each room. She even sewed the duvet covers for the down comforters, curtains, dust ruffles and fancy pillows. The garden is very pretty with nearly 1200 varieties of plants, many of them brought from England and lovingly planted in California. To start each day, a Continental breakfast is brought to each room on a tray. In the evening, guests congregate in the lounge for complimentary sherry or port. This is a very lovely little inn with a great bonus of excellent management: Susan is not only a gracious hostess, but also an excellent housekeeper—everything is spotlessly clean. *Directions:* Driving south from San Francisco on Highway 101 take the University Avenue (Palo Alto) exit west then turn right at Middlefield and left on Lytton.

THE VICTORIAN ON LYTTON
Innkeepers: Susan & Maxwell Hall
555 Lytton Avenue
Palo Alto, CA 94301
tel: (415) 322-8555, fax: (415) 322-7141
10 bedrooms with private bathroom
Double from $98 to $175
Open all year
Credit cards: all major
Children accepted over 15

When the last of Janet Marangi's four children left the nest, she fulfilled her dream of opening a small bed and breakfast. Just two blocks from the colorful center of South Pasadena, she found an 1895 Victorian-style farmhouse, built by a settler from Indiana for his family. The house is painted a pretty buttercup-yellow, accented by white trim. A white picket fence and old-fashioned swinging gate enclose a perfectly groomed front lawn. Eighty-four rose bushes line the fence and border the path leading to the spacious front porch. Janet's goal was to instill a totally comfortable, homey ambiance, recreating happy memories of visits to grandmother's house. She has succeeded. The furnishings are mostly pieces lovingly collected over the years by Janet while antique-browsing. The living room is painted a rich green that sets off the white wicker furniture and rich floral fabrics. The four bedrooms are appealingly decorated, each representing an artistic period. The Eighteenth Century English, is a sunny, cheerful room with windows on three sides, king-sized bed, old-fashioned rose patterned wallpaper, antique desk, dressing table, and white lace curtains. *Directions*: Fifteen minutes from downtown Los Angeles. Take Highway 110 (the Pasadena Freeway). Exit at the Orange Grove off-ramp. Turn right on Orange Grove. Go two blocks and turn left on Magnolia.

THE ARTISTS' INN
Owner: Janet Marangi
Innkeepers: Barbara & Phil Bennett
1038 Magnolia Street
South Pasadena, CA 91030
tel: (818) 799-5668, fax: (818) 799-5668
4 bedrooms with private bathroom
Double from $90 to $100
Open all year
Credit cards: none accepted
Children accepted over 8

Petaluma is a charming agricultural town situated on the Petaluma River that feeds into the San Francisco Bay. On a pretty residential street the Cavanaugh Inn is within walking distance of the historic downtown area with its multitude of antique shops and the river. Accommodations are in two neighboring neo-classic Victorian homes that share a lawn shaded by a large Magnolia tree and enclosed by a white picket fence. The main home was built in 1903 as a private residence and the cottage was added on in 1912 to accommodate the sisters. The main home is lovely, handsome and rich with all redwood floors and walls. Just off the entry is the library and parlor with chairs set in front of an open fireplace and a back dining room that opens onto the back porch and garden. Climb a beautiful staircase to reach a stunning octagonal redwood paneled landing. Four guestrooms open onto the landing where you can select from a library of books or find a forgotten item in the thoughtfully provided "basket of remembers". The guestrooms in the house are very comfortable and homey and all are with private bath or shower. The three rooms in the cottage enjoy a welcoming sun porch, are smaller, more calico than Victorian in decor and two of the rooms share a bath. A country breakfast is offered to all in the dining room of the main house or in pretty weather on the back porch. *Directions:* Traveling Highway 101 north, take Petaluma Boulevard South, follow it to Western Avenue. Turn left, go two blocks to Keller, make another left on Keller.

CAVANAUGH INN
Innkeeper: Billie Erkel
10 Keller Street
Petaluma, CA 94952
tel: (707) 765-4657
7 bedrooms, 5 with private bathroom
Double from $65 to $115
Open all year
Credit cards: all major
Children accepted

Thirty-nine Cypress is not old; it is not brimming with antiques; it is not decorator-perfect; it is not cutesy country: but it radiates warmth. A winding cobbled path leads through a profusion of happy flowers to the entry of the weathered-wood low building which blends into the landscape. The main room features a large fireplace encased with well-worn books. Facing the fireplace a comfortable sofa invites you to snuggle down with a good book and cup of tea. The country-style kitchen shows all the touches of someone who loves to cook. A patio leads out to the back where an idyllic view spreads before you with cattle grazing in the fields below. There are only three bedrooms: two have a private washbasin and toilet plus an outdoor nook with a shower stall with a terry cloth robe hanging conveniently near. The third bedroom has a bathroom off the hallway and if guests feel uncomfortable showering outdoors, they can use this bathroom's shower. Julia calls the furnishings "Family-Illinois" since most came with her when she moved out to California. There is no particular style, but everything is combined to exude a comfortable, appealing ambiance. An added bonus is a hot tub installed halfway down the bluff, a great way to relax and bird watch. *Directions:* Drive north through Point Reyes Station. on Highway 1 to the far side of town. As the road curves right, go left on Mesa Road for one mile, then left onto Cypress.

THIRTY-NINE CYPRESS
Innkeeper: Julia Bartlett
39 Cypress, Box 176
Point Reyes Station, CA 94956
tel: (415) 663-1709
3 bedrooms, 2 with private bathroom
Double from $105 to $120
Open all year
Credit cards: MC VS
Children accepted

The East Brother Light Station, snugly sitting on its own tiny island, dates back to 1873 when it was built to guide ships through a two-mile wide strait connecting San Francisco Bay and San Pablo Bay. Adjoining the tower beacon, a small house with gingerbread trim was built for the lightkeepers and their families. This nostalgic lighthouse was doomed for destruction until a group of concerned citizens banded together, raised the funds and rescued it. As a boy, one of the saviours, Walter Fanning, spent many happy hours at the East Brother Light Station where his grandfather was the lighthouse keeper. Today, a few lucky guests enjoy the island in far more commodious circumstances than the keepers of old. Guests are brought by boat in the afternoon, treated to a champagne tour and delicious four-course dinner with wines, then lulled to sleep by the sound of a fog-horn. There are four guest rooms, not large nor luxurious, but pleasantly decorated with antiques and all with a view of the bay. The innkeepers, Lore and John, live on the island, prepare the meals and graciously tend to the needs of their guests. Because all the water is caught from the rain and is limited, only guests staying more than one night may use the showers. *Directions:* The East Brother Light Station, located in San Pablo Bay, is reached by boat. When you call for reservations, ask for further information.

EAST BROTHER LIGHT STATION
Innkeepers: Lore Hogan & John Barnett
117 Park Place
Point Richmond, CA 94801
tel: (510) 820-9133, fax:(510) 232-5325
4 bedrooms, 2 with private bathroom
Double from $295
Rate includes breakfast & dinner
Open all year Thursday to Sunday
Credit cards: none accepted
Inappropriate for children

The known history of the Rancho Santa Fe property dates back to 1845 when an 8,842 acre land grant was given to Juan Maria Osuna. Then in 1906 the Santa Fe Railroad purchased the land grant, changed the name to Rancho Santa Fe and planted about three million eucalyptus seedlings with the idea of growing wood for railroad ties. The project failed: the wood was not appropriate. So the railroad decided instead to develop a planned community and built a lovely Spanish-style guest house for prospective home buyers. This became the nucleus for what is now the Inn at Rancho Santa Fe and houses the lounges, dining rooms, offices and a few of the guest rooms. The lounge is extremely appealing, like a cozy living room in a private home, with a large fireplace, comfortable seating, impressive floral arrangements and a roaring fire. The dining rooms are more "hotel-like" in ambiance. The bedrooms, most tucked away in cottages scattered throughout the property, are attractively decorated with traditional fabrics and furnishings and many have fireplaces. The grounds are lovely, filled with flowers and shaded by fragrant eucalyptus trees. The inn's greatest asset is the Royce family, who own the hotel and give what first appears to be a slick commercial resort, the warmth and friendliness of a small inn. *Directions:* From San Diego go north for twenty-five miles on Highway 5 and take the Lomas Santa Fe Drive turnoff, travel four and two tenths of a mile to the inn.

INN AT RANCHO SANTA FE
Innkeeper: Duncan Royce Hadden
Linea del Cielo at Paseo Delicias
P.O. Box 869, Rancho Santa Fe, CA 92067
tel: (619) 756-1131, fax: (619) 759-1604
75 bedrooms with private bathroom
Double from $90 to $225 (without breakfast)
Suite from $250 to $475 (without breakfast)
Open all year
Credit cards: all major
Children accepted

On two hundred fifty-six sprawling acres, Meadowood, an attractive complex of sand-gray gabled wooden buildings with crisp white trim, is a resort community in a secluded, quiet valley sheltered by towering Ponderosa pines and Douglas firs. Wooded areas open up to a golf course, two croquet courts and seven tennis courts. Centrally located, the clubhouse, a rambling, three-story structure that overlooks the golf course, houses the country elegant Restaurant at Meadowood, the less formal Grill, golf shop, conference facilities and the inviting reception lodge with a wonderful fieldstone fireplace. There are thirteen guest rooms in the Croquet Lodge which overlooks the perfectly manicured croquet lawn. Other guest rooms are found in clusters of lodges scattered about the property. The atmosphere, relaxed, informal, unpretentious, is accurately described as "California casual." Although expensive, the accommodations are luxuriously appointed and attractively furnished, reflecting an incredible attention to detail. Concern for a guest's comfort and satisfaction is foremost and service is carried out with a friendly and professional flair. Meadowood is a luxurious resort with every amenity, including a new state-of-the-art health spa and a most caring staff. *Directions:* From St. Helena take Pope Street east from Highway 29 to the Silverado Trail, cross the Silverado Trail, jog to the left and then right on Howell Mountain Road following Meadowood signs.

MEADOWOOD RESORT HOTEL
Director: Maurice Nayrolles
900 Meadowood Lane
St. Helena, CA 94574
tel: (707) 963-3646, fax: (707) 963-3532
82 bedrooms with private bathroom
Double from $215 to $445
Suite from $265 to $680
Open all year
Credit cards: all major
Children accepted, under 12 free

With an entry tucked off a small shopping arcade on St. Helena's delightful main street, the Hotel St. Helena affords an ideal location for those who want to stay within walking distance of shops and a wide range of interesting restaurants. The attractive lobby, decorated in rich tones of burgundy, mauve and brown, sets an inviting ambiance that is carried through to the decor in the bedrooms. A few steps up off the lobby is an extremely cozy wine bar whose intimate tables are set against rose-colored walls and dressed with pink cloths. Here you can sample by the glass fine Napa Valley wines and accompany your tasting with tempting appetizers or cheese plates. In addition, the wine bar serves a large selection of imported beers, coffees and teas. A Continental breakfast of croissants, cereal, fresh fruit and hot beverages is also served in the wine bar and on sunny days you can carry a tray out into the lovely garden courtyard. The hotel's seventeen bedrooms and one suite are located up a narrow flight of stairs decorated with attractive prints on the walls. While the guestrooms are on the small side, most have private bathrooms and all are delightfully decorated and furnished with Victorian antiques including some brass headboards and bent willow furniture. *Directions:* Located on the west side of Main Street in downtown St. Helena.

HOTEL ST. HELENA
Innkeeper: Athena Martin
1309 Main Street
St. Helena, CA 94574
tel: (707) 963-4388, fax: (707) 963-5402
17 bedrooms, 14 with private bathroom
Double from $100 to $150; Suite from $190
Open all year
Credit cards: all major
Children accepted

Just off Highway 29 at the corner of El Bonita, on the outskirts of St. Helena, the Vineyard Country Inn backs onto an expanse of vineyards. Newly constructed to resemble a French country manor, the attention to detail and the quality of appointments is impressive. Handsome slate roofs dotted by whimsical brick chimneys top the inn's complex of buildings. A path winds from the main building that houses the lobby and attractive breakfast room past the enclosed pool and jacuzzi, through patches of flowering garden to the guestrooms. Accommodations are all suites which enjoy a sitting area in front of a wood-burning fireplace, a game table or work area and then a bedroom furnished with either a four poster king bed or two queen sleigh beds. The decor is clean and elegant in its simplicity. Bathrooms are lovely in their tile and wallpaper and are beautifully fresh and modern. Under beamed ceilings the downstairs rooms (with the exception of two) open onto patios and under vaulted ceilings, all the upstairs rooms open onto private decks. The Vineyard Country Inn offers guestrooms that are spacious and priced well in comparison to other luxury accommodation offered in the valley. A bountiful breakfast buffet is offered mornings. *Directions*: Just on the south approach to St. Helena, travelling Highway 29, the Vineyard Country Inn is located on the left hand side at the intersection of El Bonita.

VINEYARD COUNTRY INN
Innkeepers: Gene & Ida Lubberstedt
201 Main Street
St. Helena, CA 94574
tel: (707) 963-1000, fax: (707) 963-1794
21 suites with private bathroom
Suite from $155 midweek to $175 weekends
Open all year
Credit cards: all major
Children accepted

The Wine Country Inn is a new complex of buildings built of wood and stone, fashioned after the inns of New England, settled on a low hillside and surrounded by acres of vineyards. The inn has twenty-five rooms which have been oriented to enjoy the tranquil and scenic setting: fifteen rooms are housed in the main building, six in the Brandy Barn and four in the Hastings House. Many of the rooms have private patios, balconies and fireplaces that are usable mid-October to mid-April. Each room, unique in its appeal and character, has its own bath and is individually decorated with country furnishings. Many of the quilts were handmade by the owner. The setting is peaceful, the mood relaxing and the staff knowledgeable and friendly. Public areas include a lovely lobby that opens onto a large expanse of deck and a pool on the terraced hillside bounded by a patio and colorful gardens. *Directions:* Two miles north of St. Helena on Highway 29 turn right onto Lodi Lane. The Wine Country Inn is in a quarter of a mile on the left.

THE WINE COUNTRY INN
Innkeeper: Jim Smith
1152 Lodi Lane
St. Helena, CA 94574
tel: (707) 963-7077, fax: (707) 963-9018
25 bedrooms with private bathroom
Double from $96 to $161
Suite from $152 to $217
Open all year
Credit cards: all major
Inappropriate for children

Heritage Park Bed and Breakfast crests the top of a lovely pedestrian street just steps from San Diego's popular tourist destination "Old Town." This authentically restored 1889 Queen Anne-style home, shares seven acres of English gardens with six other handsome Victorian beauties. Each gingerbread house was relocated from downtown San Diego to create this charming hillock village. You enter off the cobblestone, pedestrian-only street into a parlor that looks straight out of a Victorian novel. The inn has nine antique-filled guest rooms, most with puffy down mattresses. Some enjoy views of the city; some have fireplaces. In the adjacent Victorian home, the downstairs can be reserved for private parties while side-steps lead up to an ever-so-pretty suite with hand-stenciled walls, a four poster bed, spacious sitting area and a large bathroom with jacuzzi tub. (If travelling with children, this suite also has a separate room with trundle beds—perfect for the little ones.) In the morning, a delicious, home-made breakfast is served buffet-style from a large table in the parlor. During the summer, guests eat outside on the front porch where tables are set with fresh flowers and pretty linens. The extremely gracious owners, Nancy and Charles Helsper, are wonderful in advising guests of the best places to dine and ways to enjoy San Diego to the fullest. *Directions:* Take Highway 5 north from San Diego, exit on to Old Town Avenue and follow signs to Old Town and Heritage Park.

HERITAGE PARK BED & BREAKFAST
Innkeepers: Nancy & Charles Helsper
2470 Heritage Park Row
San Diego, CA 92110
tel: (619) 299-6832, fax: (619) 299-9465
9 bedrooms, 5 with private bathroom
Double from $80 to $120
Suite from $200 to $280
Open all year
Credit cards: MC VS
Children accepted over 12

This guide supposedly features small hotels with charm, so how could we even remotely consider including a resort hotel? Especially one with over 700 rooms! The reason is quite simple. There is just nothing else in California to compare with the marvelously whimsical Hotel del Coronado. If you are looking for a secluded hideaway or subdued elegance, this is definitely not your cup of tea. But if you want a hotel with boundless action, plenty of pizzazz, fabulous architecture, and an incredible creamy-white sandy beach, the Hotel del Coronado is tops. Its history dates back to 1887 when Elisha Babcock and H.L. Story purchased Coronado Island. They reserved the prime thirty-three acres of real estate for their extravagant venture, then sold off the remainder of the land to finance the building of one of the world's largest wooden structures. Within a year, their dream came true. The Hotel del Coronado, a white Victorian, gingerbread-hotel—a fantasy of turrets, wrap-around porches, funny little towers, and perky gables—was ready to open. Over the years, two modern wings have been added, but the original old hotel remains much as it was over a hundred years ago (except of course for a computer game arcade and a virtual shopping paradise discreetly tunneled beneath the building). If you want a modern beachfront room, opt for the new section, but if you value nostalgia, ask to be in the original building (be well-aware that some of the rooms are very small). *Directions:* Highway 5 to the Coronado Bridge. Turn left on Orange Avenue.

HOTEL DEL CORONADO
Manager: Dean Nelson
1500 Orange Avenue
Coronado, CA 92118
tel: (619) 435-6611, fax: (619) 522-8262
700 bedrooms with private bathroom
Double from $149 to $359 (without breakfast)
Suite from $399 to $1,275 (without breakfast)
Open all year
Credit cards: all major, Children accepted

Archbishops Mansion Inn is located on Alamo Square in an historic Victorian district of the city saved from fires after the 1906 San Francisco earthquake, just six blocks from the Opera House. Impressive in structure as well as in its role in San Francisco's history, the mansion since its construction in 1904 has served as the residence for three Archbishops and as a Catholic boys' school. The careful and artful supervision of Jonathan Shannon and Jeffrey Ross has now transformed it into a small luxury-class hotel. Extravagant furnishings have been selected to match the sophisticated elegance of the building. Crystal chandeliers illuminate the high, intricately sculpted ceilings, marble encases many of the fourteen working fireplaces and, of the fifteen guest rooms, even the smallest is large by standard hotel offerings. A grand staircase winds up three stories to the bedrooms, exposed to a large stained glass skylight. Each room is named for an opera whose theme stages a mood for the decor. Copies of the libretto are left in each room. In the ornate parlor complimentary wine is served accompanied by piano selections played on a 1904 Bechstein once owned by Noel Coward. An especially elegant Continental breakfast is brought to your room in a French picnic basket. *Directions:* From the south take 101 to Fell Street, go five blocks, then turn right onto Steiner: continue three blocks to Fulton.

THE ARCHBISHOPS MANSION INN
Owners: Jonathan Shannon & Jeffrey Ross
Manager: Kathleen Austin
1000 Fulton Street
San Francisco, CA 94117
tel: (415) 563-7872, fax: (415) 885-3193
15 bedrooms with private bathroom
Double from $115 to $185
Suite from $195 to $285
Open all year
Credit cards: all major
Children accepted

It is a joy to visit the Inn at the Opera and see how with imagination, excellent taste and (of course) money, a mediocre hotel can be converted into a real gem. Stepping into the intimate lobby is like walking into a lovely home. Comfortable chairs slipcovered in muted green, a superb carpet with a rose design, an antique cabinet, potted palms, soft lighting and beautiful floral bouquets add to the mood of quiet elegance. From the reception area a hallway leads to one of San Francisco's most appealing small restaurants and cocktail lounge. Here, in the Act IV lounge, the ambiance changes from light and airy to cozy and romantic. Dark paisley-like print wallpaper, rich paneling, subdued lighting, leather upholstered chairs, green plants, beautiful flower arrangements, a baby grand piano softly playing and the open fireplace create the perfect rendezvous. The guest rooms maintain the same tasteful decor promised by the public rooms. Most have traditional furnishings in dark woods which contrast pleasantly with pastel walls, carpeting and drapes. The least expensive rooms are quite small, but even these have terry cloth robes in the armoire, a small refrigerator, microwave oven, direct-dial telephone and chocolates on the pillow. *Directions:* As you might guess from the name, the Inn at the Opera is located in the heart of San Francisco's Performing Arts Complex—a perfect hotel choice for patrons of the opera, ballet and symphony.

INN AT THE OPERA
Innkeeper: Thomas R. Noonan
333 Fulton Avenue
San Francisco, CA 94102
tel: (415) 863-8400, fax: (415) 861-0821
48 bedrooms with private bathroom
Double from $110 to $155
Suite from $165 to $205
Open all year
Credit cards: all major
Children accepted

The Inn at Union Square has an absolutely perfect location, smack in the heart of San Francisco—just steps from Union Square, the theaters and shopping. But it is not just its strategic position that makes this inn so appealing: it is a winner in every respect. The charm is apparent from the moment you enter into the cozy, book-lined lobby which looks more like a small library in a country home than a lobby in a commercial hotel. An elevator takes guests to the upper floors. As you step off the elevator, each floor has its own little sitting area where chairs are grouped comfortably around a fireplace and where complimentary tea is served each afternoon from 4:00 p.m. to 6:00 p.m. with sandwiches and cakes, followed in the early evening from 6:00 p.m. to 8:00 p.m. by wine and cheeses. Newspapers are left outside each door in the morning. Guests can either go to the lounge (the same one where tea and wine are served) for Continental breakfast or else they can have a tray brought to their room. The decor in each of the rooms is most attractive, with a traditional mood created by the use of beautiful fabrics and fine furniture. Some of the rooms have their own fireplaces and the penthouse suite has a jacuzzi tub. Every room, from the least expensive small room to the deluxe suites, is spotlessly maintained and very appealing. *Directions:* Located one block off Union Square on Post Street.

THE INN AT UNION SQUARE
Owners: Nan & Norman Rosenblatt
Innkeeper: Brooks Bayly
400 Post Street
San Francisco, CA 94102
tel: (415) 397-3510, fax: (415) 989-0529
30 bedrooms with private bathroom
Double from $120 to $180
Suite from $170 to $400
Open all year
Credit cards: all major
Children accepted

The Marina Inn is not a typical country inn. In fact, it is a large, four-story building whose boxy exterior is made more lively by tiers of bay windows. But as soon as you enter, the successful effort to achieve the warmth of a homey inn is immediately apparent. The lobby is small and intimate, with light pine furniture, a pair of handsome upholstered chairs, green potted plants and off-white walls. The staff is friendly and eager to be helpful. An elevator leads upstairs to the bedrooms, each similar in decor with two-poster country beds, pastel print wallpaper, comfortable chairs, light pine armoires and forest green carpeting. In addition to being pleasantly decorated, the rooms offer all the amenities of a proper hotel: television in each room, comfortable queen-sized beds, direct-dial telephones and modern bathrooms with marble sinks and a basket of toiletries. On the second floor a sitting room is provided where in the morning a buffet Continental breakfast is served and in the afternoon complimentary sherry. One of the nicest merits of this hotel is its excellent price—a real value for such a spiffy place. Another plus: cribs are provided for babies and children under five are free of charge. The hotel is located just a brisk walk from Fisherman's Wharf, Ghirardelli Square and the St. Francis Yacht Club. *Directions:* Take Van Ness Avenue north to Lombard Street. Turn left and go three blocks to Octavia.

MARINA INN
Innkeeper: Suzie Baum
3110 Octavia
San Francisco, CA 94123
tel: (415) 928-1000, fax: (415) 928-5909
40 bedrooms with private bathroom
Double from $65 to $85
Open all year
Credit cards: all major
Children accepted

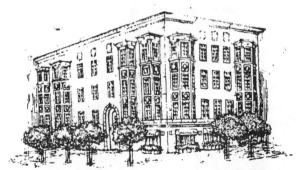

The Petite Auberge and the White Swan are two lovely little hotels sitting side by side on Bush Street in the heart of San Francisco. Both are owned and managed by the extremely clever "Four Sisters," a family run company that overseas a prestigious chain of delightful little hotels in northern California. Whereas the White Swan has an English flavor, the Petite Auberge is like a romantic French country inn snuggled at the heart of the city, just steps from the famous theater district and exclusive shopping and fine dining. The facade is most appealing—a narrow four-story building with a double column of bay windows bordered by narrow windows decorated with flower boxes. An antique carousel horse, burnished woods and soft pastel colors of peach and blue give a warm welcome to the cozy entry. Each guest room is attractively decorated with delicate colors. All have private baths, many have fireplaces, and each evening the linens are turned down and chocolates placed on the pillow. Wine and tea are served every afternoon to those guests who want a quiet moment after a busy day. A delicious breakfast is served buffet style each morning and includes a selection of teas and coffee, homemade breads, fruit, a hot dish, cereals and pastries. *Directions:* Take Van Ness Avenue north to Bush Street. Turn right on Bush and go approximately one mile. The inn is between Taylor and Mason.

PETITE AUBERGE
Owners: Roger & Sally Post
Innkeeper: Rich Revaz
863 Bush Street
San Francisco, CA 94108
tel: (415) 928-6000, fax: (415) 775-2465
26 bedrooms with private bathroom
Double from $110 to $160, Suite from $220
Open all year
Credit cards: all major
Children accepted

The Sherman House is an oasis of luxury and provides San Francisco with some of its most exceptional accommodation and personalized and attentive service. This French Italianate three-story mansion was built in 1876 for Leander Sherman, founder of the Sherman Clay Music Company and host to a number of famous musicians who performed within its walls. A soaring, three-story music hall is now a stunning salon for hotel guests. The main house contains eleven rooms or suites, while the carriage house, set in the middle of the gardens designed by Thomas Church, offers three spectacular suites. Armoires, mirrors, desks, chairs, paintings and chandeliers have been carefully selected for each room. Each room has a grand canopy bed, sumptuously draped in luxurious fabrics with feather-down mattresses and a magnificent private bath finished in black granite with the exception of one in Chinese slate. The restaurant is open only to hotel residents and is spectacular when compared to any of the world's finest restaurants. The chef shops every day to obtain only the freshest and finest ingredients and plans his menu accordingly. *Directions:* From the south, take Highway 101 to Franklin Street, bear left up the hill and continue for eighteen blocks to Green Street. Turn left onto Green and continue five and a half blocks to the Sherman House on the right.

SHERMAN HOUSE
Owner: Manou Mobedshahi
2160 Green Street
San Francisco, CA 94123
tel: (415) 563-3600, fax: (415) 563-1882
14 bedrooms with private bathroom
Double from $235 to $750 (without breakfast)
Open all year
Credit cards: all major
Children accepted

The Spencer House does not look like a hotel and there is no sign in front of the beautiful old Victorian to give any clue that guests are welcome. Yet within this stately, immaculately maintained mansion is one of San Francisco's most personalized, delightful places to stay. The owners, Barbara and Jack Chambers, have converted a woefully neglected charmer back to its original glory—the attention to detail and the amount of love, labor and money that must have gone into the project is astounding: the floors gleam again as when first installed, Lincresta Walton wall coverings have been restored to their original perfection, the living room and bedrooms have been padded and "papered" with beautiful fabric to soften any distracting noises, the kitchen looks straight out of *Gourmet*, the original gas lights are still operable. Barbara took advantage of Jack being a commercial airline pilot and flew to London to pick out all of the exquisite fabrics and many of the gorgeous antiques used throughout. It is like being in a private home with each guest room exuding its own personality, but all, even the smallest, are most inviting. One of the greatest assets of the inn is Barbara, a superb hostess and a fabulous cook. Breakfast is always a memorable, gourmet event and dramatically presented using the finest china and silver. *Directions:* From Van Ness take Sutter Street west to Divisidero, turn left, continue on to Haight turn right.

SPENCER HOUSE
Innkeeper: Barbara Chambers
1080 Haight Street
San Francisco, CA 94117
tel: (415) 626-9205, fax: (415) 626-9208
6 bedrooms with private bathroom
Double from $95 to $155
Open all year
Credit cards: none accepted
Children accepted over 16

The Washington Square Inn, one of San Francisco's most appealing hostelries, is located in the North Beach area, facing historic Washington Square. Within easy strolling distance is a wealth of wonderful little places to eat and a bit farther, but an interesting walk through Chinatown, are the theaters and shops of the Union Square area. From the moment you enter, the ambiance of the French countryside surrounds you—an antique dining table, mellowed with age and surrounded by country chairs, stretches in front of large windows framed with tie-back drapes. A superb armoire, large gilt mirror, baskets of flowers and a fireplace with an antique wooden mantel add to the country appeal. In the afternoon guests have tea in front of the fire and in the morning Continental breakfast is served here (if guests prefer, breakfast will be brought to their room). Two staircases lead to the guest rooms, each individually decorated with fine English and French antiques by the famous San Francisco designer Nan Rosenblatt (who, with her husband Norm, owns the inn). From the simplest room with "bath down the hall" to the most luxurious suite, each of the rooms exudes a lovely, elegant country charm. Beautiful coordinating fabrics dramatize the rooms, a couple with cozy bay windows accented with inviting sitting nooks. Each of the rooms has its own telephone. There is a new restaurant next door, Moose's, serving fine Italian cuisine. *Directions:* On Washington Square.

WASHINGTON SQUARE INN
Owners: Nan & Norm Rosenblatt
Innkeeper: Brooks Bayly
1660 Stockton Street
San Francisco, CA 94133
tel: (415) 981-4220, fax: (415) 397-7242
15 bedrooms, 10 with private bathroom
Double from $85 to $190
Open all year
Credit cards: all major
Children accepted

The White Swan Inn, a small, London-style hotel, has a splendid location just steps from a wide selection of quaint restaurants and a five-minute walk from San Francisco's fabulous Union Square shopping and theater district. Or, if you are heading for Fisherman's Wharf, the cable car is close by. But the appeal of the White Swan is far greater than its setting: from the moment you enter, you will know immediately that this is not a standard commercial hotel. A small sitting area greets you as you enter, with a reception desk to your right, but the heart of the inn is down a flight of stairs where a spacious lounge awaits with one section set up with tables and chairs for breakfast—a hearty meal of coffee, muffins, a hot entree, juices and cereals. Beyond the eating area is a pretty living room with a fireplace and comfortable lounge chairs. Next door is the library, another cozy area for relaxing. Although the inn is in the center of the city, French doors open out onto a small English-style garden where guests can sit outside on pleasant days. The bedrooms are beautifully decorated with pretty coordinating fabrics. Each room has a separate sitting area, fireplace (which can be turned on by a bedside switch), small refrigerator, wet bar, direct dial telephone and color television. *Directions:* Take Van Ness Avenue north, turn right on Bush and go approximately one mile. The inn is between Taylor and Mason.

WHITE SWAN INN
Owners: Roger & Sally Post
Innkeeper: Rich Revaz
845 Bush Street
San Francisco, CA 94108
tel: (415) 775-1755, fax: (415) 775-5717
26 bedrooms with private bathroom
Double from $145 to $160
Suite from $195 to $250
Open all year; Credit cards: all major
Children accepted

The Cheshire Cat is comprised of two lovely beige and white Victorians sitting side by side near the center of Santa Barbara and connected by a tranquil bricked patio (where breakfast is served on all but grim days). Behind the patio a jacuzzi is sheltered by a lacy white gazebo. In the foyer a grouping of "Alice in Wonderland" figurines placed on a small table beside the guest book immediately sets the whimsical theme of the inn: each of the rooms is named for an Alice in Wonderland character with the exception of two rooms—Jean's (named for the owner Chris' mother) and the Eberle Suite (named for the previous owners). Laura Ashley coordinated prints and wallpapers are used throughout with different color schemes, from plums and creams in the Mad Hatter room to smoke-blue and cream in the Dormouse's Room. Each bedroom is different; some are dramatic with a large jacuzzi bath in the bedroom, some have cozy bay windows, others an intimate private balcony. Loving touches make each guest feel special: fresh flowers in the rooms, individual bottles of Baileys Cream, and delicious chocolates. The Cheshire Cat room has the added features of TV and VCR. Mountain bikes are available for guests with suggestions on where to pedal when exploring Santa Barbara. *Directions:* Exit Highway 101 at Mission Street. East on Mission Street for five blocks. Turn right on State Street and go three blocks. Turn right on Valerio.

THE CHESHIRE CAT
Owner: Christine Dunstan
Innkeeper: Margaret Goeden
36 West Valerio Street
Santa Barbara, CA 93101
tel: (805) 569-1610, fax: (805) 682-1876
14 bedrooms with private bathroom
Double $79 to $139; Suite from $129 to $249
Closed Christmas
Credit cards: MC VS
Children accepted over 8, mid-week

The El Encanto Hotel has the rare privilege of being the only hotel in an exclusive residential area in the foothills above Santa Barbara. From the entrance the driveway circles around a fountain to the front of the main building. In addition to the reception area, this building also houses the lounges, the dining room, a spacious bar and outdoor terrace, all graced by spectacular views of the distant ocean. The guest rooms are in clusters of cottages dotted spaciously about the park-like grounds. Most of the rooms have been recently renovated and are decorated in a somewhat bland, country-French. The styles of the buildings reflect various stages of development: those built in the 1930s featuring heavy tiled roofs and dark wood-framed windows are our favorites. The cottages are linked by a brick path which winds through the beautifully tended gardens leading to fountains, swimming pool, wisteria-covered arbors and reflecting pools—in summer the fragrance of jasmine scents the balmy air. El Encanto is larger and more commercial than most of our recommendations, but it is a beautiful property whose clusters of cottages achieve a certain hide-away ambiance. *Directions:* Take Mission Road to the Mission Santa Barbara and where the road forks, continue to the right a short distance. Turn left at Lasuen Road and follow signs to the hotel.

EL ENCANTO HOTEL
Owner: Friden Hotels Company
Innkeeper: Jorge Plaza
1900 Lasuen Road
Santa Barbara, CA 93103
tel: (805) 687-5000, fax: (805) 687-3903
85 cottages & villas with private bathroom
Double from $120 to $500 (without breakfast)
Open all year
Credit cards: all major
Children accepted

The Simpson House Inn, a handsome, rosy-beige Victorian landmark with white and smoke blue trim, is superbly located on a quiet residential street only two blocks from the main shopping attractions of State Street. Surrounded by an acre of lawn, the back garden is especially appealing, with beautifully maintained flower beds and mature shade trees. One of the most irresistible features of the inn is a cheerful back porch under an arbor of draping wisteria with white wicker chairs and comfy pillows: a perfect niche to enjoy the garden. In the main house the lounges and dining room are quite formal—some museum-quality chairs are roped to prevent guests using them. However, the formality disappears upstairs in the charming guest chambers, each individually decorated to suit different tastes—some are lacy and frilly, others have a more tailored look. All are most attractive and enjoy such niceties as terry-cloth robes, fresh flowers, bottled water and sherry. Off the lawn in the back garden are three cottages that are beautifully decorated in rich fabrics and intimate with a jacuzzi tub nestled right into the room. The barn also offers spacious accommodations, light and airy, whose pine furnishings are perfect against the exposed beams of the original barn. *Directions:* From downtown take Santa Barbara Street heading northeast toward the Mission and turn left onto Arrellaga.

SIMPSON HOUSE INN
Owners: Glyn & Linda Davies
Innkeeper: Gillean Wilson
121 East Arrellaga Street
Santa Barbara, CA 93101
tel: (805) 963-7067, fax: (805) 564-4811
13 bedrooms with private bathroom
Double from $105 to $165
Suite from $195 to $250
Open all year
Credit cards: all major
Children accepted

The Tiffany Inn is an especially handsome old Victorian separated by a lawn from a rather busy street in Santa Barbara's residential area. Although the traffic in front is a bit distracting, the back garden is very charming and gives a quiet retreat for guests with an attractive lattice-covered verandah set with prettily-covered wicker chairs. If you are a fan of beautifully decorated Victorians, you will thoroughly enjoy a stay at the Tiffany Inn. Carol has done a lovely job of decorating, with romantic, old-fashioned antiques accented by well-chosen, colorful fabrics. The living room with its grouping of sofas and chairs around a fireplace is just the perfect place to sit and relax while planning sightseeing adventures. Each comfortable bedchamber exudes its own charm and character and several have the added bonus of a cozy log-burning fireplace. For those who crave privacy, one of the rooms has its own outside entrance and the added bonus of breakfast delivery each morning. Other guests enjoy a hearty breakfast of an entree, fresh fruits, muffins and coffee served in the dining room or on sunny days in the peace and quiet of the lattice-covered porch in the back garden. Joining you for breakfast might be Tiffany, the perky black spaniel with a "diamond" collar. *Directions:* Exit Highway 101 in Santa Barbara at Mission Street, drive east to De La Vina, turn left and the inn is on your right.

TIFFANY INN
Innkeepers: Carol & Larry MacDonald
1323 De la Vina Street
Santa Barbara, CA 93101
tel: (805) 963-2283
7 bedrooms, 5 with private bathroom
Double from $105 to $145
Suite from $175 to $190
Open all year
Credit cards: all major
Children accepted

The foundations of The Babbling Brook Inn date back to the 1790s when padres from the Santa Cruz Mission built a grist mill on the property, taking advantage of the small stream to grind corn. In the late 19th century a tannery powered by a huge water wheel was constructed. A rustic log cabin remains today as the "heart" of the inn with a small lobby where guests congregate around a roaring fire with hot coffee and homemade cookies. The historic wheel was recently returned to the brook pond. Most of the guest rooms are in shingled chalets nestled in the garden surrounded by pines and redwoods and overlooking the idyllic little meandering brook. Each of the rooms is decorated in European country style with an individual flair. Although calling itself a "bed and breakfast," the Babbling Brook is actually wonderfully sophisticated—each of the twelve guest rooms has a private bathroom, telephone, radio with alarm, and television. Most have a cozy fireplace, private deck and an outside entrance—four have deep, soaking, jet bathtubs. Helen King, who is the owner and manager, adds greatly to the warmth and charm of her appealing little inn. Helen, who has won many awards for her cooking, not only keeps guests well supplied with cookies, but also serves a delicious full breakfast each morning. *Directions:* From San Jose or San Francisco take Highway 17 to Santa Cruz. Turn north on Highway 1; then left on Laurel for one and a half blocks to the inn

THE BABBLING BROOK INN
Innkeeper: Helen King
1025 Laurel Street
Santa Cruz, CA 95060
tel: (408) 427-2437, fax: (408) 427-2457
12 bedrooms with private bathroom
Double from $85 to $150
Open all year
Credit cards: all major
Children accepted over 12

Tucked in the wooded hills above Santa Cruz is a charming bed and breakfast. Painted a soft yellow, the property is referred to and signposted both as Lemon Yellow Farm and Wayfarer Station. Cecil Carnes, a gracious hostess and a gourmet cook, is an attentive innkeeper. Shadowed by her ever present companions, Ingrid, Ajax and Tortu, Cecil is responsible for the marvelous renovation and offers two distinctly different accommodations. Set apart in its own building, The Wayfarer enjoys the spaciousness of an entry, a lovely living room arrangement in its bedroom (twin or king bed) and an additional downstairs, dainty and cleverly appointed sleeping area with both daybed and sleeping alcove. The furnishings in the Wayfarer are quietly elegant, set against a backdrop of gracefully arched doorways and windows. The Tower, appealing in its intimacy and coziness, adjoins Cecil's residence. The Tower enjoys two sitting areas one that opens onto a lovely deck and a second warmed by a woodburning stove. A narrow flight of stairs leads up to the small sleeping nook, a double bed with a beautiful hand carved headboard set under the vaulted beams of the tower. From the bed it is possible to look out to the trees and evening stars. Overlooking a lovely expanse of lawn banded by a babbling brook the setting at Wayfarer Station is romantic and poetic. Perfect for weddings. *Directions:* Follow Vine Hill Road for two miles off Highway 17.

WAYFARER STATION
Innkeeper: Cecil Carnes
Lemon Yellow Farm
111 Vine Hill Road
Santa Cruz, CA 95065
tel: (408) 425-5949
2 bedrooms with private bathroom
Double from $125 to $195
Open all year
Credit cards: none accepted
Children accepted over 12

The Channel Road Inn dates back to 1910 when Thomas McCall, a Scotsman who made a fortune in Texas oil and cattle, moved to California where he built an elaborate wood-shingled home for his family of six daughters. Although large to begin with, a third story was later added giving plenty of space for fourteen guest rooms. The house has an interesting location: just on the fringe of the elegant suburb of Pacific Palisades yet on a busy street that leads through the somewhat honky tonk neighborhood to the beach. But, oh what a beach. The wide sandy stretch of the Santa Monica beach is a wonderful playground. Even if the super location were not a factor, the Channel Road Inn would be a winner. The downstairs lounge and dining areas are sedately decorated, beautifully in keeping with the style of the home. The guest rooms are tucked throughout the large home. Each is individually decorated and has its own personality. My favorite rooms were No. One, one of the less expensive rooms but delightful with fresh white and blue the color scheme, and a more expensive room, No. 11 with stripped-pine furniture looking so pretty against the dark green carpet. Ask when you make a reservation and Kathy can help you pick out a room. *Directions:* From Highway 405 take 10 west, then Route 1 north about two miles. Turn right on West Channel Road.

CHANNEL ROAD INN
Owner: Susan Zolla
Innkeeper: Kathy Jensen
219 West Channel Road
Santa Monica, CA 90402
tel: (310) 459-1920, fax: (310) 454-9920
14 bedrooms with private bathroom
Double from $95 to $225
Suite from $179 to $225
Open all year
Credit cards: MC VS
Children accepted

With the opening in 1993 of Shutters on the Beach, a stunning, deluxe hotel emerged in the Los Angeles area. The property fronts directly onto the superb Santa Monica beach. Although of new construction, the mood created is delightfully nostalgic. The attractive, Cape-Cod-like whisper-gray, wood-shingled building is enhanced by white gingerbread trim. I am not sure how it is accomplished, but there is an engaging, home-like ambiance throughout—perhaps it is the low ceiling, or the cozy groupings of plump comfy sofas, or the fireplaces. The designer's goal was to create an inn where guests would feel that they were staying at a friend's beach house rather than a commercial hotel: the goal has certainly been achieved. My favorite rooms are in the two-story building that fronts the sea. A garden terrace (where white lounge chairs are grouped around an attractive swimming pool) spans a small street to connect the beach house with a more traditional-looking hotel section. All of the guest rooms are attractive: pastel blues, aquas, beiges, and peach colors accent a predominately white color scheme. An uncluttered, simple yet elegant, mood prevails, enhanced by fine linens and excellent-quality furniture. Every room has heavy wooden, white louvered shutters—setting the theme and name for the hotel. *Directions*: West on Highway 10 (Santa Monica Expressway) to Santa Monica. Take the 4th Street exit, south to Pico Boulevard. Located just south of downtown Santa Monica.

SHUTTERS ON THE BEACH
Director: Klaus Mennekes
One Pico Boulevard
Santa Monica, CA 90405
tel: (310) 458-0030, fax: (310) 458-4589
198 bedrooms with private bathroom
Double from $195 to $350 (without breakfast)
Open all year
Credit cards: all major
Children accepted

The Gables is a fine example of a bed and breakfast whose owners' love, dedication and caring enhance the comfort and welcome and make it a very special place to stay. Judy and Mike selected the Gables, an aristocratic Victorian home, on the outskirts of Santa Rosa with a dream of opening a bed and breakfast. Although, the Gables enjoys an expanse of three acres at back, with a wonderful old barn that creaks with age, the home sits just off Petaluma Hill Road. A little traffic can be heard from the front guest rooms, but the rooms at back overlooking the garden fully enjoy the quiet of the country meadow setting. The decor throughout the inn is in keeping with the grandeur of the home. Guestrooms are spacious and pretty in a country Victorian theme. Accommodation is also offered in a dear side cottage that enjoys its own little sitting area, fireplace, kitchenette, jacuzzi tub and cozy upstairs sleeping loft. Judy is quite an accomplished cook and her *casual* afternoon tea features homemade cookies and brownies. Breakfasts are quite a repast with freshly squeezed juice, fruit and a main course—a bounty that will take one right through to dinner. Mike is a talented craftsman and he is responsible for many of the fine finishes throughout the inn, and most notably a wonderful bird cage, home to some beautiful finches, that sits on the inn's back deck. *Directions:* From San Francisco travel Highway 101 north to Sonoma County. Exit at Rohnert Park Expressway. Turn right off the exit ramp and travel two and a half miles. Turn left on Petaluma Hill Road.

THE GABLES
Innkeepers: Judy & Mike Ogne
4257 Petaluma Hill Road
Santa Rosa, CA 95404
tel: (707) 585-7777, fax: (707) 584-5634
7 bedrooms, all with private bathroom
Double from $103 to $189
Open all year
Credit cards: all major
Children accepted in the cottage

Sausalito is a quaint waterfront town with fabulous views across the bay to San Francisco. Alongside the harbor runs one main street from which small roads spider-web up the steep hillside checkered with many Victorian houses. Among these is a lovely home, built in 1885, with marble fireplaces, stained glass windows, wrought-iron grillwork and lacy wood trim, which has now been converted to a wonderful hotel. The dining room and a few of the guest rooms are in the original home, while the rest of the rooms are in clusters of small buildings which step down the hill to the main street. The guest rooms in the original Victorian have been refurbished in Victorian style with all the behind-the-scenes amenities added for modern comfort. The newer rooms (all with views) are larger and each has its own style of decor—to mention just a few: Casa Cabana has a southwest look; Misia's Lilac and Lace is all fancy with eyelet and laces; La Belle Provence is very French, done in blues and whites; The Summer House is light and airy with light woods and wicker furniture; the Artist's Loft is most appealing with a fresh, uncluttered New-England look. The restaurant, with its large glassed-in porch, is a favorite, not only for guests of the hotel, but also for San Franciscans who come over for dinner or lunch. *Directions:* Ferry from San Francisco or drive Highway 101 over the Golden Gate Bridge. Take the Alexander exit which becomes Bridgeway.

CASA MADRONA HOTEL
Innkeeper: John W. Mays
801 Bridgeway
Sausalito, CA 94965
tel: (415) 332-0502, fax: (415) 332-2537
34 bedrooms with private bathroom
Double from $105 to $195
Open all year
Credit cards: all major
Children accepted

The recently renovated El Dorado Hotel is located on the Spanish Plaza in the town of Sonoma, directly opposite from another recommendation in this guide, the old Sonoma Hotel, but each hotel has its own personality. Built in 1843 by Salvador Vallejo, the stately El Dorado Hotel offers twenty-seven rooms with private bath and balcony. It is owned by a by a corporation, but managed by an efficient, professional staff. The decor throughout the hotel is clean, fresh, and attractive with tile floors, cream colored walls and white trim. The entry just off the square serves as the reception and also as the passageway to the hotel's highly regarded Ristorante Piatti (specializing in regional Italian cuisine) and two retail shops (a women's clothing store and antique store). Most of the guestrooms are found by climbing the stairs from the reception area, although, there are four rooms with enclosed patios located off the courtyard by the pool. The guest rooms are comfortable in size and identical in their decor with four-poster pewter beds, color television, sliding shuttered windows and soft pastel colors. Request an interior room overlooking the vine-covered courtyard; these are preferable to those opening onto the bustle and noise of the street. *Directions:* The town of Sonoma is located sixty miles to the north of San Francisco and fifteen miles south of Santa Rosa. The El Dorado Hotel is located on the northwest corner of the town's main square.

EL DORADO HOTEL
Innkeeper: Craig Clark
405 First Street West
Sonoma, CA 95476
tel: (707) 996-3030, fax: (707) 996-3148
27 bedrooms with private bathroom
Double from $80 to $140
Open all year
Credit cards: all major
Children accepted

The town of Sonoma is a gem and a wonderful base for exploring the region, its wineries and points of historical interest. Because of the part it played in California's history it is a fascinating destination for children, and the Sonoma Hotel, located on a corner of the main plaza, is one of the few hotels in the area that welcomes them. The Sonoma Hotel is also a historical landmark, housed in a century-old building which has offered overnight accommodation for decades. You can enter the hotel through its attractive lobby or into a delightful old-fashioned saloon. Casual dining is possible in the restaurant set with antique oak tables or, when weather permits, on the shaded garden patio. A steep flight of stairs leads to the upstairs bedrooms. Hallways are papered to capture a feeling of yesteryear and decorated with lovely antiques, mementos and plants. All of the seventeen bedrooms have been thoughtfully furnished with antiques to enhance both the flavor and history of the hotel. The five rooms with private bath have deep, clawfoot tubs. In the European tradition, all other rooms have private washbasins and share bathrooms on the hallways. The inn's owners oversee every aspect of innkeeping. *Directions:* From San Francisco take Highway 101 north: travel east on Highway 37 to Highway 121 and then north on Highway 12 to the northwest corner of Sonoma's plaza.

SONOMA HOTEL
Owners: Dorene & John Musilli
Innkeeper: Judy Versis
110 West Spain Street
Sonoma, CA 95476
tel: (707) 996-2996, fax: (707) 996-7014
17 bedrooms, 5 with private bathroom
Double from $70 to $115
Open all year
Credit cards: all major
Children accepted

The Casa del Mar, a Mediterranean-style home crowning a maze of lovely terraced gardens, is a pastel peach, three-story stucco building with a red tile roof. Refreshingly different from most California bed and breakfasts, there are no fussy frills to the decor of Casa del Mar: fresh white interior walls, furnishings of light pine and wicker, terra cotta tiled floors, and colorful fabrics. For accent, the owner, Rick Klein, has selected bright and dramatic paintings and sculptures from local talent. The guestrooms are modest in size, with just enough space to accommodate a queen mattress set upon a custom- made wood platform and a corner chair or two. The closet is a functional alcove with a free-standing chest of drawers. Four guest rooms (Passion Flower, Shell, Hummingbird and Heron) have subtle decorative touches to match their name, and balconies where canvas director's chairs can be relocated from the bedroom to enjoy the view. Although spartan, the decor is clean and fresh and fitting for a beach and park setting. Just steps from the bed and breakfast is an entrance to the park that accesses hundreds of miles of trails, or two blocks down the road is the justifiably famous white sandy stretch of Stinson Beach. *Directions:* As you drive into town from the south, the first building on the right is a small firehouse. Turn right at the firehouse onto Belvedere Avenue. Casa del Mar is located one hundred yards just up the street on the left.

CASA DEL MAR
Innkeeper: Rick Klein
37 Belvedere Avenue, P.O. Box 238
Stinson Beach, CA 94970
tel: (415) 868-2124
4 bedrooms with private bathroom
Double from $100 to $225
Open all year
Credit cards: all major
Children accepted over 6

Sutter Creek is a charming gold country town whose main street is bordered at either end by New-England style residences surrounded by green lawns and neatly clipped hedges. Occupying one of these attractive homes is The Foxes, an idyllic hideaway put together with great flair and taste by Pete and Min Fox. The symbol of the inn is the fox and the perky little fellow pops up everywhere. Yet this is not an inn with a cutesy theme, but an unsnobbish, sophisticated inn where everything has been done with exquisite flair. Three suites are in the main house and three new suites have been added to the rear. The Honeymoon Suite is the largest, most elegant bedchamber where a large brick fireplace overlooks a magnificent bed and gorgeous Austrian armoire. Sparkling crystal chandeliers light the enormous bathroom. In the Foxes' Den a border of foxes, hunt prints, a hunting horn, leather-bound books and leather chairs set before the fireplace give the room an inviting study feel. Each suite has a sitting area with a table to accommodate breakfast. Pete and Min discuss with you what you would like for breakfast and then it is brought to your room on silver service accompanied by a large pot of coffee or tea. You feel thoroughly pampered by a stay here. *Directions:* Sutter Creek straddles Highway 49, four miles north of Jackson. The Foxes is at the north end of Main Street.

THE FOXES
Innkeepers: Min & Pete Fox
77 Main Street, P.O. Box 159
Sutter Creek, CA 95685
tel: (209) 267-5882, fax: (209) 267-0712
6 suites with private bathroom
Suite from $100 to $140
Closed Christmas
Credit cards: all major
Inappropriate for children

My idea of a holiday at Lake Tahoe is to rent a cabin in the pines and catch up on my reading. One can do just that at The Cottage Inn which captures the mountain-cabin atmosphere while adding the comforts of fresh linens and a scrumptious breakfast. Built as a resort by the Pomin family in 1938, the cottages (which recently received a major overhaul without sacrificing their knotty pine paneling) are grouped under the pines a few steps from the shore of the lake. In the guest rooms Swedish-pine furniture and a variety of beds (brass, willow or pine) are complemented by the use of rich colors. The Fireplace Room has the added attraction of a wood-burning fireplace. The Pomin House, the original home on the property, contains the reception area, a large sitting room with games, books and comfortable furniture before a blazing log fire, and the breakfast room. In summer you can happily while away the hours sunning yourself on the dock and swimming in Lake Tahoe's cool, clear waters; the more energetic can take advantage of the lovely bicycle trail that passes behind the inn. Vikingsholm, Emerald Bay and D. L. Bliss Park are a short car-ride south. Ski resorts are between a five minute and twenty minute drive distant. *Directions:* From the Bay Area take Highway 80 to 89 Tahoe City exit, follow the river to Tahoe City and continue south on 89 following West Lake Boulevard: the inn is two miles on your left.

THE COTTAGE INN
Owners: Patti & Terry Giles
Innkeeper: Dawn R. Bliss
1690 West Lake Boulevard, P.O. Box 66
Tahoe City, CA 96145
tel: (916) 581-4073, fax:(916) 581-0226
15 bedrooms with private bathroom
Doubles: $120; Suite from $130
Open all year
Credit cards: MC VS
Children accepted

Having just visited a nearby inn where we were made to feel thoroughly unwelcome, it was with some trepidation that we knocked on the door of Mayfield House. But after a most gracious greeting from the resident innkeeper, our mood once again was "up." The experience was a good one—emphasizing so personally the great importance of an innkeeper's warmth of reception. Mayfield House is a cozy wood and stone building just a short walk from Lake Tahoe and the center of Tahoe City. The living room with its dark pine paneling, beamed ceiling, large fireplace and sofas is very comfortable and inviting. There are only six bedrooms sharing the facilities of three bathrooms (bathrobes are provided). Bedrooms are priced according to the size of the room and the bed. The innkeepers do live at the inn, but if you arrive late in the day you will be left a key and a friendly welcoming note explaining how things work. A full breakfast and a hot beverage is served every morning in the breakfast room or on the patio. Guests are encouraged to make themselves hot beverages in the tiny kitchen. A shed on the patio is used for storing ski equipment—Squaw Valley and several other ski resorts are just a ten-minute drive away. *Directions:* From the Bay Area take Highway 80 to the 89 Tahoe City exit and follow the river to Tahoe City: Grove Street is on your left.

MAYFIELD HOUSE
Innkeepers: Cynthia & Bruce Knauss
236 Grove Street
P.O. Box 5999
Tahoe City, CA 95730
tel: (916) 583-1001
6 bedrooms sharing 3 bathrooms
Double from $75 to $115
Open all year
Credit cards: MC VS
Children accepted

Lake Tahoe is an exquisite, crystal-clear blue lake ringed by pines and backed by high mountains. The only outlet for this enormous body of water is the Truckee River, and standing on a broad river bend some three miles downstream is River Ranch. This lodge exudes the air of a mountain resort, and the circular bar with its picture windows opening onto the river is particularly popular with the winter apres-ski crowd. The bedrooms are most attractively decorated in soft pastels with matching drapes and bedspreads in country check fabrics—all the rooms have phones, televisions and river views. The very nicest have queen-size beds and private balconies, while one very inexpensive tiny room has bunk beds. The ski resorts of Squaw Valley and Alpine Meadows are close at hand for winter fun, with sightseeing, hiking, trout fishing and river rafting as favorite summer pastimes. If you are not inclined to physical endeavors, you can confine yourself to the patio and watch rafters hurtle down the last stretch of their river ride and scramble ashore. Rafting the gentle Truckee river is a fun family outing. A basic Continental breakfast of sweet rolls, muffins and beverages is served in the bar. *Directions:* From the Bay Area take the Highway 80 to the 89 Tahoe City exit and follow the river to River Ranch.

RIVER RANCH
Innkeeper: Peter Friedrichsen
P.O. Box 197; 2285 River Road
Tahoe City, CA 96145
tel: (916) 583-4264, fax: (916) 583-7237
21 bedrooms with private bathroom
Double from $90 to $110
Suite from $140 to $175
Open all year
Credit cards: all major
Children accepted

The Country House Inn is located on the main street of Templeton, a pretty, small, western-style town, about midway between Los Angeles and San Francisco. The building, a large, white Victorian farmhouse accented by a dusty rose trim, is surrounded by a wide, grassy lawn dotted with shade trees and set off by an old-fashioned white picket fence. The inn is simple, not decorated with the polish of an expensive interior designer, yet abounding with the warmth and good taste of the owner, Dianne Garth, who bought the property a few years ago and has been pouring love and money into it ever since. Roses climbing over the porch set the mood as you enter the comfortable house. The dining room, a bright and airy room with flower-sprigged wallpaper and French doors leading to the garden, is the heart of the inn, with light wooden chairs and an antique country table. Country accents abound, especially a wonderful collection of hobbyhorses. Many of the very attractive handmade items are for sale. Each of the guest rooms is individually decorated and has its own personality. The front parlor room is decorated in shades of pink with Laura Ashley fabrics. The porch room, decorated in happy yellows, has its own private entrance. *Directions:* Twenty miles north of San Luis Obispo on Highway 101, turn off 101 at Vineyard, turn right to Main Street, then turn left, the inn is about eight blocks on the right.

COUNTRY HOUSE INN
Innkeeper: Dianne Garth
91 Main Street
Templeton, CA 93465
tel: (805) 434-1598
6 bedrooms, 4 with private bathroom
Double from $75 to $95
Open all year
Credit cards: all major
Children accepted

The Lost Whale, a gray-wash Cape Cod house with blue trim set on the windswept coast of northern California, was literally built by Susanne and Lee Miller who make their home in the inn and manage it with a refreshing, bountiful enthusiasm. The decor is delightful: fir floors are warmed by pretty throw rugs, lace curtains dress the windows and Laura Ashley comforters deck the beds. Four rooms capture magnificent views out through the towering pine trees to the ocean beyond, while two rooms overlook the front yards. The distant sound of barking sea lions tempts guests down to the Miller's private beach. (There are also numerous other beaches nearby to explore). Each morning a bountiful, delicious feast is served family-style at long pine tables. Susanne and Lee have two daughters and welcome children into their own kitchen for a simpler fare enhanced by crayons and toys. Outdoors their children's playhouse, barn and goat yard are also made available to young guests. Whereas most bed and breakfasts traditionally discourage children, here at the Lost Whale they are genuinely welcome. The Lost Whale is a very relaxed, lovely inn in a spectacular setting. *Directions:* North from Trinidad: take the Seawood Drive exit, cross under the freeway, and then travel one and eight tenths of a mile north on Patrick's Point Drive. South from Oregon: exit Patrick's Point Drive and continue south one mile.

THE LOST WHALE
Innkeepers: Susanne Lakin & Lee Miller
3452 Patrick's Point Drive
Trinidad, CA 95570
tel: (707) 677-3425
6 bedrooms with private bathroom
Double from $90 to $130
Open all year
Credit cards: MC VS
Children accepted

234   *Places to Stay*

The Trinidad Bed & Breakfast is a Cape Cod-style home constructed in 1949, painted barn-red with crisp white trim, located just across the road from the Trinidad Memorial Lighthouse. Although neither the building nor the furnishings are old, this small inn is very inviting. You enter into a cheerful family room with a brick fireplace faced by a sofa and flanked by two wooden rockers. A table is set prettily for breakfast which consists of homemade jams, hot baked bread and muffins, and fresh fruit. Upstairs are two double rooms, each with an alcove in the dormer with views of the coast. Above the garage is a suite with the best view from its long strip of windows overlooking the harbor. The fourth room, a suite on the ground floor, has a wrap-around window, king sized bed and a fireplace for cozy evenings. Both suites enjoy the luxury of breakfast delivered to the room. There is nothing outstanding in the decor, but then there is no pretense: this is just a homelike inn, but immaculately clean with everything shining with a "just scrubbed" look. The best part of all is the location: overlooking Trinidad Bay, whose old wharf still looks like a proper wharf should and where the trails along the magnificent headlands still maintain their unspoiled splendor. *Directions:* Twenty-five miles north of Eureka on Highway 101. Take the Trinidad exit west to Trinidad Bay Memorial Lighthouse—the inn is across the street.

TRINIDAD BED & BREAKFAST
Innkeepers: Carol & Paul Kirk
560 Edwards Street, P.O. Box 849
Trinidad, CA 95570
tel: (707) 677-0840
4 bedrooms with private bathroom
Double from $102 to $112
Suite from $130 to $140
Closed Mondays & Tuesdays off season
Credit cards: MC VS
Children accepted

The Carrville Inn, located in the Trinity Alps, began its history as a wayside inn for stagecoaches on their way to Oregon. The inn has great architectural appeal, a simple, white, wooden building with a two-tiered porch stretching across the front where guests sit in old-fashioned wicker furniture to soak in the view of the meadow and hills. A shady lawn with a lazy swing hung from the tree, a swimming pool enclosed by a white picket fence, and the miniature horses and sheep grazing in the pasture complete the scene of tranquillity. Downstairs the mood is "light" Victorian. The furnishings are appropriate to the era, but are not dark and oppressive—especially in the dining room, the mood is bright, with large windows overlooking the rose garden. Upstairs there are five bedrooms, three with private bathrooms and two sharing a large bathroom. Each room is most attractively decorated and has its own personality. The inn is very professionally run and guests are pampered from the time they come down to Barbara's hearty country breakfast (featuring farm-fresh eggs) until they retire at night to bed linens turned down, the lamps softly lit, a pitcher of ice water beside the bed and chocolates on the pillow. *Directions:* To reach the Carrville Inn, take Highway 3 north from Weaverville and continue six miles past Trinity Center to the Carrville Loop Road (the first paved road you will come to on your left).

CARRVILLE INN BED & BREAKFAST
Innkeepers: Barbara & Ray Vasconcellos
Carrville Loop Road, Rt. 2, Box 3536
Trinity Center, CA 96091
tel: (916) 266-3511
5 bedrooms, 3 with private bathroom
Double from $110 to $140
Open April to late October
Credit cards: none accepted
Children accepted over 16

Contra Costa County by and large comprises bedroom communities for San Francisco commuters. Walnut Creek is one of its more attractive towns, having the advantages of both freeways and the fast, high-tech BART trains (Bay Area Rapid Transit) to whisk you into San Francisco. Surprisingly, this urban enclave has a perfect hideaway inn for those who want to get away from San Francisco and yet cannot travel very far. The Mansion at Lakewood is a lovely Victorian estate sitting behind high, white, wrought-iron gates in a quiet residential neighborhood of ranch-style homes. Sharyn and Mike McCoy bought the then dilapidated home and wrangled with the city council to be able to restore it and open it as a country inn. Their battle won, The Mansion has received a new lease on life with luxurious appointments and inviting decor. The bedrooms range from the cozy Attic Hideaway to the opulent Estate Suite where an extraordinary antique four-poster brass bed draped with lace and soft pink damask sits center stage. The suite's enormous bathroom has every luxurious amenity: jacuzzi tub, extra large shower, his and hers vanities, oodles of soft towels and fluffy robes. A breakfast of hot, flaky, homemade croissants and fresh fruit is exquisitely presented. *Directions:* From Highway 680 take Ygnacio Valley Road north, turn right on Homestead and left on Hacienda: downtown Walnut Creek is just a quarter of a mile away.

THE MANSION AT LAKEWOOD
Innkeepers: Sharyn & Mike McCoy
1056 Hacienda Drive
Walnut Creek, CA 94598
tel: (510) 945-3600, fax:(510) 945-3608
7 bedrooms with private bathroom
Double from $125 to $275
Open all year
Credit cards: all major
Children accepted over 13

The Ahwahnee with 123 bedrooms hardly qualifies for inclusion in a country inn guide. It is a large, bustling resort with a level of activity in its lobby that is comparable to that at many airports, yet it merits inclusion because it is the most individual of hotels, with all the sophistication of a grand European castle, surrounded by the awesome beauty of Yosemite Valley. The lofty vastness of the lounge dwarfs the sofas and chairs and its huge windows frame magnificent views of the outdoors. The dining room has to be the largest in the United States: it is gorgeous with its massive floor-to-ceiling windows framing towering granite walls, cascading waterfalls and giant sugar pines. In contrast to the surrounding wilderness the dining room wears an air of sophistication in the evening when guests dress for dinner and flickering candlelight casts its magical spell. Bedrooms are in the main building or in little cottages in a nearby woodland grove. There is a small swimming pool just off the back patio and it is not unusual to see deer grazing on the lawn. This is undeniably a grand old hotel but if the price tag is a little rich for your blood, less expensive accommodations in Yosemite Valley are briefly outlined on pages 48 and 49. *Directions:* The Ahwahnee is located in Yosemite Valley just east of Yosemite Village.

THE AHWAHNEE
Innkeeper: Curt Abramson
Yosemite National Park, CA 95389
tel: (209) 372-1407
Reservations: (209) 252-4848
123 bedrooms & cottages,
  all rooms with private bathroom
Double from $201 to $208 (without breakfast)
Suite from $259 to $409 (without breakfast)
Open all year
Credit cards: all major
Children accepted

While the attractions of staying in Yosemite Valley cannot be denied, a more serene, country atmosphere pervades the Wawona Hotel, located within Yosemite Park about a twenty-seven mile drive south of the valley. With its shaded verandahs overlooking broad, rolling lawns and a nine-hole golf course, the hotel presents a welcoming picture that invites one to while away the afternoon beside the pool, fondly referred to as the swimming tank. Bedrooms are in several scattered buildings and private bathrooms are at a premium. Bedrooms without private facilities use two blocks of men's and women's bathrooms, which can be situated a long walk from your bedroom. The hotel was refurbished in 1987 in a most attractive decor. This is the kind of wonderful old hotel that attracts lots of families: people who came as children now return with their children and grandchildren. Advance dinner reservations are required. In the summer rangers give interpretive presentations on such topics as bears, climbing and photography and there are carriage rides, wonderful Sunday brunches, Saturday-night barbecues and barn dances. *Directions:* Wawona is in Yosemite National Park, twenty-seven miles south of Yosemite Valley on Highway 41.

WAWONA HOTEL
Innkeeper: Mark Merrill
Yosemite National Park, CA 95389
tel: (209) 375-6556, fax: (209) 372-1362
Reservations: (209) 252-4848
104 bedrooms, 52 with private bathroom
Double from $63 to $86 (without breakfast)
Closed mid-week January to Easter
Credit cards: MC VS
Children accepted

Located high above the Napa Valley, where the Yountville Cross Road meets the beautiful
Silverado Trail, the Cross Roads Inn is what I have always imagined the ideal Napa
Valley retreat to look like—with redwood siding, large windows and a multitude of
decks from which to soak in and breathe the beauty of the wine country. The view, once
your car negotiates the steep driveway, is truly breathtaking—a panorama of peaceful
vineyards and the Mayacamas mountains as far as you can see. This contemporary home,
which was built as an inn, is situated so that every one of its four suites can fully appreciate
the commanding view. Their decor is light and airy, reminiscent of romantic children's
books. The wine bar and jacuzzi spas in each room, without the intrusion of phone or
television, provide just the right accompaniments for a sybaritic getaway. A full breakfast,
taking advantage of the many in-season fruits available to the area, is served in your
spacious room or on the deck right outside. Your gracious innkeeper, Nancy Scott, is more
than happy to arrange for dinner reservations, hot air balloon rides and other diversions.
Twenty-three acres with hiking trails surround the inn where you can enjoy native flora
and fauna. *Directions:* Highway 29 north, turn right onto Madison Street into Yountville.
Turn left up Yount Street and then right onto Yountville Cross Road to the Silverado Trail.
Take another right turn and then a very quick left into the inn's driveway.

CROSS ROADS INN
Innkeepers: Nancy & Sam Scott
6380 Silverado Trail
Yountville, CA 94558
tel: (707) 944-0646
4 suites with private baths
Suite from $175 to $200
Closed Christmas
Credit cards: MC VS
Children accepted over 16

The Vintage Inn is a large hotel complex nestled between Highway 29 and the main street of Yountville. The eighty rooms are housed in an attractive mix of two story green and blue, wood sided and red brick buildings that are connected by meandering paths. We recommend the Vintage Inn as an alternative to bed and breakfast accommodation, if you seek a bit more anonymity, privacy and the full services of a luxury hotel. A concierge is present for assistance, a limited menu is offered poolside and through room service, and the stretch limousine parked at the front entry is available for hire. Guestrooms are very attractive in their decor, spacious and comfortable, equipped with television, fireplace (duraflame logs), coffee maker, a complimentary bottle of wine, tub-shower with jacuzzi jets and terry cloth robes. Turn down service is offered each evening and appreciated touches such as a fresh supply of towels and bedside chocolates are thoughtfully provided. Mornings, an appetizing champagne breakfast buffet of juice, hot beverages, fresh baked pastries, cereals, yogurt and fruit are set out in the front lobby and one can either dine inside or at tables on the patio. The Vintage Inn has a capable management team that extends a courteous welcome and strives to please. *Directions:* Take the Yountville exit off Highway 29, turn right at the bottom of the exit and then a quick left on Washington Street. The Vintage Inn is just off Washington Street beyond Vintage 1870.

VINTAGE INN
Innkeeper: Nancy Lochman
6541 Washington Street
Yountville, CA 94599
tel: (707) 944-1112, fax: (707) 944-1617
80 rooms with private bathroom
Double from $144 to $204
Open all year
Credit cards: all major
Children accepted

Key Map

Map 1

OREGON

Crescent City

Ft. Jones · Yreka · Mt. Shasta

Etna

McCloud

Trinity Center

Trinidad

Eureka · 101

Weaverville

Burney · Cassel

Redding

Ferndale

Lassen Volcanic National Park

Scotia

Garberville

Drakesbad

Leggett

PACIFIC OCEAN

Willits

Ft. Bragg

Mendocino · Little River

Albion · 128

Elk · Boonville · Ukiah

Gualala · Cloverdale · Geyserville · Healdsburg

Ft. Ross · Guerneville · Santa Rosa · Occidental

Pt. Reyes Station · Petaluma

Inverness

Muir Beach · SAN FRANCISCO

Chico

SACRAMENTO

299 · 101 · 5 · 3 · 1 · 116

★ Places to Stay
● Points of Reference

245

Map 2

Lakeport Clear Lake

Elk

128

101

Cloverdale

128

29

Gualala

Geyserville

Healdsburg

Calistoga

St. Helena

1

Guerneville

Santa Rosa

PACIFIC
OCEAN

116

Occidental

Glen Ellen

Yountville

29

101

12

Sonoma

Napa

116

★ Places to Stay
● Points of Reference

Petaluma

121

to Sacramento

37

Vallejo

80

1

101

Inverness

Pt. Reyes Station

Point Richmond

Muir Beach

Sausalito

SAN FRANCISCO

Map 3

★ *Inverness*

★ *Petaluma*

★ *Sonoma*

★ *Napa*

★ *Pt. Reyes Station*

● *Novato*

1

101

● *San Rafael*

★ *Pt. Richmond*

● *Vallejo*

Stinson Beach ★

80

Muir Beach ★

Sausalito

● *Berkeley*

SAN FRANCISCO ★

80

★ *Walnut Creek*

24

680

★ *Places to Stay*
● *Points of Reference*

1

280

101

● *Oakland*

880

680

Moss Beach ★

Half Moon Bay ★

● *San Mateo*

92

● *Pleasanton*

PACIFIC OCEAN

280

● *Fremont*

Palo Alto ★

101

● *San Jose*

Map 4

Grass Valley ★ ★ Nevada City
20
I-80

to San Francisco
I-80
Sacramento

Auburn
Coloma ★ ★ Georgetown
Tahoe City ★
Lake Tahoe
50

Placerville
Amador City ★ Sutter Creek
Jackson

I-5

SAN FRANCISCO ★

49

NEVADA

★ Arnold

Stockton
205
to San Francisco
580
120

Angels Camp ★ Murphys
★ Columbia
Jamestown ★
Groveland ★
Yosemite National Park
★ Yosemite Valley

49
49
Wawona ★

140

Merced ●
99
★ Oakhurst
41

★ Places to Stay
● Points of Reference

Fresno ●
to Los Angeles

251

Map 5

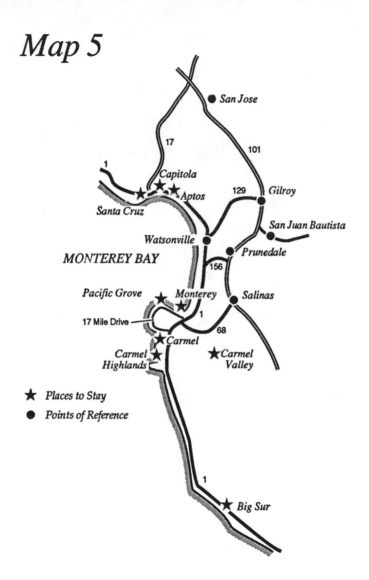

San Jose

17

101

1

Capitola

Aptos

129

Gilroy

Santa Cruz

San Juan Bautista

Watsonville

Prunedale

MONTEREY BAY

156

Pacific Grove

Monterey

Salinas

17 Mile Drive

1

68

Carmel

Carmel
Highlands

Carmel
Valley

★ Places to Stay

● Points of Reference

1

Big Sur

253

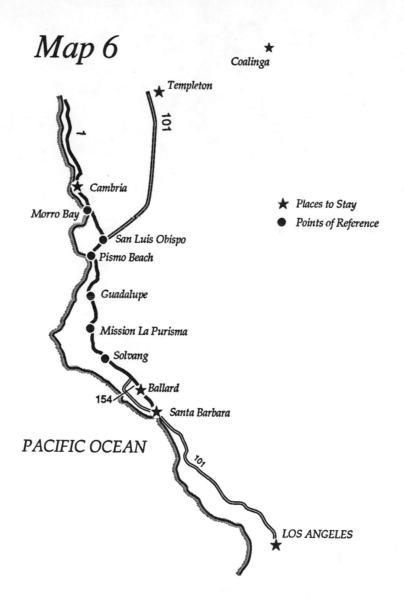

Map 6

Coalinga ★

Templeton ★

101

1

★ Cambria

Morro Bay ●

● San Luis Obispo

● Pismo Beach

● Guadalupe

● Mission La Purisma

● Solvang

★ Ballard

154

★ Santa Barbara

★ Places to Stay
● Points of Reference

PACIFIC OCEAN

101

★ LOS ANGELES

Map 7

Lake Arrowhead

Pasedena

LOS ANGELES South Pasedena

Santa Monica

Manhattan
Beach

18

18
330

10

30

Redlands

Banning

Big Bear Lake

10

111

Palm Springs

243

Idyllwild

74

405

5

Anaheim
Disneyland

Newport Beach

371

Temecula

Aguanga

Laguna Beach

San Juan Capistrano

Pala

76

Dana Point

76

79

Avalon

CATALINA

Rancho Santa Fe

Santa Ysabel

Julian

PACIFIC OCEAN

79

La Jolla

SAN DIEGO

★ Places to Stay

● Points of Reference

Coronado

Dulzura

8

Tijuana

MEXICO

257

INDEX

A

Academy of Sciences, 15
Adventures Aloft, 80
Aerial Tramway, 43
Afternoon Tea, 6
Ahwahnee, The, 48, 238
Air Conditioning, 4
Albion, 68
    Albion River Inn, 94
Albion River Inn, 94
Alcatraz, 12
Amador City, 54
    Imperial Hotel, 95
Amador County Museum, 53
American River Inn, 139
Anderson Valley, 68
Angel's Camp
    Cooper House, 96
Angels Camp, 52
Año Nuevo State Reserve, 18
Applewood, 145
Aptos
    Mangels House, 97
Archbishops Mansion Inn, The, 207
Arnold
    Lodge At Manuel Mill, 98
Artists' Inn Bed & Breakfast, The, 196
Avalon
    Garden House Inn, 122
    Inn On Mt Ada, 123
Avenue Of The Giants, The, 70

B

Babbling Brook Inn, The, 220
Balboa, 35

Balboa Island, 35
Balboa Park, 36
Ballard
    Ballard Inn, The, 99
Ballard Inn, The, 99
Barnabey's Hotel, 171
Bathrooms, 4
Beaulieu Vineyards, 83
Bed & Breakfast Inn at La Jolla, The, 161
Belle de Jour Inn, 149
Beltane Ranch, 88, 141
Benbow Inn, 138
Beringer Vineyards, 85
Big Bear Lake
    Gold Mountain Manor, 100
Big Oak Flat, 50
Big Sur, 23
    Post Ranch Inn, 101
    Ventana, 102
Blackthorne Inn, 154
Blue Heron Inn, 173
Blue Lantern Inn, 128
Blue Whale, The, 110
Bolinas Lagoon, 65
Breakfast, 5, 6
Brookside Farm B & B Inn, 131
Buelleton, 27
    Andersen's Restaurant, 27
Buena Vista Winery, 90

C

Cable Cars, 12
Calaveras Big Trees State Park, 52
Calistoga, 86
    Christopher's Inn, 103
    Larkmead Country Inn, 104

Calistoga, 86
    Meadowlark Country House, 105
    Quail Mountain Bed & Breakfast, 106
    Scarlett's Country Inn, 107
    Silver Rose Inn, 108
    Zinfandel House, 109
Calistoga Gliders, 87
Calistoga Spa and Hot Springs, 87
Cambria
    Blue Whale, The, 110
    Olallieberry Inn, 111
Campbell Ranch Inn, 140
Cancellation Policies, 5
Cannery Row, 20
Capitola
    Inn At Depot Hill, The, 112
Car Rental, 2
Carmel, 21
    Cobblestone Inn, 113
    Happy Landing, The, 114
    Mission Ranch, 115
    San Antonio House, 116
    Sea View Inn, 117
    Vagabond's House Inn, 118
Carmel Highlands
    Tickle Pink Inn, 119
Carmel Valley
    Stonepine, 120
Carriage House, The, 164
Carrville Inn Bed & Breakfast, 74, 236
Carson City, 60
Carter House, The, 135
Casa Cody, 191
Casa Del Mar, 228
Casa Madrona Hotel, 225

Cassel
    Clearwater House, 121
Castroville, 20
Catalina Island
    Garden House Inn, 122
    Inn On Mt Ada, 123
Cavanaugh Inn, 197
Channel Road Inn, 222
Château Du Lac, 165
Château Du Sureau, 187
Château St Jean, 88
Chaw'se Indian Grinding Rock State Park, 53
Check-in, 5
Cheshire Cat, The, 216
Children, 6
Chili Bar, 54
Chinatown, 13
Chinese Camp, 50
Christopher's Inn, 103
City Hotel, 52, 126
Clearwater House, 121
Clos Du Val, 79
Cloverdale, 68
    Ye Olde Shelford House, 124
Cobblestone Inn, 113
Coit Tower, 13
Coloma, 55
    Coloma Country Inn, 125
Coloma Country Inn, 125
Columbia, 51
    City Hotel, 126
    Fallon Hotel, 127
Cooper House, 96
Corona Del Mar, 35
Coronado, 37

Cottage Inn, The, 230
Country House Inn, 233
Credit Cards, 6
Cross Roads Inn, 240
Cuyamaca Rancho State Park, 40
Cypress Inn, 148

D

Daffodil Hill, 54
Dana Point
    Blue Lantern Inn, 128
    Ritz-Carlton Laguna Niguel, The, 129
De Young Museum, 15
Disneyland, 31
Domaine Chandon, 80
Donner Lake, 57
Donner Pass, 57
Dorado Hotel, El, 226
Dory Fleet, 34
Doryman's Inn, 186
Drakes Bay, 66
Drakesbad
    Drakesbad Guest Ranch, 130
Drakesbad Guest Ranch, 130
Driving Times, 2
Drytown, 54
Dudley's Bakery, 41
Dulzura
    Brookside Farm B & B Inn, 131
Dunbar House, 182

E

Eagle's Landing, 166
Eagle Falls, 59
East Brother Light Station, 199
Eiler's Inn, 163

Elephant Seals, 18
Elk, 69
    Griffin House, 132
    Harbor House—Inn By The Sea, 133
    Sandpiper House Inn, 134
Embarcadero, The, 37
Emerald Bay, 59
Empire Mine State Park, 55
Encanto Hotel, El, 217
Eureka, 70
    Carter House,The, 135

F

Fallon Hotel, 127
Fanny Bridge, 58
Felton, 19
Fern Valley Inn, 152
Ferndale
    Gingerbread Mansion, The, 136
Fisherman's Wharf, 13, 20
Fitzgerald Marine Reserve, 17
Forbestown Inn, 168
Fort Bragg, 69
    Noyo River Lodge, 137
Fort Point, 14
Fort Ross, 67
Foxes, The, 229

G

Gables, The, 224
Garberville
    Benbow Inn, 138
Garden House Inn, 122
Gatekeeper's Cabin, 58
Georgetown, 54
    American River Inn, 139

Geyserville
  Campbell Ranch Inn, 140
Ghirardelli Square, 14
Gingerbread Mansion, The, 136
Glacier Point, 50
Glen Ellen, 88
  Beltane Ranch, 141
Glen Ellen Winery, 88
Glendeven, 169
Gloria Ferrer Winery, 92
Gold Mountain Manor, 100
Golden Gate Park, 14
Gosby House, 189
Grandmere's, 185
Grass Valley, 55
  Murphy's Inn, 142
Green Gables Inn, The, 190
Griffin House, 132
Groveland, 50
  Groveland Hotel, The, 143
Groveland Hotel, The, 143
Guadalupe, 26
Gualala
  Old Milano Hotel, 144
Guerneville, 67
  Applewood, 145

H

Half Moon Bay, 17
  Cypress Inn, 148
  Old Thyme Inn, 146
  Zaballa House Bed & Breakfast, 147
Half Moon Bay Stores, 17
Hanns Kornell Winery, 85
Happy Landing, The, 114

Harbor House—Inn By The Sea, 133
Headlands Inn, The, 174
Healdsburg, 68
  Belle de Jour Inn, 149
  Healdsburg Inn On The Plaza, 150
  Madrona Manor, 151
Healdsburg Inn On The Plaza, 150
Hearst Castle, 24
Heart's Desire Inn At Occidental, 188
Helena's Library and Museum, 84
Heritage Park, 37
Heritage Park Bed & Breakfast, 205
Hop Kiln Winery, 68
Hotel Del Coronado, 206
Hotel Saint Helena, 202
Hotel Saint. Helena, 202
Humboldt Redwoods State Park, 70
Huntington Library, Gallery, Gardens, 32

I

Idyllwild, 42
  Fern Valley Inn, 152
  Strawberry Creek Inn, 153
Imperial Hotel, 95
Inglenook Winery, 81
Ingleside Inn, 192
Inn At Depot Hill, The, 112
Inn at Rancho Santa Fe, 200
Inn at The Opera, 208
Inn At Union Square, The, 209
Inn On Mt Ada, 123
Inverness, 65
  Blackthorne Inn, 154
  Manka's Inverness Lodge, 155
  Ten Inverness Way, 156
Itinerary Maps, 2

J

J. Paul Getty Museum, 32
J. Rochioli Winery, 68
Jack London, 88
Jack London State Park, 89
Jackson, 53
    Wedgewood Inn, The, 157
Jamestown, 50
    Jamestown Hotel, 158
Jamestown Hotel, 158
Japanese Tea Garden, 14
Jenner, 67
Johnson Oyster Company, 66
Joshua Grindle Inn, 175
Joss House, 73
Julia Pfeiffer Burns State Park, 23
Julian, 40
    Julian Hotel, 159
    Julian White House, The, 160
Julian Hotel, 159
Julian White House, The, 160

K

Kenwood Vineyards, 88
Key Overview Map, 243
Korakia Pensione, 193
Korbel Winery, 67

L

La Jolla, 37
    Bed & Breakfast Inn at La Jolla, The, 161
    Valencia Hotel. La, 162
Lachryma Montis, 91

Laguna Beach
    Eiler's Inn, 163
Lake Arrowhead
    Château Du Lac, 165
    Eagle's Landing, 166
    Saddleback Inn, 167
    The Carriage House, 164
Lake Arrowhead Village, 44
Lake Tahoe, 57
Lakeport
    Forbestown Inn, 168
Larkmead Country Inn, 104
Lassen National Park
    Drakesbad Guest Ranch, 130
Leggett, 70
Little River, 68
    Glendeven, 169
Living Desert Outdoor Museum, 44
Lodge At Manuel Mill, 98
Lombard Street, 15
Los Angeles
    Salisbury House, 170
Lost Whale, The, 234
Louis Honig Winery, 83

M

Madrona Manor, 151
Maggie's Attic, 42
Malakoff Diggins, 56
Mangels House, 97
Manhattan Beach
    Barnabey's Hotel, 171
Manka's Inverness Lodge, 155
Mansion At Lakewood, The, 237

Maps:
    Key Overview Map, 243
    Map 1 - Hotel Locations, 245
    Map 2 - Hotel Locations, 247
    Map 3 - Hotel Locations, 249
    Map 4 - Hotel Locations, 251
    Map 5 - Hotel Locations, 253
    Map 6 - Hotel Locations, 255
    Map 7 - Hotel Locations, 257
    Overview of Itinerary Maps, 3
Marin Headlands, 64
Marin Mammal Center, 64
Marina Inn, 210
Mariposa Grove, 50
Marshall Gold Discovery State Historic Park, 55
Mayfield House, 231
McCloud
    McCloud Guest House, 172
McCloud Guest House, 172
Meadowlark Country House, 105
Meadowood Resort Hotel, 201
Mendocino, 68
    Blue Heron Inn, 173
    Headlands Inn, The, 174
    Joshua Grindle Inn, 175
    Mendocino Farmhouse, 176
    Stanford Inn By The Sea, The, 177
Mendocino Farmhouse, 176
Mercer Caverns, 52
Mexico, 38
Mill Valley, 64
Miramar Beach
    Cypress Inn, 148
Mission Carmel, 22
Mission La Purisma Concepcion, 26

Mission Ranch, 115
Mission San Antonio de Pala, 41
Mission San Diego de Alcala, 38
Mission San Francisco De Assisi, 15
Mission San Francisco Solano De Sonoma, 90
Mission San Juan Capistrano, 36
Mission Santa Barbara, 28
Mission Santa Ysabel, 41
Moaning Cavern, 52
Monterey, 20
    Old Monterey Inn, 178
    Spindrift Inn, 179
Monterey Bay Aquarium, 20
Moss Beach, 17
    Seal Cove Inn, 17, 180
Muir Beach, 64
    Pelican Inn, 181
Muir Woods, 64
Mukulumne Hill, 53
Murphy's Inn, 142
Murphys, 52
    Dunbar House, 182
Myers Flat, 70

N

Napa
    Oak Knoll Inn, 183
    Residence, La, 184
National Maritime Museum, 16
Navarro Winery, 68
NBC Television Studios, 33
Nepenthe, 23
Nevada City, 56
    Grandmere's, 185
Nevada State Museum, 60

Newport Beach, 34
    Doryman's Inn, 186
North Bloomfield, 57
Norton Simon Museum Of Art, The, 33
Noyo River Lodge, 137

O

Oak Knoll Inn, 183
Oakhurst
    Château Du Sureau, 187
Oakville, 81
Oakville Grocery, 81
Occidental
    Heart's Desire Inn At Occidental, 188
Olallieberry Inn, 111
Old Faithful Geyser, 87
Old Milano Hotel, 144
Old Monterey Inn, 178
Old Stonewall Mine, 40
Old Thyme Inn, 146
Old Timer's Museum, 52
Old Town, 20
Once In A Lifetime, 87
Overview Map of Driving Itineraries, 3

P

Pacific Grove, 20
    Gosby House, 189
    Green Gables Inn, The, 190
Pacific Lumber Company, 71
Pacifica, 17
Pala, 41
Palm Springs, 42
    Casa Cody, 191
    Ingleside Inn, 192

Palm Springs, 42
    Korakia Pensione, 193
    Villa Royale, 194
Palo Alto
    Victorian On Lytton, The, 195
Palomar Observatory, 41
Pasadena, South
    The Artists' Inn Bed & Breakfast, 196
Pelican Inn, 64, 181
Petaluma
    Cavanaugh Inn, 197
Petite Auberge, 211
Pfeiffer Big Sur State Park, 23
Pigeon Point Lighthouse, 18
Pine Ridge, 79
Pismo Beach State Park, 26
Placerville, 54
Planetarium, 15
Pocket Canyon
    Applewood, 145
Point Lobos State Reserve, 22
Point Reyes Lighthouse, 65
Point Reyes National Seashore, 65
Point Reyes Station, 66
    Thirty-Nine Cypress, 198
Point Richmond
    East Brother Light Station, 199
Post Ranch Inn, 101
Princeton, 17
Prunedale, 20
Pueblo de Los Angeles, 33

Q

Quail Mountain Bed & Breakfast, 106
Queen Mary, The, 33

R

Railtown 1897 State Historic Park, 51
Rancho Santa Fe
    Inn At Rancho Santa Fe, 200
Reservations, 7
Residence, La, 184
Ritz-Carlton Laguna Niguel Hotel, The, 129
River Ranch, 57, 232
Roaring Camp Railroad, 18
Robert Louis Stevenson Park, 84
Robert Mondavi Winery, 81
Rockerfeller Forest, 71
Room Rates, 7
Russian River, 67
Rutherford Hill Winery, 83

S

Saddleback Inn, 167
Saint Helena
    Meadowood Resort Hotel, 201
    Saint Helena, Hotel, 202
    Vineyard Country Inn, 203
    Wine Country Inn, The, 204
Salisbury House, 170
Sam Brannan, 86
San Andreas, 53
San Antonio House, 116
San Diego
    Heritage Park Bed & Breakfast, 205
    Hotel Del Coronado, 206
San Diego Old Town, 39
San Diego Visitors' Bureau, 36
San Diego Zoo, 36
San Diego Zoo Museums, 37

San Francisco, 11
    Archbishops Mansion Inn, The, 207
    Inn at The Opera, 208
    Inn At Union Square, The, 209
    Marina Inn, 210
    Petite Auberge, 211
    Sherman House, 212
San Francisco, 11
    Spencer House, 213
    Washington Square Inn, 214
    White Swan Inn, 215
San Francisco Stores, 16
San Francisco Theater, 16
San Francisco Visitors' Bureau, 12
San Juan Bautista, 19
San Juan Capistrano, 36
San Luis Obispo, 26
Sandpiper House Inn, 134
Santa Barbara, 27
    Cheshire Cat, The, 216
    Encanto Hotel, El, 217
    Simpson House Inn, 218
    Tiffany Inn, 219
Santa Barbara Chamber of Commerce, 28
Santa Cruz, 18
    Babbling Brook Inn. The, 220
    Wayfarer Station, 221
Santa Cruz Boardwalk, 18
Santa Monica
    Channel Road Inn, 222
    Shutters On The Beach, 223
Santa Rosa, 87
    Gables, The, 224
Santa Ysabel, 41
Sausalito
    Casa Madrona Hotel, 225

Scarlett's Country Inn, 107
Schramsberg Vineyards, 84
Scotia, 71
Scripps Institution of Oceanography, 37
Sea View Inn, 117
Sea World, 39
Seal Cove Inn, 17, 180
Seaport Village, 39
Seventeen Mile Drive, The, 21
Sherman House, 212
Shutters On The Beach, 223
Silver Rose Inn, 108
Silverado, 79
Simpson House Inn, 218
Skunk Railroad, 69
Smoking, 8
Solvang, 27
Sonoma, 89
    Dorado Hotel, El, 226
    Sonoma Hotel, 227
Sonoma Barracks, 90
Sonoma Cheese Factory, 90
Sonoma Hotel, 227
South Pasadena
    The Artists' Inn Bed & Breakfast, 196
Spencer House, 213
Spindrift Inn, 179
Stag's Leap Wine Cellars, 79
Stanford Inn By The Sea, The, 177
Steinhart Aquarium, 15
Sterling Vineyards, 85
Stinson Beach, 65
    Casa Del Mar, 228
Stonepine, 120
Strawberry Creek Inn, 153
Sugar Pine State Park, 59

Sutter's Sawmill, 55
Sutter Creek, 54
    Foxes, The, 229

T

Tahoe City, 58
    Mayfield House, 231
Tahoe City, 58
    Cottage Inn, The, 230
    River Ranch, 232
Templeton
    Country House Inn, 233
Ten Inverness Way, 156
The Gingerbread Mansion, 72
Thirty-Nine Cypress, 198
Tiburon, 16
Tickle Pink Inn, 119
Tiffany Inn, 219
Tijuana, 38
Tomales Bay, 66
Toscano Hotel, 90
Trefethen Vineyards, 79
Trinidad, 72
    Lost Whale, The, 234
    Trinidad Bed & Breakfast, 235
Trinidad Bed & Breakfast, 235
Trinity Alps, 74
Trinity Center, 74
    Carrville Inn Bed & Breakfast, 236
Truckee River, 57

U

Union Square, 16
Union Street, 17
Universal Studios, 34

V

V. Sattui Winery, 84
Vagabond's House Inn, 118
Valencia Hotel, La, 162
Vallejo's Home, 91
Valley Of The Moon, 88
Ventana, 102
Victorian On Lytton, The, 195
Vikingsholm, 59
Villa Royale, 194
Vineyard Country Inn, 203
Vintage 1870, 80
Vintage Inn, 241
Virginia City, 59
Volcano, 54

W

Walnut Creek
        Mansion At Lakewood, The, 237
Washington Square Inn, 214
Wawona Hotel, 49, 239
Wayfarer Station, 221
Weather, 4
Weaverville, 73

Wedgewood Inn, The, 157
White Swan Inn, 215
Wild Animal Park, 39
Williams Grove, 70
Willits, 69
Wine Country Inn, The, 204

Y

Ye Olde Shelford House, 124
Yosemite National Park, 48
        Ahwahnee, The, 238
        Half Dome, 49
        Wawona Hotel, 239
        Yosemite Lodge, 49
        Yosemite Valley, 48
Yosemite Park and Curry Company, 48
Yountville, 80
        Cross Roads Inn, 240
        Vintage Inn, 241

Z

Zaballa House Bed & Breakfast, 147
Zinfandel House, 109

DISCOVERIES FROM OUR READERS

If you have a favorite hideaway that you would be willing to share with other readers, we would love to hear from you. The type of accommodations we feature are those with old-world ambiance, special charm, historical interest, attractive setting, and, above all, warmth of welcome. Please send the following information:

Your name, address, and telephone number.

Name, address, and telephone number of your discovery.

Rate for a double room including tax, service, and breakfast

Brochure or picture (we cannot return material).

Permission to use an edited version of your description.

Would you want your name, city, and state included in the book?

Please send information to:

KAREN BROWN'S GUIDES
Post Office Box 70, San Mateo, CA 94401, USA
Telephone: (415) 342-9117   Fax: (415) 342-9153

Karen Brown's Country Inn Guides

The Most Reliable & Informative Series on Country Inns

Detailed itineraries guide you through the countryside. Every recommendation, from the most deluxe hotel to a simple B&B, is personally inspected, approved and chosen for its romantic ambiance and warmth of welcome. Our charming accommodations reflect every price range, from budget hideaways to the most luxurious palaces.

Order Form for Shipments within the U.S.A.

Please ask in your local bookstore for KAREN BROWN'S GUIDES. If the books you want are unavailable, you may order directly from the publisher.

California Country Inns & Itineraries $14.95

English Country Bed & Breakfasts $13.95

English, Welsh & Scottish Country Hotels & Itineraries $14.95

French Country Bed & Breakfasts $13.95

French Country Inns & Itineraries $14.95

German Country Inns & Itineraries $14.95

Irish Country Inns & Itineraries $14.95

Italian Country Bed & Breakfasts $14.95

Italian Country Inns & Itineraries $14.95

Portuguese Country Inns & Pousadas (1990 edition) $6.00

Spanish Country Inns & Itineraries $14.95

Swiss Country Inns & Itineraries $14.95

Name _____ Street _____

City _____ State ___ Zip _____ Tel: _____

Credit Card (MasterCard or Visa) _____ Exp: _____

Add $3.50 for the first book and .50 cents for each additional book for postage & packing. California residents add 8.25% sales tax. *Order form only for shipments within the U.S.A.* Indicate number of copies of each title; send form with check or credit card information to:

KAREN BROWN'S GUIDES
Post Office Box 70, San Mateo, California, 94401, U.S.A.
Tel: (415) 342-9117   Fax: (415) 342-9153

KAREN BROWN wrote her first travel guide, *French Country Inns & Chateaux*, in 1979, now in its seventh edition. Thirteen other books have been added to the series which has become known as the most personalized, reliable reference library for the discriminating traveller. Although Karen's staff has expanded, she is still involved in the publication of her guide books. Karen, her husband, Rick, their daughter, Alexandra, and son, Richard, live on the coast south of San Francisco at their own country inn, Seal Cove Inn, in Moss Beach.

JUNE BROWN, CTC, born in Sheffield, England, has an extensive background in travel, dating back to her school-girl days when she "youth hosteled" throughout Europe. When June moved to California, she worked as a travel consultant for several years before joining her friend Karen to research, write, and produce travel guides. June lives in San Mateo with her husband, Tony, their son, Simon, and daughter, Clare.

CLARE BROWN, CTC, has many years of experience in the field of travel and has earned the designation of Certified Travel Consultant. Since 1969 she has specialized in planning itineraries to Europe using charming small hotels in the countryside for her clients. The focus of her job remains unchanged, but now her expertise is available to a larger audience—the readers of her daughter's country inn guides. Clare lives in the San Francisco Bay area with her husband, Bill.

BARBARA TAPP, the talented artist responsible for all of the hotel sketches and delightful illustrations in this guide, was raised in Australia where she studied in Sydney at the School of Interior Design. Although Barbara continues with freelance projects, she devotes much of her time to illustrating the Karen Brown guides. Barbara lives in the San Francisco Bay area with her husband, Richard, their two sons, Jonothan, Alexander, and daughter, Georgia.

JANN POLLARD, the artist responsible for the beautiful painting on the cover of this guide, has studied art since childhood, and is well-known for her outstanding impressionistic-style water colors which she has exhibited in numerous juried shows, winning many awards. Jann travels frequently to Europe (using Karen Brown's guides) where she loves to paint historical buildings. Jann lives in the San Francisco Bay area with her husband, Gene, and their two daughters.

SEAL COVE INN—LOCATED IN THE SAN FRANCISCO AREA

Karen Brown Herbert (best known as author of the Karen Brown's Guides) and her husband, Rick, have put seventeen years of experience into reality and opened their own superb hideaway, Seal Cove Inn. Spectacularly set amongst wild flowers and bordered by towering cypress trees, Seal Cove Inn looks out to the ocean over acres of county park: an oasis where you can enjoy secluded beaches, explore tide-pools, watch frolicking seals, and follow the tree-lined path that traces the windswept ocean bluffs. Country antiques, original-watercolors, flower-laden cradles, rich fabrics, and the gentle ticking of grandfather clocks create the perfect ambiance for a foggy day in front of the crackling log fire. Each bedroom is its own haven with a cozy sitting area before a wood-burning fireplace and doors opening onto a private balcony or patio with views to the distant ocean. Moss Beach is a 35-minute drive south of San Francisco, 6 miles north of the picturesque town of Half Moon Bay, and a few minutes from Princeton harbor with its colorful fishing boats and restaurants. Seal Cove Inn makes a perfect base for whale-watching, salmon-fishing excursions, day trips to San Francisco, exploring the coast, or, best of all, just a romantic interlude by the sea, time to relax and be pampered. Karen and Rick look forward to the pleasure of welcoming you to their hide-away by the sea.

Seal Cove Inn, 221 Cypress Avenue, Moss Beach, California, 94038, U.S.A.
telephone: (415) 728-7325   fax: (415) 728-4116